More Novels and Plays

More Novels and Plays

Thirty Creative Teaching Guides for Grades 6–12

Janet E. Worthington

Albert B. Somers

2000
Teacher Ideas Press
A Division of
Libraries Unlimited, Inc.
Englewood, Colorado

TEACHER IDEAS PRESS
A Division of
Libraries Unlimited, Inc.
P.O. Box 6633
Englewood, CO 80155-6633
1-800-237-6124
www.lu.com/tip

Library of Congress Cataloging-in-Publication Data

Worthington, Janet E., 1942-
More novels and plays : thirty creative teaching guides for grades six through twelve / Janet E. Worthington, Albert B. Somers.
p. cm.
Both this vol. and its companion vol. Novels and plays (published 1997) constitute a rev. ed. of: Candles and mirrors. 1984.
Includes bibliographical references and index.
ISBN 1-56308-691-3 (pbk.)
1. American literature--Study and teaching (Secondary) 2. English literature--Study and teaching (Secondary) I. Worthington, Janet Evans, 1942- II. Somers, Albert B., 1939- Candles and mirrors. III. Title.

PS41 .S66 2000
820.9'00071'273--dc21

99-089777

Contents

Grades 9–10

Grades 9–11

Grades 10–11

Grade 11

Grades 11–12

Grade 12

Preface

There are two ways of spreading light; to be
The candle or the mirror that reflects it.
—Edith Wharton, *Vesalius in Zante*

In 1984, Libraries Unlimited published the first edition of *Candles and Mirrors*, a collection of guides for teaching thirty-five novels and plays in middle and high schools. The intent of that book was to provide suggestions for teaching those thirty-five popular works in a single volume.

Our primary purpose was to provide an array of useful ideas to the thousands of talented English language arts teachers who are very committed to their students but lack planning time. When we asked ourselves the question: "What would be helpful?" our answer for each of the guides included the following components:

- a brief summary of the plot
- an appraisal of the work's reputation and its place in the curriculum
- lists of themes and literary concepts
- related titles for outside reading
- a section on reading problems and opportunities (including vocabulary enrichment)
- lists of selected media and print resources
- thought-provoking questions to promote discussion
- a variety of initiating activities to prepare readers for the work
- creative and other types of writing activities to accompany and follow up the reading
- activities that focus on language skills, such as role playing, debating, and interviewing
- activities that integrate other components of the curriculum, such as history, art, science, and geography

Novels and Plays: Thirty Creative Teaching Guides for Grades 6–12, and *More Novels and Plays: Thirty Creative Teaching Guides for Grades 6–12,* present a revised version of *Candles and Mirrors.* Like the original book, each of the two volumes of *Novels and Plays* assumes that teachers often look for help, but want many choices. Teachers know the needs and interests of their students and the concerns of their communities better than anyone. Their experience and intelligence enable them to select not only books but also questions and activities based on what they believe is important. Recognizing this important consideration, we prepared these guides not as a cookbook of rigid recipes for success but rather as a sourcebook of possibilities. We knew good teachers would use a given guide as they saw fit, some selecting perhaps an initiating activity they liked, others a sequence of questions, and others drawing from the list of resources. Perhaps a few teachers (especially beginners) might rely on a guide more heavily to jump-start a unit and save time. To whatever extent it is used, we've always envisioned the book being passed around a school from teacher to teacher.

Novels and Plays, then, is a newer version of *Candles and Mirrors,* based on the same concept. In this second volume (the first was published in 1997), guides for thirty novels and plays are presented. Ten titles have been retained from *Candles and Mirrors,* but as in the first volume, the guides have been updated with new suggestions in Related Readings, new Selected Teaching Resources (including, in most cases, appropriate related Internet listings), and revised questions and activities. Twenty guides are new:

Tuck Everlasting by Natalie Babbitt
Bridge to Terabithia by Katherine Paterson
Shiloh by Phyllis Reynolds Naylor
Sign of the Beaver by Elizabeth George Speare
Where the Lilies Bloom by Vera Cleaver and Bill Cleaver
Hatchet by Gary Paulsen
The Cay by Theodore Taylor
Number the Stars by Lois Lowry
Moves Make the Man by Bruce Brooks
The Goats by Brock Cole
Nothing but the Truth by Avi
Fahrenheit 451 by Ray Bradbury
Fences by August Wilson
Their Eyes Were Watching God by Zora Neale Hurston
The Crucible by Arthur Miller
A Lesson Before Dying by Ernest Gaines
Things Fall Apart by Chinua Achebe
The Great Gatsby by F. Scott Fitzgerald
Julius Caesar and *Hamlet* by William Shakespeare

Eight of these works—those by Naylor, Paulsen, Lowry, Brooks, Cole, Avi, Wilson, and Gaines—were written since *Candles and Mirrors* was published. The titles were selected on the basis of quality, variety, frequency of use, potential appeal to a wide variety of students, and a need to enhance cultural and ethnic diversity in the works taught in the English language arts curriculum.

The literature was chosen for its potential to "spread light" into the lives of students; we hope that this second volume of *Novels and Plays* will help teachers reflect and extend that light in many ways. Ultimately, we hope that by offering questions, activities, and experiences that involve students in an active response to literature, the book will play a part in broadening the influence that literature can have upon our students and increase the likelihood that they will continue to enrich their lives through reading.

Introduction

Like *Novels and Plays*, *More Novels and Plays* is written for teachers. As former public school teachers, we want this book to be practical, timely, affordable, and easy to use. For this reason, we have chosen works that teachers often teach, including both established classics and titles published in the 1990s. We have developed questions and activities that address multiple intelligence, promote critical thinking, and integrate the curriculum. Also, rather than writing and marketing individual guides (two or three of which are often as expensive as this single volume), we have compiled thirty into a single book.

In this companion volume to *Novels and Plays* we again emphasize the idea of *students responding actively to books.* By offering higher-level questions for discussion and a variety of activities, we hope that teachers will actively engage their students in the works they teach by talking, writing, drawing, debating, role playing, viewing, exploring the Internet, reporting, interviewing, creating collages and mobiles ... the possibilities are almost limitless.

The thirty response guides in *More Novels and Plays* use the same format featured in *Novels and Plays.* The standard publication information is followed by a brief Summary, an Appraisal that comments on the work's reputation and the grade level(s) at which it is most commonly taught, lists of suggested Themes and Literary Concepts for teaching, and a Related Reading section containing suggested selections for further reading. For each book there is also an extensive discussion of Reading Problems and Opportunities. These problems include such matters as the dialect of the character Joseph in *Wuthering Heights,* the archaic language and obscure word play in *Julius Caesar* and *Hamlet,* and the Appalachian dialect and words related to plant life in *Where the Lilies Bloom.* The opportunities mostly take the form of lists of vocabulary words that may be useful for study. As we noted earlier, while we don't believe that the teaching of a book should be bogged down in vocabulary work, we do feel that the best way for students to increase their fund of words is through reading. We suggest, in particular, that teachers emphasize the words that appear more than once because reinforcement is one key to vocabulary development.

The bulk of the book consists of questions and activities. The Discussion Questions are designed to promote higher-level thinking. In any given response guide, a few questions focus on responses at the "knowledge" or "recall" level, but the great majority aim higher, urging students to compare, apply, analyze, predict, generalize, synthesize, and evaluate. We realize that all teachers will want to supplement these questions with their own and will use reader-response approaches that capitalize on questions that students themselves ask.

We hasten to emphasize one other point regarding the questions: Because the great majority of them require critical thinking, many could be used as essay questions for a unit-ending test. Two examples among many are the final questions for *A Lesson Before Dying* (To what extent is Grant Wiggins a different person at the end of the book? What has he learned? Is he more, or less, confused? Is he more, or less, hopeful? Does he have faith? What was the "the lesson before dying"?); and the final questions for *The Sign of the Beaver* (How are Matt's views different from the views of his parents? In what ways might these views affect the rest of his life?)

The first activities, Initiating Activities, offer opportunities for teachers to involve students in some of a work's ideas and issues before they begin reading the work. The activities anticipate conflicts or themes and thus usher young readers into the work. One Initiating Activity might have students, before reading *Tuck Everlasting*, write what they think they would do if they knew they could live forever; another might have students conduct research that would provide a background on the setting of the book, for example, researching the Nazi invasion and the resistance movements in Denmark during World War II before reading *Number the Stars.*

The Writing Activities are numerous and varied. Some invite a personal response, such as having students write about a time in their lives when they learned "it is not good to want a thing too much" (*The Pearl*). Others call for rhetorical writing, for example, having students write the speech that Brother Leon might have given to the student assembly after the successful completion of the chocolate sale (*The Chocolate War*). Others call for poems (a list poem on friendship based on *The Moves Make the Man*), eulogies or obituaries, letters, ads, stories, critiques, folk tales, myths, parables, bumper stickers, and wills.

As with everything else in these guides, our idea is to offer teachers options, as they, in turn, would offer choices to their students. The Other Activities obey the same rule. For the most part, these offerings reach out to other areas of the curriculum and the culture: to history and music, to science and art, to geography, economics, and sometimes even mathematics and dance (like the activity for *The Great Gatsby* in which students are encouraged to learn the dance steps of the Charleston).

Finally, the last section presents Selected Teaching Resources. Here are not only cassettes, videos, articles, books, and teaching aids, but also CD-ROMs and even home pages on the Internet. (Just one example of a website: Anyone teaching *The Red Badge of Courage* would surely find the home page *The United States Civil War Center* to be useful and interesting.) Users of *Novels and Plays* will realize, of course, that the Internet is an extremely fluid phenomenon: Home pages here today are often gone tomorrow, or at least altered. Most of the ones we've included, however, seem substantial enough to remain in place for more than a few years.

Teachers interested in any of the resources can inquire about or order them from the appropriate companies listed in Appendix B. (Appendix A explains a form of poetry called *diamante,* which we have recommended for several writing activities.)

We hope this second volume will be helpful. However it is used—by one teacher as the source of a single activity, by another as the first item in an extensive file on the teaching of a favorite work—our purposes will be realized if the book plays a small role in spreading the light that only literature can cast, leading students to find in books the same joy and excitement and heightened awareness that all of us have found.

We want to thank Gary Worthington, Rachael Walker, Kate Chilton, and Dr. Priscilla Myers for offering ideas and encouragement in the preparation of this second volume. A very special thanks goes to Lee Zanistowski for her assistance in research and editing.

Bridge to Terabithia

Katherine Paterson
New York: Avon, 1978
Available in paperback from HarperTrophy.

SUMMARY

Jess Aarons looks forward to the beginning of his fifth-grade year because he hopes to be the fastest runner in his class, but, to his chagrin, he is beaten by Leslie Burke, a new girl who has adopted the attitudes and dress of her unconventional mother and father. Soon Jess and Leslie become soul mates and establish Terabithia, their special hideaway where they reign as king and queen. Leslie encourages Jess's artistic efforts and Jess helps Leslie understand and fit in somewhat with the local children. Unfortunately, one rainy day, Leslie goes off alone to Terabithia, falls into a creek, and dies. Jess must then cope with her loss and come to an understanding of the courage and wisdom he gained from her.

APPRAISAL

Winner of the 1978 Newbery Medal, *Bridge to Terabithia* is a great favorite of students and teachers. Like other works by Katherine Paterson, its characters ring true, its themes touch the hearts of young readers, and its message has staying power. The strong friendship established between two children with very different backgrounds is the uniting thread of the novel. The presentation of this relationship serves as a model for young people today. While the book speaks to all ages, it is most appropriate for grades five through six.

THEMES

friendship, death, imagination/creativity, self-worth, following the crowd, child-parent relationships

LITERARY CONCEPTS

characterization, foreshadowing, onomatopoeia, omniscient third-person point of view

RELATED READING

Other novels that focus on the tragic deaths of young people include *Beat the Turtle Drum* by Constance Green, *The Outsiders* by S. E. Hinton, *Of Love and Death and Other Journeys* by Isabelle Holland, *Mick Harte Was Here* by Barbara Park, and *Walk Two Moons* by Sharon Creech.

Other novels by Katherine Paterson that have received wide acclaim include *The Great Gilly Hopkins*, *The Master Puppeteer*, and *Jacob Have I Loved.*

READING PROBLEMS AND OPPORTUNITIES

Basically an easy book to decode, *Bridge to Terabithia* does have several opportunities for vocabulary expansion, many of which come from Leslie's life and her imagination. Vocabulary includes (chapter numbers are in parentheses):

hippie (2),
peacenik (2),
pandemonium (2),
hypocritical (2),
proverbial (2),
repulsive (3),
conspicuous (3),
prissily (4),
ominously (4),
regicide (5),
parapets (5),
foundling (6),
dregs (7),
predator (7),
wheedling (8),
complacent (8),
sporadically (9),
piteously (13),
constricting (13), and
traitorous (13).

INITIATING ACTIVITIES

1. Research the word "Terabithia." Where would you look for information? With your classmates, make a list of possible resources. Divide up the list of resources and search for a definition. Compare the information you and your classmates collect and prepare a definition.
2. For what reasons are students ridiculed by their classmates? Consider clothes, language, habits, family background, and hobbies. Consider why some behavior is accepted while other behavior causes a student to be left out of groups and activities.
3. Imagine what your favorite hiding place would look like—a place that just you and your best friends go. Prepare a sketch or a computer drawing of this place. Save it for later activities.

DISCUSSION QUESTIONS

1. *Chapter 1:* List three adjectives to describe Jesse Oliver Aarons, Jr. Support your choices with details and events from chapter 1. What is his relationship with the other members of his family? Why isn't Jess excited about the arrival of new people at the Perkins Place? How do you know this is an important event?
2. *Chapter 2:* How does Jess feel about the drawings he does? In what ways have others caused him to feel this way? What other people do you know (both famous and not-so-famous) who have had their talents overlooked or ridiculed in a similar manner? What are Jess's first impressions of Leslie? On what does he base these impressions?
3. *Chapter 3:* In what ways does Leslie fail to follow the unwritten codes of conduct for fifth-graders at Lark Creek Elementary? Why does Jess stand up for Leslie? How does he feel as a result of this?
4. *Chapter 4:* Why does Jess change his mind about Leslie? In what other ways does Leslie break the codes of conduct at Lake Creek? How does Jess attempt to rescue her from these missteps? How does Terabithia draw Leslie and Jess together? Since Jess and Leslie come from such different backgrounds, how is it possible that they could be friends?

5. *Chapter 5:* Why is Janice Avery such a terror to the other children? How are Leslie and Jess able to trick Janice into making a fool of herself? What traits in her character do they exploit? Why is May Belle satisfied that the wrong done her by Janice has been appropriately punished?

6. *Chapter 6:* What is the relationship between the cost of the Christmas gifts and the pleasure they provide the recipients? Why is Jess's free gift so much better than the too-expensive racing car set his father gave him?

7. *Chapter 7:* How does helping the Burkes remodel their home improve Jess's self esteem? How is Leslie able to help Janice Avery? What events show how important Leslie's friendship is to Jess?

8. *Chapter 8:* Why do each of the following characters go to church on Easter Sunday: Mrs. Aarons, Ellie, Jess, and Leslie? Why does Jess believe what the Bible says? Why doesn't Leslie believe it?

9. *Chapter 9:* How do Leslie and Jess deal with the continuing rain? What frightens Jess about the rain and the woods?

10. *Chapter 10:* What makes the trip to Washington a perfect day for Jess? What makes the day a terrible day for Jess?

11. *Chapter 11:* Why doesn't Jess's father comfort him? How does Jess manage to deal with Leslie's death? Is this a normal reaction to tragedy? Why or why not?

12. *Chapter 12:* How does P. T. ease the pain of Leslie's death for Leslie's parents and Jess? Why does Jess hit May Belle so hard? Why can't he say he is sorry?

13. *Chapter 13:* How does Jess know what to do to commemorate Leslie's life? What new understanding of Mrs. Myers does Jess achieve? In what ways do you change your opinion of her? Do you think that May Belle can be the new queen of Terabithia? Why or why not?

WRITING ACTIVITIES

1. Prepare a definition of a hippie, using the dictionary, the Internet, and interviews with people who were involved in the movement or knew others who were. Using your definition, write an evaluation of Miss Julie Edmunds as a hippie. In what ways does she fit the traditional portrait of a hippie; in what ways does she not fit? Compare your evaluation with those written by others in your class.

2. Imagine that you are with the local board of education. Prepare a report for the board on the conditions at Lark Creek Elementary. Some of these conditions are described directly in the novel, for example, the number of students in the class, while others you must infer, such as what kind of equipment was available on the playground. At the end of your report, make recommendations about needed changes at this school. Work with your teacher to conduct a similar survey of your school.

3. Take out your drawing of your secret place. Then reread the sections of the novel that describe Terabithia. Write a comparison and contrast paper about these two special locations. List all the differences first, then explain why each one occurs. For example, maybe your special place is in the basement of your apartment building because there are no woods or other secluded places near your home. Then list all the similarities and why they occur. Try to draw generalizations about young people's hiding places based on your

comparisons; for example, hiding places must offer shelter and a place for storing secret, precious objects because these are very important to young people.

4. Symbols are words, objects, or persons that represent something larger and more complex than themselves. For example, the flag is a symbol of its country and the people in that country. What is Terabithia a symbol for? Discuss this with your classmates and come up with as many ideas as possible. Then attempt to narrow the list to between two and four that seem most appropriate. Write a one- to two-page paper explaining what you believe Terabithia stands for.

5. Why is the last chapter of the novel entitled "Building a Bridge?" Write a letter to a classmate explaining why that title is appropriate for the last chapter of the book. Share your letter with other classmates and also review what they may have written. Do you all agree about why it is given that title? Why or why not?

OTHER ACTIVITIES

1. Research the stages of dealing with grief over the loss of a loved one. Prepare a chart of these stages and, in a second column, list examples of Jess's behavior that fit in each stage. Post your chart on the bulletin board so your classmates can understand how Jess's behavior is typical or not typical.

2. With several classmates, improvise the scene in which Jess goes to Leslie's house after her death and meets with her father. After you have played that scene, try it again, this time with Leslie's spirit there guiding Jess as to what he should do and what he should say. How are the two scenes different? Why are they different?

3. Jess would draw pictures in his head but could not always produce them because he did not have the proper art supplies to create them. Review his description of how he would like to portray Hamlet in chapter 5 and how he would like to prepare a Christmas book for Leslie in chapter 6. Try your hand at bringing to life one of Jess's mental pictures. In the first attempt, use only the pencils and crayons that Jess normally had access to, but in the second picture, select any medium that you think would appropriately portray these images. Compare the two final products. Was Jess right that having good art supplies makes it possible to re-create mental images more accurately? Why or why not?

4. Compare the values of Jess's family with the values of Leslie's family. Prepare a chart of your findings that includes how much each family valued each of the following: family time, material possessions, knowledge, fun, imagination/creativity, as well as other categories that you think are needed. Using this chart as a starting point, discuss with your classmates how Jess and Leslie could be friends even though their families differed in their values.

5. Choose key events from the novel that could be used to trace Jess's development from self-doubt to self-understanding and self-confidence. Place these events on a timeline. Ask your classmates to examine this timeline and add their suggestions to it.

6. Leslie kept several cans in Terabithia. Each contained items that were needed for Jess's and Leslie's reign in this magic kingdom. Put together your own can (a coffee can or other similar large can will do) containing items you think would be helpful and desirable for either Jess, Leslie, or both of them. Prepare a small tag for each item with an explanation of why it was included in the can. Ask your classmates to review the contents of your can and comment on your choices.

7. *Bridge to Terabithia* is one of the books for young people that is most frequently banned. Search the Internet for lists of banned books to see if *Bridge to Terabithia* is included. Imagine that *Bridge to Terabithia* has been banned in your school. Stage a mock trial to rescue the book. You need at least five parties: a team of lawyers for the defense, a team of lawyers for the prosecution, a judge, a parent who wants the book banned, and a teacher who wants students to read the book. Present the trial to the rest of the class.

SELECTED TEACHING RESOURCES

Media Aids

Internet

Official Katherine Paterson Web Site. Available: http://www.terabithia.com (Accessed March 10, 2000).

A helpful site featuring book covers, a list of books, answers to frequently asked questions, and awards.

Video

Bridge to Terabithia. 58 min., color. Wonderworks Video series. Perma-Bound, Clearvue/eav, and Sundance, 1985.

Printed Resources

Article

Paterson, Katherine. "Newbery Award Acceptance." *The Horn Book Magazine* LIV (August 1978): 361–367.

Teaching Aids

Bridge to Terabithia. Bookwise Literature Guides. Christopher-Gordon Publishers, Inc.

Bridge to Terabithia. Novel/Drama Curriculum Units. The Center for Learning.

Bridge to Terabithia. Novel-Ties. Learning Links.

Bridge to Terabithia. Reading Beyond the Basal Plus series, Portals to Reading series, and Portals Plus series. Perfection Learning Corporation.

Test

Bridge to Terabithia. Alternative assessment version. Perfection Learning Corporation.

Shiloh

Phyllis Reynolds Naylor
New York: Atheneum, 1991
Available in paperback from Bantam Doubleday Dell.

SUMMARY

Eleven-year-old Marty Preston lives with his mother, father, and two sisters in a house in rural West Virginia. When he discovers that a beagle dog is being mistreated by its owner, Judd Travers, Marty determines to rescue and keep the dog, which he names Shiloh. He hides the dog from even his parents and weaves a web of lies to keep his secret. When Shiloh is discovered, Marty learns that lies are complicated and rarely left unfound, that solutions to problems like this are difficult to reach, and that life in general is far less simple than he had thought.

APPRAISAL

As a novel most appropriate for fifth and sixth graders, *Shiloh* offers a suspenseful story based on a difficult, complex moral dilemma. The book addresses such questions as: What is the nature of truth and honesty? Is it ever acceptable to lie? and What are our responsibilities to animals? *Shiloh* won the 1992 Newbery Medal and won additional recognition as an American Library Association Notable Book for Children.

THEMES

honesty, decisions, responsibility, treatment of animals, secrets

LITERARY CONCEPTS

characterization, first-person narration, plot, dialect, irony, simile

RELATED READING

In 1996, Atheneum published a sequel to *Shiloh* by Phyllis Reynolds Naylor entitled *Shiloh Season*, which was followed a year later by *Saving Shiloh*. There are many other books about the relationships of young people and animals, dogs in particular. These include *Where the Red Fern Grows* by Wilson Rawls, *Big Red* by Jim Kjelgaard, *The Dog Who Wouldn't Be* by Farley Mowat, *Old Yeller* by Fred Gipson, and *Windsong* by Lynn Hall. One of the best comparable novels about a young boy's wrestling with secrets and the truth is Marion Dane Bauer's *On My Honor*.

READING PROBLEMS AND OPPORTUNITIES

Narrated by the pre-adolescent Marty, *Shiloh* offers few reading difficulties to early middle school students. Opportunities for vocabulary enrichment are minimal, but do include such words as (numbers in parentheses are page numbers):

slinks, *slinking* (13, 17),
groveling (13),
loping (20),
flustered (23),
commence (51),
humble (58),
devilment (61),
suspicious, *suspicions* (63, 82),
envy (66),
enthusiasm (99),
generous (103),
antibiotics (102),
allergic (115),
intention (120),
slogs (120),
regulation (122),
edgy (125),
lying by omission (130), and
jubilation (132).

INITIATING ACTIVITIES

1. For each of the five statements below, have students indicate whether they *Strongly agree*, *Agree*, *Disagree*, or *Strongly disagree*.
   a. It is always wrong to lie.
   b. People should never interfere in the business of others.
   c. Harming a helpless animal is just as bad as harming a human being.
   d. One lie always leads to another.
   e. Some people are by their nature mean and uncaring.

   Have students discuss their responses and attempt to come to a consensus.
2. Engage the class in a discussion of the following dilemma: You are shopping at a local store when you happen to see the mother of your best friend ahead in the personal care department. As you approach her to say hello, you see her look around quickly and then stuff several bottles of deodorant into her handbag. She then walks off. You are aware of the fact that your friend's family is having financial problems (the father was recently laid off at work), but this behavior shocks you. You are hurt and disappointed, and as you walk back to the store's entrance, you see a security guard at the door. What do you do?

DISCUSSION QUESTIONS

1. *Chapter 1:* What do we learn about Marty early in the chapter? What are some of his qualities? What do we learn about his family? What tells us they are not wealthy?
2. *Chapter 2:* How does Marty's dad feel about Shiloh? About relating to neighbors (like Judd)? What reasons does Marty give for not liking Judd Travers? Are the reasons all equally important? Elaborate. Do you agree with Dad that no one should interfere with how another person treats his or her animals? Why or why not?
3. *Chapter 3:* Are Marty's father and mother different from each other or similar? In what ways are they smart people? In what ways are they caring and sensitive? Why do the people on the mail route value the Sears catalog so much? By the end of the chapter, what do we know about Judd? Do you think that Marty's feelings about him are justified? Why or why not?

4. *Chapter 4:* Is Marty's dad an admirable man? In what ways? Do you think Marty's determination to keep Shiloh is realistic? Why or why not? Do you think he's doing the right thing?

5. *Chapter 5:* At the beginning of the chapter, Marty mentions three problems. Can you think of others that he is overlooking? When Judd Travers arrives, does Marty succeed in avoiding a lie? Explain. Is his avoidance the same thing as lying? How do you think Marty's dad feels about Judd?

6. *Chapter 6:* In this chapter, Marty argues with himself about lying. Do you think he is being honest with himself? Explain. What happens in the chapter to complicate things for Marty? Marty thinks, "Funny how one lie leads to another." Has this ever happened to you? Does your feeling toward Judd change in any way in this chapter? Explain.

7. *Chapter 7:* What are some different ways in which Marty begins to figure out how to get food for Shiloh? Can you predict what might happen as a result of these actions that he hasn't thought of? Who begins to notice how much time he's spending up on the hill? If Dara Lynn is noticing, who else might be noticing?

8. *Chapter 8:* How does Marty's secret become increasingly complicated? What do you think has led Ma to suspect Marty and thus discover the dog? In this chapter and others, how does the author build suspense for the reader?

9. *Chapter 9:* What else do we learn about Marty's mother in this chapter? Do you think she is more—or less—strict than Marty's father?

10. *Chapter 10:* At Doc Murphy's, why does Marty's dad make Marty do the talking? Describe the difference in the ways Marty and his dad see the problem involving Shiloh and Judd Travers. Why is the situation so complicated? At this point, can you think of a way Marty might convince his dad to keep Shiloh?

11. *Chapter 11:* Early in the chapter, what does Marty begin to realize? What does this realization tell us about him? Do you agree that "a secret is just too big for a little kid"? Why or why not?

12. *Chapter 12:* For the Prestons, what is the danger in having Shiloh around the house too long? When Judd Travers arrives, do you think it was fair for Marty's dad to make Marty explain the situation? Why or why not? How does Judd take advantage of the situation?

13. *Chapter 13:* At this point, the possibility of Marty's actually getting Shiloh from Judd Travers seems remote. Can you think of any approach he might use?

14. *Chapter 14:* When Marty stands next to Judd, why does he feel taller than he really is? Marty thinks to himself, "Way we're raised around here, children don't talk back to grown folks." Do you think this is a good idea? Why or why not? As Marty and Judd argue about Shiloh and the dead doe, do you think Marty is too willing to strike a bargain? Why or why not? Why doesn't he feel as good as he thought he would?

15. *Chapter 15:* How does Judd's behavior toward Marty begin to change? Why do you think this happens? What lessons does Marty think they are out to teach each other? Are the lessons equally important? Do they change? Why do you think Marty decides to keep his end of the bargain? And finally, why does Judd decide to keep his as well? By the end of the book, do we feel any different at all toward Judd? Has he changed at all? How has Marty changed? What does he mean at the end by "nothing is as simple as you guess—not right or wrong, not Judd Travers, not even me or this dog I got here"?

WRITING ACTIVITIES

1. Marty uses lots of similes when he describes Shiloh, especially the dog's tail: "tail sticking up like a flagpole," "tail going like a propeller," and "tail going like a windshield wiper." Write a description of your own pet in which you use at least three similes.
2. To Marty, a dog's name is important: He names Shiloh with care and later criticizes Judd Travers for naming his dogs Git, Scram, Out, and Dammit. Do some research on names that people pick for dogs and other animals. What are the most popular dog names in America? Cat names? Horse names? Check animal or pet encyclopedias in the library or on the Internet.
3. Write about a time in your life when one lie led to another. Be sure to tell what the lies were, how they built upon each other, and what the results were.
4. In chapter 2, Marty and his dad argue briefly over Judd's treatment of Shiloh, with Marty asking, "What if it was a child?" Write a short paper explaining your views on animal abuse versus child abuse. How are they similar? How are they different?
5. Find out about how your community deals with animals that are reportedly abused. Is your county like Tyler County, with not enough money to investigate such cases? Write up your findings in a two- to three-page paper.
6. In the last chapter, Marty comments on his community's belief that it's always wrong to report one's neighbor to the authorities even if a law is broken: "That's the way it's always been around here." Another example of a tradition that most communities uphold is that it's wrong to criticize someone else's religious practices. With one other student, make a list of several other similar traditions or accepted beliefs in your community. Indicate the degree to which the two of you agree with each of them.
7. In chapter 9, Marty's mother sings a stanza from a country love song ("It's you I wanna come home to . . ."). Using the same pattern and rhythm, write a similar song that Marty might have written that expresses his love for Shiloh. Try to write at least two stanzas.
8. Marty speaks a version of nonstandard English, the dialect of much of small-town and rural America. A good example of this is on page 43 (second paragraph from the top). Read the paragraph and note any words or expressions that are different from the way you talk. How might the expressions differ if Marty were, for example, the son of a doctor or a teacher? Rewrite the paragraph in standard English. Does the rewritten version "lose" anything?

OTHER ACTIVITIES

1. With two other students, role play the scene that Marty remembers in the grocery store when Judd cheats Mr. Wallace out of ten dollars. First act it out as Marty remembers it. Then act out a different version in which the student playing Marty responds differently by continuing to challenge Judd.
2. Marty's family is obviously very important to him. Design a coat of arms for the Preston family, taking into consideration the apparent values and interests of the family.
3. Conduct a class debate on the pros and cons of the following statement: Animals have no rights.

4. Pretend that Marty decides that he has to tell his parents about Judd's killing the doe. Role play the scene where he explains this to his parents. How would they react? Would they have required Marty to return the dog?
5. Much is made in the novel of the complications involving laws and how they are or might be interpreted. Pretend that Judd Travers refuses at the end of the book to let Marty have Shiloh and that Marty and his parents decide to take the matter to court. Conduct some preliminary research on how laws and courts in your community deal with such matters. Then role play a mock trial or hearing involving Marty and his parents, Judd Travers, a judge or magistrate, and other required participants.
6. Based on the limited descriptions of setting in the novel (especially in chapter 1), draw a map of the parts of Tyler County that are prominently mentioned: the Preston house, the hill where Shiloh is hidden, Judd Travers's trailer, the Shiloh schoolhouse, the river, and the towns of Friendly and Sistersville. Don't be overly concerned with complete accuracy; just try to convey a sense of where these places might be, especially in relationship to each other.

SELECTED TEACHING RESOURCES

Media Aids

Cassettes (2)

Shiloh. Unabridged, 183 min. Bantam Audio Publishing and Perma-Bound, 1992.

Internet

Kramer, Laurie. 1996–1998. *Beagles on the Web*. Available: http://www.beagles-on-the-web.com/ (Accessed March 10, 2000).

A jumping-off place for over 250 home pages on the breed, including photos, adoption sites, and beagle FAQs.

Video

Shiloh. 93 min., color. Perfection Learning Corporation, 1997.

Printed Materials

Articles

Naylor, Phyllis Reynolds. "Newbery Acceptance Speech." *The Horn Book Magazine* 68 (July/August 1992): 404–411.

Naylor, Phyllis Reynolds. "The Writing of *Shiloh*." *The Reading Teacher* 46 (September 1992): 10–12.

Teaching Aids

Shiloh. Novel Unit Guide and Novel Units Student Packet. Perma-Bound.

Shiloh. Novel-Ties. Learning Links.

Shiloh. Reading Beyond the Basal Plus series. Perfection Learning Corporation.

Tuck Everlasting

Natalie Babbitt

New York: Farrar, Straus & Giroux, 1975

Available in paperback from Farrar, Straus & Giroux.

SUMMARY

A ten-year-old girl named Winnie is kidnapped by a family of friendly folk named the Tucks, who harbor an awesome secret: In a nearby wood, they long ago drank from a magic fountain that gave them eternal life. Convinced that the water is more curse than blessing, they spirit Winnie away from her family. Their well-intentioned deed, however, is complicated by a mysterious man in a yellow suit, who overhears the secret being told by the Tucks and tries to take advantage. His plan to get rich by marketing the magic water to "the most deserving people," however, is thwarted by Mae Tuck, who kills him with a blow to the head and then escapes from jail with the help of Winnie and the other Tucks. All of this leaves Winnie faced with her own eventual decision: whether or not to drink the water when she turns seventeen, then marry the Tucks' son Jesse and live happily ever after.

APPRAISAL

Since its publication in 1975, *Tuck Everlasting* has become a favorite fantasy among students and teachers in grades five and six, if not earlier. The book's compelling premise and plot, its beautiful descriptions of setting, and its picturesque characters and dialogue combine to make a unique reading experience that promotes much thought and discussion. This is one of those books that might be best read aloud to a class, for two reasons: Its rhythms and language lend themselves beautifully to oral reading, and oral reading allows the teacher to prevent children from reading ahead and thus undermining the effect that thoughtful questions can have on the discussion of the carefully developed series of events and the provocative themes.

THEMES

immortality, death, change, the purpose of living, right and wrong behavior

LITERARY CONCEPTS

setting, figurative language (especially simile and metaphor), imagery, plot, foreshadowing, characterization, recurring symbol, personification, fantasy

RELATED READING

Students who like Natalie Babbitt's whimsical style and characters might want to read her other books for young adolescents, including *The Search for Delicious*, *Kneeknock Rise*, *Goody Hall*, and *The Eyes of the Amaryllis*. If they haven't read it before, some might consider the classic *Alice's Adventures in Wonderland* by Lewis Carroll.

READING PROBLEMS AND OPPORTUNITIES

With its very short chapters and approachable style, *Tuck Everlasting* is easy to read. Still, like the best books for children and young adults, the novel challenges its readers with many words that are often colorful, wonderfully used, and often definable by their context. They include the following (numbers refer to chapters):

balmy (Prologue),
tangent (1),
ambled (1),
tranquil (1),
bovine (1),
contemplation (1),
infinite (1),
oppressive (1),
forlorn (1),
accessible (1),
melancholy (2, 9),
rueful (2),
hysterical (3),
intrusions (3),
resentful (3, 5, 20),
exasperated (3),
jaunty (4),
self-deprecation (4),
retorted (4),
reluctant (4, 5, 23),
galling (5),
disheartened (5),
consolingly (5),
irrelevantly (5),
primly (5),
plaintive (5, 23),
perversely (6, 25),
dismay (6),
implored (6),
distractedly (6),
faltered (6),
scornful (8),
elated, elation (8, 11),
receded (8, 24),
vanity (9),
vigorous (9),
revived (9),
embankment (9),
homely (9, 10),
pitiless (10),
indomitable (10),
perilous (10),
lolled (10),
aimlessly (10),
cavernous (10),
disarray (10),
luxurious (11),
anguish (12),
earnestly (14),
barbarian (15),
illiterates (15),
companionable (16),
grudgingly (16),
cantering (16),
absently (17),
alien (18),
petulance (19),
ghastly (19),
unflinchingly (20),
acrid (21),
exertion (22),
ponderous (23),
remorseless (23),
gentility (23),
prostrate (23),
protruding (24),
exultant (24),
sedately (25),
profoundly (25),
unwittingly (25),
constricted (25),
apprehension (25),
wistful (25),
staunchly (25),
revulsion (25),
catholic (Epilogue), and
imposing (Epilogue).

INITIATING ACTIVITIES

1. Bring to class a jar of sweetened, colored water. Tell the class that you want them to imagine that it has a very special power: If someone drinks it, he or she will live forever. Pour some of the water in a glass or cup and pass it around. Ask the students to take a sip *if* they feels they would like to have this power. After everyone has had the opportunity to choose, have them talk about why they decided as they did.
2. Have students discuss (or write about) what they would do—how they would live—if they knew they would live forever. How might it change their lives?

DISCUSSION QUESTIONS

1. *Prologue:* How does the author make us feel about autumn? What are the three events that seem to have no connection? What are some things in this chapter that turn? (Think about the obvious—and the not-so-obvious.) What are some unanswered questions in the prologue?
2. *Chapter 1:* What kind of mood is created by the setting of the road, the first house, and the wood? In this chapter, Natalie Babbitt makes us think about the nature of property. What are some other questions the author raises? Why do you think noticing the spring hidden by pebbles beneath the ash tree at the center of the wood would have been so disastrous?
3. *Chapter 2:* What are the Tucks like? How do Mae and Tuck seem to differ? What seems a little mysterious about them? What is their clothing like? What is finally confirmed about them at the end of the chapter?
4. *Chapter 3:* Why is Winnie unhappy? Why does she think of running away?
5. *Chapter 4:* What do you make of the stranger? Does he seem kind? Pleasant? Odd in any way? How does Winnie react to him? Why do you think he asks so many questions? Are his questions harmless? How does Winnie's grandmother seem to feel about him? What do you think the elf music might be? By the end of chapter 4, we have been introduced to the book's main characters: Winnie, the Tucks, and the man in the yellow suit. How do you think they will connect with each other later?
6. *Chapter 5:* What is Winnie afraid of? In the clearing in the wood, why is she so struck by the sight of the boy? What is he like? Why do you think Jesse—and then his mother and brother—seem to believe that "the worst is happening at last"?
7. *Chapter 6:* How does Winnie feel about the kidnapping? Is she afraid? Why doesn't she call out to the man in the yellow suit? Why does the music calm her?
8. *Chapter 7:* Often we hear someone say, "I wish I could live forever." From the Tucks' account, what problems do we begin to see about being in such a state? Can you think of other problems that might develop?
9. *Chapter 8:* Do all of the Tucks feel the same about the power they have? How do Winnie's feelings toward her predicament begin to change, and why? At this point, how do you think she feels about the water? What effect do you think the eavesdropping of the man in the yellow suit will have on the story? Why does he smile?
10. *Chapter 9:* Natalie Babbitt writes beautiful description. Find some examples of this in the first few pages of this chapter. (Looking ahead, find other examples in chapter 10.)

11. *Chapter 10:* What more do we learn about Winnie's upbringing in this chapter? Aside from their immortality, how do the Tucks differ from Winnie's family? Which do you think you would prefer? Why? What are some good things about order? About disorder? What do all the details of the cottage tell us about the Tucks? Throughout, what have we learned about how Miles and Jesse differ?

12. *Chapter 11:* How and why does Winnie's attitude toward the Tucks change during the meal? Why do you think Angus Tuck wants to be the one who takes Winnie out on the pond? In what way does the author remind us of a possible lingering threat? How does Winnie now view the man in the yellow suit?

13. *Chapters 12 and 13:* What does Tuck compare the water to? How does he broaden the comparison? (Compare this with the things that turn in the Prologue.) What does he compare the stuck rowboat to? Why does he see living forever as, at best, a mixed blessing? Why do you think he thinks most people would "trample each other, trying to get some of that water?" At the end of the chapter why might the theft of the horse be such a problem? In all likelihood, what has happened? Why do you think the author made chapter 13 so short? What do you think the man in the yellow suit is planning to do?

14. *Chapter 14:* Why are the Tucks so attentive to Winnie? Why do you think Natalie Babbitt chose to portray Jesse as one in favor of drinking the water? Do you think Jesse's suggestion to Winnie about returning to marry him is a good idea? Why or why not?

15. *Chapter 15:* Why do you think Natalie Babbitt chose not to give the man in the yellow suit a name? Does he seem evil to you, or just greedy? Do you like his courteous manner? Why or why not? Why don't the family members respond to him?

16. *Chapter 16:* The constable asks the man in the yellow suit what he plans to do with the land. What do you think his plans are?

17. *Chapter 17:* How does the time fishing with Miles affect Winnie's thoughts about living and dying? Why is it all so complicated?

18. *Chapter 18:* Why does Winnie love the Tucks? Are her thoughts about them, especially about Jesse, realistic? Why or why not? Why is Angus Tuck to her "the dearest of them all"?

19. *Chapter 19:* How do you feel about the man in the yellow suit's plan to sell the water only "to people who deserve it"? What kind of people does he think these are? Are some people or kinds of people more deserving of such a "blessing" than others? How do you feel about similar issues in our own times involving cloning or genetic engineering? At the end of the chapter, does Mae Tuck overreact to the situation?

20. *Chapter 20:* Why does Tuck look enviously at the man in the yellow suit? Why does he react the way he does when the constable mentions the gallows for Mae?

21. *Chapter 21:* Why don't Winnie's parents and grandmother want to believe her? How does Winnie feel she is different now? "Now *she* would have to do something. She had no idea what, but something." What do you think Winnie might do to resolve the situation? Now that the man in the yellow suit has died, how do you feel about what Mae did?

22. *Chapter 22:* "At midnight she would make a difference in the world." How do you feel about such a statement? Is wanting to make such a difference a good thing? How might it not be good? Even if you wanted to make a positive difference, might there be ways in which making it would be bad?

23. *Chapter 23:* How would a "lapse from gentility" make one more interesting? What kinds of mixed feelings does Winnie have as she waits in her room? Do you feel she is planning to do the right thing? Why or why not?

24. *Chapter 24:* Why does Winnie keep thinking about the old poem about "stone bars"? Does it possibly have larger meanings? (In what ways is Mae Tuck a prisoner?) Why does Winnie wonder if Miles will put the nails back in? Do you think she is disappointed to find that he has not?

25. *Chapter 25:* On the basis of the opening paragraph, what do you think has happened between chapters 24 and 25? This chapter once more repeats the reference to August and to "the wheel turning again." How does this image reinforce one of the major ideas in the book? What is about to happen in Treegate and elsewhere? Why do Winnie's parents forgive her? Does Winnie's giving the toad the water suggest what her future decision will be regarding herself? At this point, what do you think she will decide—and why?

26. *Epilogue:* What do we learn about the span of years covered by this story? When Tuck finds Winnie's gravestone, why is he sad? Why does he say, "Good girl"? Do you think the brief incident with the toad at the end is an effective way to end the book? Why or why not? Why do you think the author has the toad appear again and again throughout the book?

WRITING ACTIVITIES

1. On page 56 in the book there is a very brief description of the water cycle. Using science reference works or perhaps the Internet (or both), present a much more detailed report on this phenomenon to the class, complete with visuals.

2. There are a number of questions about the Tucks' immortality that the book does not address. For example, if Winnie drank the water at age seventeen, married Jesse, and they had a child, would the child be born with the same power? What if the Tucks refused to eat anything? Would they waste away or still not change? Try to pose answers to these questions in a brief conjectural paper to be read to the class. Consider other questions you think of as well.

3. At one point, Jesse says, "Why, heck, life's to enjoy yourself, isn't it?" At other times, Winnie and others suggest that there are other purposes for living. Write a paper in which you discuss some purposes for living and your own view of which one is the most important.

4. Winnie's father is mentioned here and there throughout the book, but we never see or hear him. Write a character sketch of what you think he was like. Also be prepared to tell the class why you think he is virtually invisible in the novel.

5. When Mae Tuck is faced with the prospect of being hanged, the Tucks are beside themselves with anxiety. Her rescue, of course, prevents this from happening. Pretend, however, that the rescue does not occur and that the hanging is about to take place. Write a page or two on what you think would have happened.

6. In the epilogue, we learn that Winnie's life covered the years between 1880 and 1950, yet we know next to nothing about it. Write a two- to three-page paper that speculates about what you think happened to her.

7. On Winnie's gravestone there is the briefest of epitaphs. Write another epitaph in the form of a rhyming couplet that reflects in some way the values she had and perhaps the decision she made.

8. Give the man in the yellow suit a name. Make sure the name fits him. A name like "John Jones" is too bland and unrevealing, whereas a name like "Snidely Snerdly" is more suggestive. (*Note to teacher:* Have a class contest for the most appropriate name, with the winner decided by class vote.)

9. One of the reasons why *Tuck Everlasting* speaks to us today as readers is that we hear more and more in the news about the role science may play in the near future in extending our lives—indeed, even in making us, in effect, immortal. Conduct some research on cloning, especially on the question and potential of cloning human beings, and report to the class.

10. The book makes a convincing case against living forever, but one could probably build an argument for the opposing point of view. Write a paper in which you present some positives about avoiding death, such as the ability to witness the historical development of one's family through the years and centuries.

OTHER ACTIVITIES

1. Paint a watercolor picture based on one of the many descriptive scenes in the book. (For example, the beginning of chapter 12 states, "The sky was a ragged blaze of red and pink and orange, and its double trembled on the surface of the pond like color spilled from a paintbox.")

2. Try to find a recording, perhaps in your public library, that represents for you the tinkling, melodic sound of the music box. Probably solo piano or harp pieces will be the best sources. Then play the piece for the class.

3. *Tuck Everlasting* is full of homey sayings or proverbs (or the raw material for them), such as "Living's heavy work" and "Never make a fortress out of duty." Choose one of these sayings that you like and write it in calligraphy. Decorate it with a border that supports the idea presented.

4. With three other students, role play the scene at the end of chapter 18 where the man in the yellow suit tells Winnie's parents and grandmother about what he has discovered. Be sure to have the family members ask questions that you think would be uppermost in their minds.

5. Write and draw a wanted poster for Mae Tuck's capture after she escapes from jail. Take into consideration the description of her in chapter 2 and elsewhere.

6. Throughout the book, but especially in chapter 12, the Tucks make fervent statements about the joy and beauty of living (even to the point of including death as a part of it). Design a collage of pictures, words clipped from magazines, and even found objects that reflect for you the joy and beauty of life.

7. Conduct a mock trial of Mae Tuck. You will need students to take on the roles of Mae and her defense attorney (with perhaps an assistant), a prosecuting attorney (and assistant), a judge, a jury, and witnesses.

SELECTED TEACHING RESOURCES

Media Aids

Cassettes (2)

Tuck Everlasting. 3 hrs. Audio Bookshelf.

Tuck Everlasting. Listening Library.

Cassettes (3)

Tuck Everlasting. 3.5 hrs. Recorded Books, Perma-Bound, and Sundance.

Internet

A + LS/Media Weaver, Elementary Novels Bundle II, *Tuck Everlasting*. Available: http://www.amered.com/curr/mwtuk.html (Accessed March 4, 2000).
Additional thinking, writing, and discussion activities related to *Tuck Everlasting*.

Video

Good Conversation! A Talk with Natalie Babbitt. 20 min., color. Tim Podell Products, 1995. Features *Tuck Everlasting*.

Printed Resources

Articles

Aippersbach, Kim. "*Tuck Everlasting* and the Tree at the Center of the World." *Children's Literature in Education* 21 (June 1990): 83–97.

Dillon, Doris, and Valerie Lewis. "Meet the Author: Natalie Babbitt." *Instructor* 102 (January 1993): 57–59.

Hartvigsen, M. Kip, and Christen Brog Hartvigsen. " 'Rough and Soft, Both at Once': Winnie Foster's Initiation in *Tuck Everlasting*." *Children's Literature in Education* 18 (Fall 1987): 176–183.

Teaching Aids

Tuck Everlasting. Bookwise Literature Guides. Christopher-Gordon Publishers.

Tuck Everlasting. LIFT series. Sundance.

Tuck Everlasting. Reading Beyond the Basal Plus series and Portals to Reading series. Perfection Learning Corporation.

Tuck Everlasting. Novel Units Student Packet and Perma-Guide. Perma-Bound.

Tuck Everlasting. Novel/Drama Curriculum Units. The Center for Learning.

Tuck Everlasting. Novel-Ties. Learning Links.

Test

Tuck Everlasting. Alternative assessment version. Perfection Learning Corporation.

Number the Stars

Lois Lowry

Boston: Houghton Mifflin, 1989

Available in paperback from Bantam, Doubleday, Dell Books for Young Readers.

SUMMARY

The year is 1943, the location is Copenhagen, Denmark, and two ten-year-old friends—AnneMarie Johansen and Ellen Rosen—enjoy their lives as much as possible given the shortages of food and clothing brought about by the Nazi invasion of their town. AnneMarie's parents try to hide the evils of war from their daughters AnneMarie and Kirsti, but when the German soldiers threaten to take Ellen and her parents away, possibly to a concentration camp, AnneMarie's parents take Ellen in, pretending she is their own daughter Lise, who died several years earlier. Ellen's parents flee, and Mrs. Johansen then steals away with all three girls to her brother's farm, where a plan is laid to take Ellen, her parents, and other Jewish refugees to Sweden by boat. When a special handkerchief treated to impair the Nazis' dogs' sense of smell is nearly lost, AnneMarie bravely faces the dangers of walking through the woods full of soldiers and delivering the handkerchief so that the Jewish people on the boats are not detected by the dogs. AnneMarie keeps Ellen's Star of David necklace, awaiting her return one day.

APPRAISAL

Number the Stars has been showered with accolades. It was the 1990 Newbery Award Winner, a School Library Journal Best Book of the Year, an American Bookseller Pick of the Lists, and an American Library Association Notable Book. This historical fiction makes very real the plight of the Danes and the Jewish people in Denmark during World War II. Lois Lowry, by drawing on her friendships, her research, and her own experiences, takes the reader back to a time of great hardships but also great determination, when the Danes helped hide and smuggle out to Sweden nearly 7,000 Jewish residents. These tales of courage and human decency, coupled with excitement and adventure, draw readers and make a lasting impression on their minds and hearts. While this book could be taught at a variety of levels, sixth and seventh graders would most readily empathize with the main characters.

THEMES

friendship, prejudice, human dignity, war, self-sacrifice, courage, faith, trust, persecution, hope

LITERARY CONCEPTS

plot, character development, symbolism, setting, historical fiction

RELATED READING

Other works that deal effectively with the Nazi terrorism include *The Diary of Anne Frank*, *The Upstairs Room* by Johanna Reiss, and *Survive: Stories of Jewish Children Rescued from the Holocaust* by Maxine B. Rosenberg. Elie Wiesel presents the story of a Jewish boy in a German concentration camp in *Night*.

READING PROBLEMS AND OPPORTUNITIES

The vocabulary of this novel poses difficulties in only a few places. German words or expressions, such as *Halte* (1), *nein* (15), or *De Frei Danske* (16), may require translation. Other possibilities for vocabulary study may include (chapter numbers are given in parentheses):

rucksack (1),
sneering (1),
defiantly (1),
obstinate (1),
crocheting (2),
trousseau (2),
dawdled (3),
haughtily (3),
unruly (3),
sarcastically (3),
swastika (3),
disdainfully (4),
imperious (5),
intoned (5),
Star of David (5),
tentatively (6),
ruefully (8),
specter (8),
deftly (9),
condescending (10),
brusque (14),
taut (14), and
warily (16).

INITIATING ACTIVITIES

1. Research the Nazi invasion and the Resistance movements in Denmark during World War II. Check specifically on key facts related to the capital city, including its products, famous authors, government, history, and famous landmarks. Share your information with your classmates and prepare a chart to show what information you have gathered. This information will help you to understand what is happening in *Number the Stars* as you read about the adventures of AnneMarie and her family.

2. How far would you go to protect a friend? Make a list of actions you would take to protect a friend from being injured physically or emotionally. Try to list at least ten actions. Save this list for an activity after reading the book.

DISCUSSION QUESTIONS

1. *Chapter 1:* What is AnneMarie's attitude toward the soldiers? Why is AnneMarie's attitude different from Kirsti's?

2. *Chapter 2:* How is the fairy tale that AnneMarie tells like her life? How is it different?

3. *Chapter 3:* Why are Mr. and Mrs. Johansen so concerned about the closing of Hirsch's store?
4. *Chapter 4:* What are the differences between the fireworks that AnneMarie remembers and those that Kirsti remembers? How could the King of Denmark be both sad and proud? Why is it necessary for AnneMarie and Ellen to pretend to be sisters? Explain the difficulties they might have in doing this.
5. *Chapter 5:* How is Mr. Johansen able to convince the soldiers that Ellen is his daughter Lise? Why is it a good thing that Kirsti remains asleep during the interrogation by the Nazi soldiers?
6. *Chapter 6:* Is Mrs. Johansen right to take the girls to her brother's house by herself? Why or why not? How do Mrs. Johansen and AnneMarie feel about Henrik's place?
7. *Chapter 7:* Why is Mrs. Johansen so afraid of contact with others?
8. *Chapter 8:* What preparations are made in the house? Why does Uncle Henrik say that they were made? Why doesn't AnneMarie believe him?
9. *Chapter 9:* Why do Uncle Henrik and Mama lie to AnneMarie? When she confronts him, why does he confess that he lied but still not tell her the truth? How does this make AnneMarie a wiser person?
10. *Chapter 10:* How does Mama trick the soldiers? Why is Peter's selection of a psalm particularly appropriate?
11. *Chapter 11:* How have the Rosens changed in appearance? How have they not changed in reality?
12. *Chapter 12:* How does AnneMarie compare the fear and the danger she faces to what her mother is facing? Is she right? Why or why not?
13. *Chapter 13:* In what ways does AnneMarie show her courage? Why doesn't she question any of her mother's directions?
14. *Chapter 14:* How is AnneMarie's journey through the woods like Little Red Riding Hood's trip? How is it different?
15. *Chapter 15:* How does AnneMarie handle the soldiers who stop her? How else might she have behaved? Does she make the right choice? Why or why not? Why do you think the handkerchief is so important?
16. *Chapter 16:* Why does Uncle Henrik answer AnneMarie's questions about the Rosens' escape?
17. *Chapter 17:* Why didn't Mr. and Mrs. Johansen know that Lise was part of the Resistance? What signs of hope do you find at the end of this novel?

WRITING ACTIVITIES

1. In chapter 2, AnneMarie tells her sister Kirsti a fairy tale, like those of Hans Christian Andersen. Review the tales of Andersen, looking for elements that are found in every tale. Then try your hand at creating your own fairy tale, making sure that you have all the key elements. Ask some of your classmates to pretend to be Kirsti. Read the tale to them and ask them to react as she would have reacted.

2. AnneMarie questions whether she is willing to die to help the Rosens. Write a letter to the editor of the local paper about a cause that you believe is worth dying for. Explain why your cause is so important and why it is worthy of the ultimate sacrifice.
3. AnneMarie is not certain what bravery is. She is confused about whether it is better to understand a situation fully or have only a bit of knowledge so others cannot trip you up. Prepare a list poem for AnneMarie using events from the novel. Begin the poem with "Bravery is ..." and list at least ten items to complete the poem. Try your hand at a second poem with the same theme, but this time, list events from the news. Compare and contrast the two poems.
4. AnneMarie goes through a scary time in her life when she knows only a part of what is happening because her relatives hide the truth from her. Gradually, she learns about the plot to help the Jews escape. Write a story about a similar time in your life when you weren't certain what was happening but you moved forward and everything eventually was revealed to you.
5. In chapter 11, Peter calls Mrs. Johansen by her first name, a sign that he is now on equal footing as an adult. Moving from childhood to adulthood often involves a rite of passage (i.e., a specific event—graduation, marriage, first job—that is symbolic of achieving adulthood). Write a description of a rite of passage that is common in your community. Give very specific details about how the rite is carried out and what symbolism is part of the ceremony.
6. Throughout the book several characters experience pride. Select one of the characters whose actions illustrate the effects that pride can have. Write a character sketch of this individual, emphasizing the effect of pride on his or her life. Illustrate your sketch with a freehand drawing or computer-prepared picture of this individual.
7. Prepare a poem on the effects of prejudice. You may choose a simple list poem or a more difficult form such as a sonnet or haiku. Share your poem with your classmates and use the class's poems as a springboard for discussion on why such hatred persists.
8. At the end of the book, Lois Lowry explains what prompted her to write this particular book about this particular young girl. Write a letter to Lois Lowry (check for her address in *Contemporary Authors* or on the Internet) and ask her any questions that you had that were not answered in the Afterword. Share any responses you get from her with your classmates.

OTHER ACTIVITIES

1. Throughout the novel, the main characters suffer from a lack of basic food and supplies because many items have been rationed. Conduct research on rationing during World War II. Look especially for the answers to questions such as: What items were rationed? Why was rationing necessary? How effective was the rationing system? What items were used as substitutes for rationed items? Prepare and post a chart of your findings. Set aside a rationing day in class. Ask everyone to agree on what items will be rationed, for example, pieces of paper, erasers, and snacks. After the day is over, discuss with your classmates your reactions to rationing.

2. Throughout the novel, the Danish people speak in code to one another. List examples of this code from the novel and write an explanation of their meaning. Evaluate the effectiveness of the code; for example, was it easy to remember but not too obvious to the enemy? Suggest other codes that you think might be equally or more effective.
3. In the time that this story is set, men and women had very distinctly defined roles. However, the war changed all that. Make a list of at least eight statements from the novel that indicate clearly how men and women were expected to behave and what their jobs were. After researching how and why men's and women's roles changed during World War II, prepare a chart listing ideas, attitudes, and occupations before and after the war.
4. Improvise the scene when the soldiers wake up the household during the night (chapter 5). To improvise, you need to be very familiar with the scene and with the character you are playing so that you can respond to a situation in the same way that he or she might have; however, you do not need to recite speeches from the novel word-for-word. In short, you need to portray the way the character would probably act. Try changing the scene in several ways; for example, Peter comes into the room while the soldiers are there, or Kirsti wakes and comes in to give the soldiers a piece of her mind. How might this change the entire plot?
5. Prepare or plan a web page for *Number the Stars*. What information would others like to have about the book? What links would you include to other sites? How would the page be organized? What other types of opportunities would you include: sign in, chat room, bulletin board for sharing ideas and responses to the novel, etc.? What graphics would you use? If possible, prepare this page and have it posted on your school's server.

SELECTED TEACHING RESOURCES

Media Aids

Cassettes (3)

Number the Stars. 3.5 hours. Recorded Books.

Internet

Hurst, Carol Otis. *Carol Hurst's Children's Literature Site.* Available: http://www.carolhurst.com./titles/numberthestars.html (Accessed March 10, 2000).
A guide to exploring the novel, including discussion topics, activities, and related books.

Learning About Lois Lowry. Available: http://www.scils.rutgers.edu/special/kay/lowry.html (Accessed March 10, 2000).
A useful site containing a brief biography, a bibliography of Lois Lowry's works, reviews of her books, and awards.

Videos

The Courage To Care. 30 min., color. PBS Video.
Presents individuals who cared enough to save the lives of many Jews during the Holocaust.

Number the Stars. 15 min., color. Read On: Cover to Cover series. PBS Video.

Printed Resources

Articles

Dobson, Dorothy. "Getting a Grip on World War II." *Instructor* 104 (March 1995): 40.

Elleman, Barbara. "Bringing a Book to Life: An Interview with Lois Lowry." *New Advocate* 11 (Summer 1998): 193–201.

Lowry, Lois. "*Number the Stars*: Lois Lowry's Journey to the Newbery Award." *The Reading Teacher* 44 (October 1990): 98–101.

Walter, Virginia A. "Metaphor and Mantra: The Function of Stories in *Number the Stars*." *Children's Literature in Education* 27 (June 1996): 123–130.

Teaching Aids

Number the Stars. Bookwise Literature Guides. Christopher-Gordon Publishers.

Number the Stars. Connect Social Studies series. Sundance.

Number the Stars. Novel Unit Guide and Novel Units Student Packet. Perma-Bound.

Number the Stars. Novel/Drama Curriculum Units. The Center for Learning.

Number the Stars. Novel-Ties. Learning Links.

Number the Stars. Reading Beyond the Basal Plus series, Portals to Reading series, and Portals Plus series. Perfection Learning Corporation.

Tests

Number the Stars. Essay, objective, and alternative assessment versions. Perfection Learning Corporation.

The Sign of the Beaver

Elizabeth George Speare

Boston: Houghton Mifflin Company, 1984

Available in paperback from Bantam Doubleday Dell Books for Young Readers.

SUMMARY

Twelve-year-old Matt must rely on his own resources to maintain his family's new home in Maine while his father returns to Massachusetts to bring out the rest of the family. Matt is too trusting and foolhardy and might have died from an attack by bees had he not been rescued by Saknis, the Indian chief, and his grandson Attean. In exchange for teaching Attean to read, Matt is given lessons on survival in the wilderness by Attean. The two gain respect for one another as Attean learns of the adventures of Robinson Crusoe and Matt learns to hunt, fish, and make provisions for himself. After months have passed and Matt's family has not arrived, Attean and his tribe move on, asking Matt to go with them. Matt, however, cannot give up hope of being reunited with his family and stays on in the company of Attean's trusty dog. Finally, Matt's family does arrive; however, he is not able to explain successfully to them the great lessons he has learned from Attean and the members of his tribe.

APPRAISAL

A Newbery Honor Book, *The Sign of the Beaver* has remained a favorite with students and teachers alike because, as well as being an exciting story of survival in the wilderness, it is a well-crafted piece of historical fiction. The novel provides great insights on cultural diversity and the importance of cultures learning from one another. The two central characters grow and mature in ways that are realistic. Elizabeth Speare has a well-deserved reputation for bringing to light historical periods while universalizing the human experience. This book is most often taught in grades six and seven.

THEMES

survival, values, Native American heritage, cultural diversity, courage, friendship, communication, understanding others

LITERARY CONCEPTS

character development, symbolism, foreshadowing, setting, literary allusions, historical fiction

RELATED READING

Students interested in novels related to the settling of America might enjoy books in the Laura Ingalls Wilder series, beginning with *Little House on the Prairie*, as well as classics such as *Caddie Woodlawn*. For those students who seek the thrills of survival in the wilderness, *Julie of the Wolves* or *The Call of the Wild* might be good choices. Check *A Bibliography of Native Americans* at http://www.ipl.org/ref/native/biblio2.html (Accessed March 10, 2000) for a variety of books on Native Americans. Finally, interested students would benefit from reading *Robinson Crusoe*, either before or after reading this book, to grasp the parallel ironies in these two works.

READING PROBLEMS AND OPPORTUNITIES

The Sign of the Beaver is an easy book for young people to read. The vocabulary is relatively simple and the sentence structure is not complex. Opportunities for vocabulary study focus on words used during the historical period and a few other terms with which students might not be familiar (chapter numbers are in parentheses):

puncheon (1),
matchlock (1),
blunderbuss (1),
passel (3),
disdainfully (7),
contemptuous (9),
incomprehensible (10),
cuff (11),
disgruntled (11),
chagrined (12),
defiant (13),
shrewdly (13),
distracted (15),
clamor (16),
boisterous (16),
contortions (16),
genial (17),
wampum (17),
warily (18),
placid (18), and
blustering (18).

INITIATING ACTIVITIES

1. If your parents left you alone for several months, how would you manage? What would you need to survive? Make a list of the items and compare your list with ones made by your classmates. As you read the novel, compare your list to the items that Matt had to help him during his parents' absence.
2. Research the settlement of the New England states. Prepare a map or chart to show when the various parts of this area were settled. Discuss with your classmates the reasons that people might have had for moving into a new area.

DISCUSSION QUESTIONS

1. *Chapter 1:* How does Matt help his father prepare for the arrival of his family? What presents does Matt's father give him? Why does his father give Matt these gifts?
2. *Chapter 2:* Why does Matt like being on his own? Why doesn't he like being on his own? What would you miss most if you were left alone in your home? What does Matt fear? What would you fear most?
3. *Chapter 3:* What clues do you find that reveal Ben's true character during his visit with Matt? Which of his past deeds does he reveal? Which are implied? What action clearly shows his nature? How do you think Matt will be able to survive?

4. *Chapter 4:* Compare Matt's encounter with the bear to his encounter with Ben. What does he lose in each case? Are either or both of these losses Matt's fault? Why or why not?
5. *Chapter 5:* What causes Matt to risk angering the bees? Is he foolish to take this chance? Why or why not? In what ways do the Indians minister to Matt? What might have happened to him if they hadn't arrived when they did?
6. *Chapter 6:* Why doesn't Matt feel that he can trust Saknis? How do the Indians know where to bring Matt? How do Saknis and Attean help Matt? How does he try to repay them? What does he fear because of the error of his gift? How do Saknis's and Attean's attitudes toward the white man differ?
7. *Chapter 7:* What is Matt's attitude toward teaching Attean to read? What is Attean's attitude toward learning to read? If you were Matt, how would you attempt to teach Attean?
8. *Chapter 8:* Is Matt's new approach to teaching Attean more effective than his previous one? Why or why not?
9. *Chapter 9:* Why doesn't Attean like the section of *Robinson Crusoe* about the rescue of the man Friday? What upsets him about this passage? Do you agree that one should die before becoming a slave? Why or why not?
10. *Chapter 10:* Why is it necessary for Matt to read selectively from *Robinson Crusoe*? How do their fishing adventures draw Attean and Matt closer together?
11. *Chapter 11:* Why does Attean keep the dog? How has the relationship between Matt and Attean changed? What is the sign of the beaver? How is it used?
12. *Chapter 12:* How is Matt's game of Indians back in Quincy different from his current experiences with Attean? What lessons does Matt learn from making a bow and arrows and learning to shoot?
13. *Chapter 13:* What are the key differences between the Indians' way of hunting and the white man's way? Explain the irony in Matt's relationship with Attean. What are the sources of irony?
14. *Chapter 14:* What are the key similarities between Attean's story of Gluskai and Matt's story of Noah?
15. *Chapter 15:* Matt feels that killing the bear was essential; Attean apologizes to the bear. Who is right? Defend your position.
16. *Chapter 16:* What mixed feelings does Matt experience as he approaches the Indian encampment? When in your life have you felt pulled in two directions? Which feeling proved stronger and moved you to action? Why doesn't Attean eat the bear stew? Why is he proud that he is not eating?
17. *Chapter 17:* How does Matt's view of the Indian village change in the morning? Describe a similar experience that you have had when a place looked one way at night and then was very different in the morning. Why was Matt invited to the feast? Support your answer with specifics from the novel regarding the values and beliefs of the characters.
18. *Chapter 18:* How is Marie like Attean? How is she different? Contrast Attean's apparent attitude toward his dog with his real feelings about him. Why does he behave in one way when he feels a different way?

19. *Chapter 19:* What does Matt learn from the Indian women? What activities does Matt enjoy during his visits? What activities make him uncomfortable? Why do they have these effects? What test does Matt feel he has passed?
20. *Chapter 20:* Explain the process that Attean must go through to become a hunter. What similar ceremonies do young men and women go through today? How will Attean's finding his manitou separate him from Matt?
21. *Chapter 21:* How has Matt changed his view of the Indians since he has been on his own?
22. *Chapter 22:* Why does Attean give his dog to Matt? How do the Indians hope to start a new life? Why does Matt fear this may not happen? What, in fact, actually did happen to the land belonging to the Indians?
23. *Chapter 23:* Why does Matt spend so much time and make such careful preparations for his parents' return?
24. *Chapter 24:* How do the snowshoes raise Matt's spirits?
25. *Chapter 25:* So much happens so quickly after Matt's family finally arrives. Which event makes Matt the most proud? the most happy? the most troubled? How are Matt's views different from the views of his parents? In what ways might these views affect the rest of his life?

WRITING ACTIVITIES

1. Write a comparison and contrast essay in which you explore the stereotypical view of the Native Americans presented in Western movies and television with the view of Native Americans presented in *The Sign of the Beaver*. Begin your writing task by identifying major characteristics that both present, such as clothing, use of language, attitudes toward white people, ways of securing food, values, etc. Then complete a chart for both the movie/television depictions and the novel's depiction. You may write your paper either by looking at each point and showing similarities and differences or by discussing all the similarities and then all the differences. At the conclusion, present your own evaluation of the two types of presentations.
2. Throughout the novel, you have learned about how the Indians felt about animals. Review the book, making a list of the various beliefs that you find. Then write up this list as Matt might have prepared it for his father, so that his father could have a better understanding of the Indians' relationship with animals (both domesticated and wild) and so that his father would not behave in a way that might offend members of the neighboring tribe.
3. Chapter 12 describes Matt's attempts at making and shooting a bow and arrow. While this was a task that Attean made look easy, Matt found out just how difficult it could be. Select another task that Attean performed or a task that you have tried and write a set of instructions for completing this task. Include in these instructions special emphasis on those steps that appear easy but are not and carefully explain the difficulties and how to overcome them.
4. Throughout the novel, Matt works at teaching Attean how to speak and read English. Using the Internet, your local library, and/or interviews with your teachers, find out how students can be taught to speak and read English. Write a letter to Matt in which you explain to him how he could have supplemented his teaching methods or used entirely

different methods. Also explain why you think these methods would be more successful or less successful.

5. Attean refers to certain jobs as "squaw work." Conduct interviews with your grandparents or members of their age group about what the term "women's work" used to mean. In addition, ask your parents or members of their age group what it used to mean to them. Finally, ask several of your friends what they think is "women's work." Prepare a chart of your findings, including Attean's ideas. In a brief written report, explain in what ways these ideas have and have not changed throughout the generations.
6. Matt has a very hard decision to make about whether he should stay at the cabin or go with the tribe. Write a letter to him to give him your ideas and reasons regarding whether he should stay or go.
7. Imagine being separated from your family for four to six months. What would you miss most about them? Write a list poem that begins "If we were apart, I would . . ." and include at least five entries that complete the sentence. Show the final version of the poem to your family and note their reactions.

OTHER ACTIVITIES

1. Throughout the novel, historic items are mentioned, such as a pewter dish, a ladle, a birch canoe, and Matt's rifle. Select one of these items and research it on the Internet or in your library. Draw a picture, either freehand or on a computer, of the object and label the various parts. Below it, write a brief explanation of its use. Combine all these illustrations into a notebook for other students to use as they read the novel.
2. Chapter 19 describes the Indian bone game. Keeping in mind what materials the Indians had available to them, create your own game that they would have enjoyed. Make the pieces necessary to play the game and write out the rules for the game. Ask several groups to play your game, evaluate how they like it, and ask them how they think Attean would have liked it.
3. Prepare a flowchart showing how Attean changed. You may focus on his change in attitude, his change in his feelings for Matt, or his change as he grew to manhood. On the flowchart list Attean's specific actions to document and support your suppositions about his growth.
4. Chapter 16 contains a description of how Attean painted his face to celebrate the feast of the bear. After researching the use of paint by Native American tribes, create a painted design for a young warrior that would show his bravery. Post your drawings on the bulletin board for everyone to see.
5. Debate the concept of land ownership as it was seen by the Indians in *The Sign of the Beaver* and as it was seen by the white people settling the country. You may choose to allow only arguments that would have been made during the eighteenth century in America or you may look at the question from a contemporary point of view. Each team should prepare its speeches and be prepared to rebut the reasons given by opponents.
6. Select a scene from *Robinson Crusoe* and a parallel scene from *The Sign of the Beaver*. Prepare a brief skit and act out these two scenes, one after the other, using simple props and bits of costumes to show the changes in time and character. Ask your classmates who watch your presentations to comment on how the two stories are similar and how they are different.

SELECTED TEACHING RESOURCES

Media Aids

Cassettes (2)

The Sign of the Beaver. Perfection Learning Corporation.

Internet

Mosley, Ann. *Signs in Speare's The Sign of the Beaver.* Available: http://scholar.lib.vt.edu/ejournals/ALAN/spring95/Mosley.html (Accessed March 10, 2000).
An interesting exploration of the different types of signs used in the novel.

Printed Resources

Articles

Hassler, Patricia Jana. "Book Strategies: The Books of Elizabeth George Speare." *Book Links* 2 (May 1993): 14–20.

Mosley, Ann. "Signs in Speare's *The Sign of the Beaver*." *The ALAN Review* 22 (Spring 1995): 19–21.

Speare, Elizabeth George. "On Writing *The Sign of the Beaver*." *Book Links* 2 (May 1993): 19.

Teaching Aids

The Sign of the Beaver. LIFT series. Sundance.

The Sign of the Beaver. Novel Unit Guide, Novel Units Student Packet, and Perma-Guide. Perma-Bound.

The Sign of the Beaver. Novel-Ties. Learning Links.

The Sign of the Beaver. Portals to Reading series, Portals Plus series, Reading Beyond the Basal Plus series, and Latitudes series. Perfection Learning Corporation

Tests

The Sign of the Beaver. Essay, objective, and alternative assessment versions. Perfection Learning Corporation.

Where the Lilies Bloom

Vera and Bill Cleaver

Philadelphia: J. B. Lippincott, 1969

Available in paperback from Harper Trophy.

SUMMARY

Mary Call Luther lives with her sisters Devola and Ima Dean, her brother Romey, and her father in Trial Valley in the Great Smoky Mountains. When her father dies, Mary Call honors his wishes and buries him secretly on Old Joshua Mountain. By pretending that he is still alive, Mary Call keeps the neighbors and the welfare workers from splitting up the family, and by engaging the family in wildcrafting, she struggles to earn the money to support her sisters and brother. Her plight is made even more difficult by Kiser Pease, the Luthers' miserly landlord, whose one desire is to wed Devola. Mary Call succeeds in keeping them apart; however, a hard winter takes its toll and Kiser finally steps in, claims Devola as his bride, and provides the finances needed to keep the Luther family together.

APPRAISAL

A Newbery Award Honor Book, *Where the Lilies Bloom* was also nominated for the National Book Award and was acclaimed "one of the year's most notable books" by the *New York Times*. It was made into a full-length motion picture with a screenplay by Earl Hamner, Jr. and released by United Artists. The character of Mary Call continues to appeal to young people because of her courage, resourcefulness, and ability to cope in the most trying of situations. This novel is most appropriate for grades six and seven.

THEMES

family values, courage, coping, nature and natural resources, love of learning, importance of charity, self reliance

LITERARY CONCEPTS

point of view, character development, figurative language (metaphors, similes, symbols), regional dialects, setting

RELATED READING

Following the publication of *Where the Lilies Bloom*, Vera and Bill Cleaver wrote a sequel entitled *Trial Valley* (1977). Popular books set in the Appalachian region include *Coal Camp Girl* by Lois Lensky, *Ida Early Comes over the Mountain* by Robert Burch, and titles by Cynthia Rylant, such as *Blue-Eyed Daisy*, *Missing May*, and *When I Was Young in the Mountains*. Selections for more mature readers include Harriette Simpson Arnow's *The Dollmaker*, Wilma Dykeman's *The Tall Woman*, and Lee Smith's *Oral History*.

READING PROBLEMS AND OPPORTUNITIES

The language in this book is basically simple; however, three opportunities for vocabulary studies are presented: (1) words related to plant life in the Appalachian area, (2) words and phrases that are part of the Appalachian dialect, and (3) words that Mary Call uses to demonstrate her learning. Words related to plant life include (chapter numbers are given in parentheses):

trillium (1, 12, 15),
shadbush (1, 15),
tamarack tea (2),
lamb's quarters (2),
coltsfoot (2),
spicewood (2),
gingseng (3),
mayapple (3),
goldenseal (3),
foxglove (4),
lobelia herb (4),
queen's delight (4),
stargrass root (4),
galax (5),
lichen (6),
whitleather (6),
rhododendron (9),
laurel (9),
wintergreen (11),
bluets (12),
lady slippers (15),
trout lilies (15),
fawn lilies (15),
blue pimpernel (15),
maypop (15),
sweet elder (15),
nettle berries (15),
catnip (15), and
sassafras (15).

Words and phrases for dialect study include:

gawk (1),
witch's keyhole (1, 12),
twice around a gimlet (1),
meanest (1),
fritter (1, 7),
divvy (1),
doesn't hold with doctors (2),
quiet us (4),
go down (4),
quested (5),
hoecake (5),
jularker (7),
claphat (8),
hog tie (8),
get shed (8),
traipsed (10),
beller (10),
hoojer (11),
toady (12),
shank's mare (13),
vittles (13),
treasoned (13), and
soared a piece (14).

Other words include:

languishing (1),
scrutinized (1),
gaunt (2),
ambiance (2),
morose (3),
countenance (5),
primeval (5),
undulating (6),
ingrates (7),
mottled (8),
bereft (8),
inscrutable (8),
wraithy (9),
convulsed (10),
acquiescent (11),
whorling (11),
dissipating (12),
abattoir (13),
tintinnabulation (13), and
hoary (15).

INITIATING ACTIVITIES

1. Imagine that your parent(s) or guardian(s) had to leave you alone for several weeks. They left so suddenly that they neglected to leave you any money, bank cards, or credit cards. You do not want your friends and neighbors to know that you are alone. How do you manage to survive? What sources of money would you find? What would be the greatest difficulties in your life? Write a brief explanation of your plan and share it with your classmates.
2. Survey your natural environment and prepare a chart of the trees and plants that are common. Using reference books, check to see which of these is edible and/or valuable for medicinal purposes. As you read the novel, add to your list the trees and plants that Mary Call and her family search for in the land surrounding their home. (See words related to plant life under "Reading Problems and Opportunities.")
3. Review the list of words and phrases from this book that illustrate the Appalachian dialect. (See "Reading Problems and Opportunities.") Make your best guess as to what each word/phrase means. As you read the novel, check your guesses and modify them, as needed, based on their use in the novel.

DISCUSSION QUESTIONS

1. *Chapter 1:* Why do the authors include the opening scene with the traveler? What does he teach Mary Call? What is Mary Call's position in the family? What are her responsibilities? Who can she call on to help her? Why doesn't she do this?
2. *Chapter 2:* What do you learn about Kiser Pease from his delirious rantings? Why does Mary Call save Kiser Pease's life? What scientific basis, if any, exists for the cure Mary Call used? Is it wrong for Romey to take food from Kiser's basement? Why or why not?
3. *Chapter 3:* How has Romey's attitude changed? Why does it change? Why is Mary Call excited about the wildcrafting book? What emotions spur Mary Call to stand up to Kiser Pease?
4. *Chapter 4:* What does Kiser Pease mean by saying, "The price of freedom comes mighty dear sometimes"? Why did Ima Dean tear the heads off the two paper dolls? Compare and contrast Mr. and Mrs. Connell's reactions to Mary Call and Romey. Should Romey be scolded for his remarks to the Connells? Why or why not?
5. *Chapter 5:* What events in this chapter reinforce your initial views on the characters of Mr. and Mrs. Connell? How do Mary Call and Romey react to Roy Luther's death? Why do they behave this way?
6. *Chapter 6:* What is Mary Call's greatest concern about burying her father? Why is Mary Call so determined to carry out her father's wishes? How has Roy Luther prepared for his own death? Mary Call compares herself to a tree battered by the wind. To what would you compare Romey? Roy Luther? How does Mary Call plan to fool the outside world into thinking Roy Luther is still alive? Why does she do this? What is Mary Call's attitude toward Kiser Pease? How does she manage to get him to do what she wants?
7. *Chapter 7:* What problems do the Luther children have when they try to drive Kiser's car? Who is the best driver? Why? How do the children continue to fool Kiser? Why are they able to do this? Why is Kiser willing to give so much to the Luther children?

8. *Chapter 8:* Why does Kiser take Devola to town? Why does Ima Dean come along? Why does Mary Call want to keep Kiser away? How does she plan to do this? Do you think this is a good plan? Why or why not? How does Mary Call feel about Miss Breathitt? Why did Mary Call shun the Graybeals? What happens to Kiser? Why is this event a blessing for the Luthers, especially Mary Call? Why can't Mary Call accept her good fortune?
9. *Chapter 9:* How are the Luther children able to survive on their own? What are the differences in the ways that Mr. and Mrs. Connell treat them? How does Romey respond to Mrs. Connell? Was he right to do so? Why or why not? How does he eventually get his revenge?
10. *Chapter 10:* Why do Devola, Ima Dean, and Romey dislike Mary Call? How else might Mary Call deal with the problems at hand? How does the weather compound the problems the Luthers face? Is Mary Call's solution to the caved-in roof a good one? What else might she have done? How does Mary Call feel after the encounter with the fox?
11. *Chapter 11:* Describe Miss Goldie Pease. Why does she want to see Roy Luther? What bad news does she give Mary Call? What alternatives does Mary Call have if her family must vacate their home? What would you advise her to do?
12. *Chapter 12:* How do the Luther children suffer from the blizzard? In what way was this a blessing? Why does Romey go out in the blizzard? What does Devola do to demonstrate her abilities to handle a problem? What is Mary Call's plan to rescue the family? Why is she willing to sacrifice herself?
13. *Chapter 13:* Why does Mary Call go to see Kiser in the hospital? Why doesn't Kiser want to marry Mary Call? What is Kiser's attitude toward his sister Gloria? Why does he feel this way? What is Mary Call's new plan? What problems do you foresee with her new plans? How has Devola changed?
14. *Chapter 14:* How has life changed for the Luther children? How has Mary Call's relationship with Kiser changed?
15. *Chapter 15:* Why does Mary Call think spring will never come? What benefits does spring have for Mary Call, Romey, and Ima Dean? What do you think the next year will be like for the Luther children? Why do you believe this?

WRITING ACTIVITIES

1. Mary Call recalls that the idea of wildcrafting was "tucked away in some forgotten pigeon-hole of my mind." After reviewing chapter 3, write a description of a time when an idea of yours came to the surface and was put into action. Ask your classmates to evaluate your idea and implementation of it.
2. In chapter 3, Mary Call explains how her father was abused by others. She says people should either hate their oppressors or pick up and get out. Write a poem that reflects this idea. It may take any form you think is appropriate.
3. Mary Call observes that, "wildcrafting is a sight easier to read about than to do." Choose an activity in your life that falls into this category. Compare and contrast the differences between reading about and actually carrying out this activity. If possible, bring in the objects needed for carrying out this activity and demonstrate the differences between reading and doing for your classmates.

4. When Roy Luther dies, Mary Call and Romey must bury him according to his wishes, even though they would have preferred a more elaborate ceremony. Write a description of a time when you did what had to be done, despite your own desires to the contrary. Compare and contrast your feelings with those of Mary Call and Romey.
5. Miss Breathitt thought lots of things wonderful. Prepare a list poem about at least ten things that you find wonderful.
6. "It's everybody's affair what they make of being here," says Mary Call in chapter 12. Select a friend or relative who has recognized that it was his or her affair to make something of being here. Write a one- to two-page biography illustrating this individual's accomplishments.
7. "It would be wrong to take notice of them in words," says Mary Call, describing Kiser's new teeth. Brainstorm with your classmates and develop a list of changes in humans that should not be discussed, such as a weight gain. List at least three generalizations your group can draw about the types of observations that shouldn't be put into words.

OTHER ACTIVITIES

1. In chapter 2, Mary Call explains that she and her family made their own toothbrushes and toothpaste. Try your hand at making either or both of these. Compare the results from these homemade dental hygiene products with those you normally use. Report to your classmates on the differences.
2. In chapter 6, Mary Call describes a "happy pappy." Using a pencil, charcoal, or markers, create a caricature of "happy pappy." Ask your classmates to review your drawing and explain what type of character they see in it.
3. In chapter 8, Miss Breathitt explains the development of the Great Smoky Mountains. Research thoroughly the evolution of these mountains and prepare a cutaway model illustrating what you have learned.
4. Research the preparation of molasses today. Compare today's methods with those used by the Graybeals in chapter 8.
5. Mary Call recounts how the hospital differs from her mental picture of a hospital. Prepare a split collage that illustrates these differences.
6. Use a reference book such as *Appalachian Speech* by Donna Christian and Walt Wolfram and *The Oxford Companion to the English Language* edited by Tom McArthur to check your modified guesses regarding the dialectical words and phrases in the novel. Prepare a glossary of terms that students in the future may use as they read *Where the Lilies Bloom*.

SELECTED TEACHING RESOURCES

Media Aids

Internet

Peterson, W. *Where the Lilies Bloom Home Page.* Available: http://www.forks.wednet.edu/ middle/ wlb.html (Accessed March 10, 2000).

This site contains worksheets and quizzes, comparison to the movie version of the novel, and information on the Great Smoky Mountains.

Appalachian Literature for Youth. Available: http://web.utk.edu/~estes/appalach.html (Accessed March 10, 2000).

Site with an extensive bibliography on a wide range of topics related to Appalachia and its literature.

Video

Where the Lilies Bloom. 97 min., color. Filmic Archives and Sundance, 1973.

Printed Materials

Article

Scales, Pat. "Book Strategies: *Where the Lilies Bloom* by Vera and Bill Cleaver." *Book Links* (May 1991): 8–10.

Teaching Aids

Where the Lilies Bloom. Connect Social Studies series and LIFT series. Sundance.

Where the Lilies Bloom. Novel/Drama Curriculum Units. The Center for Learning.

Where the Lilies Bloom. Novel-Ties. Learning Links.

Tests

Where the Lilies Bloom. Essay and objective versions. Perfection Learning Corporation.

Where the Lilies Bloom. Alert Reader Assessment. Sundance.

Hatchet

Gary Paulsen
New York: Bradbury Press, 1987
Available in paperback from Aladdin.

SUMMARY

Thirteen-year-old Brian Robeson is flying north in a small plane to spend the summer with his father in northern Canada. When the pilot suffers a heart attack, the plane crashes near a lake, leaving Brian unhurt but forced to fend for himself in the middle of a wilderness with nothing but a hatchet. For almost two months he lives in isolation off the land. In surviving, he learns to disregard the past involving his parents' ugly divorce, reject self-pity, and solve the problems of finding food and shelter before he is finally rescued and returned to civilization.

APPRAISAL

Hatchet is a classic story of survival in the wilderness. Like many other similar accounts, fictional and otherwise (see "Related Reading"), the book offers young readers a gripping account. It enables them to place themselves vicariously in Brian's situation and imagine how they would react. *Hatchet* was a Newbery Honor Book for 1988 and won recognition by many sources as one of the best novels of the year. Since it was first published, it has been extremely popular among middle-school readers. It is most appropriate for sixth through eighth grades.

THEMES

survival, courage, independence and self-reliance, problem solving, growing up

LITERARY CONCEPTS

plot (flashback, suspense), characterization, point of view (third-person limited), setting, irony

RELATED READING

This novel is one of many books about a young person's struggle to survive in the wilderness against numerous obstacles. Among the works of fiction are *My Side of the Mountain* and *Julie of the Wolves* by Jean Craighead George, *Island of the Blue Dolphins* by Scott O'Dell, *Hit and Run* by Joan Phipson, *Far North* by Will Hobbs, *A Girl Named Disaster* by Nancy Farmer, and the classics *Swiss Family Robinson* by Johann David Wyss and *Robinson Crusoe* by Daniel Defoe. Nonfiction books include *Hey, I'm Alive!* by Helen Klaben and, for mature readers, the compelling *Alive: The Story of the Andes Survivors* by Piers Paul Read. Other comparable books by Gary Paulsen are *Dogsong*, *The River* and *Brian's Winter*. The last two titles are both sequels to *Hatchet*.

READING PROBLEMS AND OPPORTUNITIES

For most middle-school readers, *Hatchet* is a quite accessible book, but it does offer opportunities for many students to strengthen their vocabularies. Possible words for a teacher to emphasize include these (numbers refer to pages):

consuming (1, 92),
drone (2),
audible (10),
spasm (10),
turbulence (13, 14),
altimeter (16),
abate (33, 38),
hummocks (39, 124),
amphibious (48),
motivated (50, 58),
diminish (57),
pulverized (58),
interlaced (65),
recede (70),
rivulets (77),
haunches (87),
exasperate (87, 138),
tendrils (88),
flammable (88),
depression (90),
gratified (92),
eddied, eddy (95, 171),
regulate (97),
dormant (99),
convulse (101),
depression (104—different meaning from p. 90),
flailing (110),
hefted (111),
telegraphed (111),
infuriating (124),
refracts (125),
exulted (126),
rectify (128),
devastating (130),
sulfurous (130),
corrosive (130),
impaired (130),
sarcasm (140),
stabilize (142),
incessant (161),
ruefully (166),
stymied (168),
frenzied (174),
oblivious (184),
unwittingly (192),
furor (194), and
predators (195).

INITIATING ACTIVITIES

1. Make a list of the ten most important items you think you would need to survive in the wilderness for two weeks. You may *not* include firearms or radio transmitters. When you have finished, meet with another student and compare your lists. Combine the lists into a single one of ten items in order of priority.
2. Complete the following "opinionnaire" by indicating whether you *Strongly agree*, *Agree*, *Disagree*, or *Strongly disagree* with each of the statements:
   a. Teenagers are more dependent on their parents than they should be.
   b. Self-pity is never good for you.
   c. Nature is cruel.
   d. If someone is faced with a problem, she can always solve it if she wants to badly enough.
   e. Being alone is often good for us.

   Discuss your responses with your classmates.

DISCUSSION QUESTIONS

1. *Chapter 1:* As the book opens, what are some things on Brian's mind? What does he like about the flight? Dislike about it? What do you think the Secret might be? How does Brian feel about being allowed to handle the controls? How does the author gradually build suspense in this chapter? As the chapter ends with Brian's sudden and awful realization, is there anything that has happened in the chapter that offers any hope at all?

2. *Chapter 2:* In what particular ways is Brian's situation precarious? Imagine yourself in his position: What do you think you would do? As he frantically tries to think of what to do, can you as the reader think of ways he could be saved from this predicament? How do you think he deals with the crisis? What would be an advantage of not waiting until the plane runs out of gas?

3. *Chapters 3 and 4:* In your view, has the author succeeded in describing how it must be to experience a plane crash? Why or why not? What do you think are Brian's most immediate needs? What more do we find out in chapter 4 about the Secret? At the end of the chapter, why do you think he seems so tired?

4. *Chapter 5:* "He had nothing." Look again at the list you compiled for "Initiating Activity" 1. If you were Brian, which single item would you choose from your list, and why? Do you agree with him that food and shelter are his most pressing needs? Discuss. When Brian makes his list of what he has, what major item does he overlook (an item that, although it is not presently visible, is still available)?

5. *Chapter 6:* At the start of the chapter, can you think of possible sources of food for Brian? If you were in his situation, can you think of TV programs you've seen or books you've read that you could draw upon for information? When the chapter ends, Brian feels somewhat reassured (" 'Good,' he said, nodding"). Do you? Why or why not?

6. *Chapter 7:* Why does Brian dwell so often on the Secret? What does the narrator mean by "long tears, self-pity tears, wasted tears?" What important understanding does Brian gain in this chapter?

7. *Chapter 8:* Do you think Brian's occasional breaking down into sobs is a weakness? Discuss. Do you agree that self-pity is *totally* pointless? What is the most important thing Brian learns in this chapter?

8. *Chapter 9:* Brian learns how to make a fire in this chapter, but what more important realization does he gain?

9. *Chapter 10:* At this halfway point in the book, how has Brian changed (if at all)? In what ways is he smarter? What does the experience with the turtle eggs teach him? Although he sees it as undesirable, in what way might Brian's forgetting about the searchers be a good thing?

10. *Chapter 11:* What changes does Brian notice in himself? Why has he changed? In what ways is it worthwhile for him to keep his mind on "things to do"?

11. *Chapter 12:* After Brian realizes the spear won't work, he decides a bow and arrow might. Can you think of any other way he might "catch" a fish? In this chapter he focuses on the bow. What might he use for string? At the end of the chapter, Brian seems to be without hope, but what in the chapter has given him reason for optimism?

12. *Chapter 13:* "But something he did not understand had stopped him." How does this "something" represent a change in Brian? Why is seeing the wolf important to him? What do we learn happened after Brian's efforts to attract the search plane's notice had failed? Does this surprise you? Why or why not? Why do you think the author chose to structure much of this chapter as a long flashback? How does Brian define "tough hope"?
13. *Chapters 14:* What would you say is the most important thing Brian is learning from his various mistakes? At this point, do you think he has completely given up on being rescued?
14. *Chapter 15:* Why does Brian crave meat so much? In chapter 15, he realizes the importance of patience. Why do you think it is often so hard in our lives to be patient?
15. *Chapter 16:* During and after the moose attack and then during the tornado, why does Brian dwell on the word *insane*? Can you think of some other word to describe these experiences?
16. *Chapter 17:* Early in this chapter, at the page break, Brian is focused on the survival pack that is in the plane. Before reading further, think of how he might rescue it from the wreckage. What are the particular problems he faces? (*Note to teacher*: This question needs to be posed before the reading of chapter 17 is assigned.) As Brian begins the plane project, what is happening in his environment that poses another threat?
17. *Chapter 18:* After Brian rescues his all-important hatchet, he knows he must be extra careful with it. What steps might he have taken to ensure that he wouldn't lose it? Why do you think the author chose to include the detail about the pilot's skull? Might it just as well have been omitted, or does it add something to the novel's overall impact?
18. *Chapter 19:* Besides its usefulness, what does all the treasure in the survival pack offer Brian? Why is he uneasy about the rifle and the lighter? What is the major irony in this chapter?
19. *Epilogue:* How has Brian changed? Do you agree that some of the changes will be permanent? How do you think you would have changed? What are the implications of the fact that Brian never tells his father about the Secret? (If you did "Initiating Activity" 2, return to the statements: Have you changed your opinion on any of them? Discuss.)

WRITING ACTIVITIES

1. In his account in chapter 5 of what he has available to him, Brian mentions fingernail clippers. With a partner, make a list of all the ways you could use fingernail clippers if you were stranded in the wilderness like Brian. Then make another list of uses if you were at home. Use your imagination: Consider not only practical uses, but more imaginative uses as well.
2. Brian recalls his teacher, Mr. Perpich, emphasizing the fact that in any given situation "*you* are the best thing you have." Write a one-page assessment of yourself in terms of your strengths. What are your best qualities? What are the particular qualities you have that you think would increase your chances for survival in a similar set of circumstances?
3. Have you ever been in a situation where you felt the kind of fear bordering on panic that Brian feels in chapter 2? Write about the occasion, what you did to deal with your feelings, how it turned out, and what you learned.

4. Much of what Brian accomplishes in his efforts to survive involves problem solving. Read a book or magazine article that explains some recommended steps for how to solve problems. Then write a paper in which you compare these steps to Brian's typical approach (e.g., in his struggle to make a fire). Possible sources include *Problem Solving Through Critical Thinking* by Ronald R. Edwards and Wanda D. Cook and *Getting Started in Problem Solving and Math Contests* by Michael W. Ecker.

5. Write a paper on edible wild foods in your part of the country. Two good sources for this are *Acorn Pancakes, Dandelion Salad, and 38 Other Wild Recipes* by Jean Craighead George and *Gather Ye Wild Things: A Forager's Year* by Susan Tyler Hitchcock. Other possible resources include magazine articles and the Internet.

6. In chapter 11, Brian is aware of the fact that he has become truly *aware*: "And when he saw something—a bird moving a wing inside a bush or a ripple on the water—he would truly see that thing. . . . He would see all parts of it." Try your hand at very close observation. For as much as twenty or thirty minutes, watch a bird or an animal up close. Try to *see* all of its parts: the colors, shape, movements, etc. Take notes and then write up your observations in a few paragraphs.

7. Read the poem "Staying Alive" by David Wagoner. (It can be found, among other places, in the collection *Some Haystacks Don't Even Have Any Needle*, edited by Stephen Dunning and others.) Write a one- to two-page paper on any ways in which the poem might have been helpful to Brian.

8. In chapter 14, Brian makes the observation that "nothing in nature was lazy." Think long and hard about this conclusion, which Brian has reached after days and days of observation and experience. Then write a paper in which you support the statement. Try to use specific examples from nature, references to animals and plants, and even events and occurrences.

9. Although the Epilogue refers to it, Brian never has to deal with winter. Given the unique demands of bitter cold and deprivation, but also Brian's resources (including the treasures in the survival pack), try to write a scenario suggesting how he might survive the upcoming winter.

OTHER ACTIVITIES

1. Using only natural materials (leaves, pebbles, stains from berries, etc.), create a collage/painting that represents one of the following:

   a. what you consider the most important awareness Brian gains during his fifty-four days in the wilderness

   b. what you think Gary Paulsen's attitude toward nature is

2. In chapters 6, 8, and 11, especially, the author gives us some details of the location of Brian's shelter. Using these specifics (e.g., the flat stone area on top of the bluff above the shelter), draw a picture of Brian's surroundings near the lake.

3. Brian never really knows exactly where he is, how far into the Canadian wilderness the plane flew and how far off course it was. Still, based on his point of departure in Hampton, New York, the general direction (northwest), and the plane's speed (as well as other important details), make a judgment about where the plane might have crashed. Using

atlases of the northern United States and Canada, draw a map of the book's overall setting from beginning to end.

4. A lot of Brian's time on the island is taken up by building and improving upon his shelter. Try to gain an appreciation of his efforts by constructing a model of a lean-to, interweaving sticks of different sizes, grasses, and so forth to create a water-resistant mesh. Use chapters 6 and 14 as points of reference.
5. In chapter 15, Brian learns to see the foolbirds, "to train his eyes to see the shape." Using a field guide as a resource, draw some silhouettes of very familiar birds (crows, robins, woodpeckers, eagles, hummingbirds, etc.). Then show them to the class to see how many are identifiable.
6. After Brian returns to civilization, we learn that he is interviewed by several TV networks. With two or three other students, conduct one of these interviews. Have the interviewers plan their questions in advance, but let the student playing Brian's part answer spontaneously.

SELECTED TEACHING RESOURCES

Media Aids

Cassettes (3)

Hatchet. Unabridged, 210 min. Bantam Doubleday Dell Audio Publishing and Perma-Bound.

Internet

Interactive Broadcasting Corporation. 1996–1998. *Wilderness Survival: Survival Basics*. Available: http://bcadventure.com/adventure/wilderness/survival/basic.htm (Accessed March 10, 2000).

Covers the effects of fear, pain, cold, thirst, hunger, fatigue, boredom, and loneliness; how to build a fire and shelter; and such other matters as clothing, equipment, survival kit, and backpacks. For other websites, type *wilderness survival* into a search engine.

Video

A Cry in the Wild. 82 min., color. Sundance, 1990.

A film version of the novel.

Printed Materials

Articles

Bressler, Jean, and Helen Howell. "Have Hatchet—Will Survive: Suggested Activities for Decision-Making Skills." *The ALAN Review* 18 (Spring 1991): 16–18.

Gale, David. "The Maximum Expression of Being Human." *School Library Journal* 43 (June 1997): 24–29.

An interview with the author.

McGillian, Jamie Kyle. "Going Down." *Creative Classroom* 12 (November/December 1997): 20–21.
Presents a readers' theater treatment of the novel.

Teaching Aids

Hatchet. Bookwise Literature Guides. Christopher-Gordon Publishers.

Hatchet. LIFT series. Sundance.

Hatchet. Novel/Drama Curriculum Units. The Center for Learning.

Hatchet. Novel Unit Guide, Novel Units Student Packet, and Perma-Guide. Perma-Bound.

Hatchet. Novel-Ties. Learning Links.

Hatchet. Portals to Reading series, Portals to Literature series, Portals Plus series, and Reading Beyond the Basal Plus series. Perfection Learning Corporation.

Tests

Hatchet. Essay, objective, and alternative assessment versions. Perfection Learning Corporation.

The Cay

Theodore Taylor
New York: Doubleday, 1969
Available in paperback from Avon Books.

SUMMARY

When Phillip and his mother set out for Virginia from Curacao to avoid German attack, their ship is bombed, leaving Phillip alone on a raft in the Caribbean with a West Indian named Timothy and a feline called Stew Cat. Matters worsen as blindness overtakes Phillip and no planes or ships find these shipwrecked souls. The three eventually come ashore on a very small island, where Timothy takes charge and makes provisions for their survival and hopefully their rescue. Phillip must cope with both his physical limitations and his initial disdain for those with black skin. Over time, Phillip grows to appreciate Timothy's wisdom and abilities to adapt and eventually owes his life to Timothy, who shields him from the pounding winds of a hurricane. After Timothy's death, Phillip finds that he is able to cope, thanks largely to the training and planning that Timothy provided. When a ship finally does rescue Phillip, he is unable to explain successfully how the old man helped him and the cat survive. Once he is home with his sight restored by surgery, Phillip sees more clearly how to judge the value of other human beings.

APPRAISAL

Highly recommended by the *Library Journal* and the *Saturday Review*, *The Cay* is an adventure story coupled with a powerful lesson in human relations. Questions of racial and socio-economic background are explored in a primitive setting where kindness, goodness, and ingenuity are most valued. This novel is most appropriate for middle school students.

THEMES

survival, friendship, growing up, dealing with a physical limitation, racial relations, coming of age, wisdom, aging

LITERARY CONCEPTS

dialect, setting, character development, first person narration

RELATED READING

Famous tales focusing on the survival of shipwrecked individuals include *The Swiss Family Robinson* and *Robinson Crusoe* by Daniel Defoe. Other popular survival tales are *Julie and the Wolves* by Jean Craighead George and *Lord of the Flies* by William Golding.

READING PROBLEMS AND OPPORTUNITIES

Basically a simple book to read, *The Cay's* only unfamiliar terms stem from German words; nautical words or phrases; names for Caribbean locations, flora and fauna; and representations of Timothy's dialect. Some possible words for vocabulary study might include (chapter numbers are in parentheses):

galleons (1),
schooners (1),
veerboots (1),
lake tanker (1),
U-boats (1),
ballast (2),
fore/aft (2),
alabaster (3),
conch (3),
calypso (3, 8),
doused (5),
fronds (8),
frangipani (9),
pampano (9),
conniving (11),
tethered (11),
receded (15), and
groped (16).

INITIATING ACTIVITIES

1. Working with a friend, blindfold yourself so that you cannot see even a crack of light through the blindfold. Using a stick or a cane, find your way around the classroom. *Note*: Your partner should stay close by to keep you out of harm's way. Write a journal entry about your experiences, focusing on how you used other senses to compensate for the lack of sight. Save this entry for comparison with Phillip's experiences described in *The Cay*.
2. Research the role of Germans in Curacao and Aruba during World War II. What activities made these areas valuable to the Germans? Why did the Germans attack these locations?

DISCUSSION QUESTIONS

1. *Chapter 1:* Compare and contrast Phillip's attitude toward the war with the attitudes of his mother and his father. Choose one word that best describes Phillip's attitude, as well as one for his father and one for his mother. Compare your choices with those made by your classmates and agree upon the best word to describe the attitudes of each of these three characters.
2. *Chapter 2:* Why does Phillip's mother want to leave Curacao? Why does his father object? How does Phillip feel? How do you think you would feel if you were in his place?
3. *Chapter 3:* Which conditions on the raft cause Phillip to be extremely sad? Why does Timothy feel he and Phillip are lucky? Do you agree with him? Why or why not?
4. *Chapter 4:* Why do you think that Timothy doesn't know much about his own background? How does Timothy care for and protect Phillip?
5. *Chapter 5:* Why is it so important to Phillip to know what could be seen from the raft?

6. *Chapter 6:* What are the advantages of the raft over the island? What are the disadvantages? If you completed "Initiating Activity" 1, compare your responses to those of Phillip. How are they the same? How are they different? Why do these similarities and differences exist?
7. *Chapter 7:* Why might this cay be a poor choice of places to make camp?
8. *Chapter 8:* What is Phillip's attitude toward Timothy? Is he appreciative of Timothy's efforts? Why or why not? In what ways does he believe he is superior to Timothy?
9. *Chapter 9:* Phillip says he doesn't know what happened to him. What do you think causes Phillip to change his mind about Timothy?
10. *Chapter 10:* Why does Phillip believe Timothy's explanation about the differences in skin color more than he believes the explanation of Herr Jonckheer?
11. *Chapter 11:* Why is Phillip afraid of Timothy? What specific events lead to this fear? Do you believe that Timothy could ever hurt Phillip or Stew Cat? Why or why not?
12. *Chapter 12:* How does Phillip know what to do to take care of Timothy's recurrence of malaria? What special problems does Phillip face because of his physical limitations?
13. *Chapter 13:* Compare and contrast the knowledge and skills that Phillip and Timothy display in this chapter. How do these two complement one another?
14. *Chapter 14:* How does Timothy know a storm is coming? How are his preparations similar to those of people today when facing a storm? How are they different?
15. *Chapter 15:* What elements threaten the lives of Phillip and Timothy? How are Phillip and Timothy able to battle these demons? What dangers does Phillip face with Timothy gone?
16. *Chapter 16:* Why do you think Timothy died? How is Phillip able to survive after the storm?
17. *Chapter 17:* Why does Phillip risk hunting for langosta? Is he foolish to do this? Why or why not?
18. *Chapter 18:* What evidence shows that Timothy had prepared Phillip to live on his own? Why are all his efforts not successful?
19. *Chapter 19:* Why are Phillip's rescuers shocked to find a naked boy and a cat? How does Phillip's life change as a result of his experiences on *The Cay*?

WRITING ACTIVITIES

1. The novel *The Cay* is written from Phillip's point of view. Select one chapter from the novel and rewrite it from a third-person point of view, that is, as an outside observer who does not allow his or her own judgments to affect the story. Compare and contrast your new version with the original chapter in the novel. What is lost by changing the point of view? What is gained? Which do you prefer? Why?
2. Select a partner to help you with this activity. Each of you select three objects from your home and bring them to school carefully concealed from your partner. Blindfold your partner and hand him or her your objects, one by one. After your partner has felt each object, conceal them again. Have your partner remove the blindfold and write a brief

description of each object. Then show the objects to your partner and have him or her write a second description. Compare the two descriptions. What is lost and what is gained when sight is not involved? Now it is your turn to describe your partner's objects. When you have both finished, compare your descriptions to those that Phillip gave when he was blind. How are they similar? How are they different?

3. In chapter 7, Phillip has the uncomfortable feeling that Timothy is not being honest and open with him. Write an essay for your classmates about being honest. You may focus on how to tell if someone is being honest or you may focus on why it is or is not important to be honest with others. Share your thoughts and those of your classmates by binding them in a book for the library or placing them on a web page.

4. In chapter 11, Timothy resorts to voodoo to try to explain why they have not been rescued. Check your library or the Internet to find out the sources and principles of voodoo. Using the information you discover, write a one-page explanation of the significance of Timothy's carving of the Stew Cat.

5. Develop a timeline to trace Phillip's growth toward independence in *The Cay*. Divide the timeline into blocks representing specific periods of times, such as months. For each block, list the skills and knowledge that Phillip gained and in a second box below that list the ways that Timothy helped Phillip to grow.

OTHER ACTIVITIES

1. Timothy guesses that they are at about 15 degrees latitude and 80 degrees longitude. Check this location on a world map and determine how accurate Timothy's guess is, keeping in mind the ship's departure point and the length of time it has been traveling. Post the map on a bulletin board and use string and push pins to show the route. If Timothy's guess is wrong, in your opinion, use a second string to show where you think they might have landed. Add brief notes to explain your map.

2. Timothy and Phillip survive on the raft because they have necessary supplies. Ships today have better-equipped life rafts. Using the Internet or other resources, research the equipment currently required on life boats. Prepare a chart of the needs you would have if you were shipwrecked in the Caribbean. After each need, such as "shelter from the sun," list the way in which Timothy and Phillip provided for themselves and then in a second column list the way in which you would be able to handle it using the equipment in your modern life raft. Prepare a drawing (freehand or using the computer) of the two rafts, with labels to show how people could survive on each of these.

3. With a partner, reenact the scene when Phillip discovers he is blind. Read chapter 4 several times and then practice enacting the scene. Do not feel compelled to repeat the dialogue word-for-word, instead focus on creating Phillip's anxiety and the tension between Timothy and Phillip.

4. Create a sketch of Timothy and Phillip's hut. Be sure to include the water catchment and the insides of the hut. Indicate the dimensions on the drawing. Label the parts and use these labels to show why this was a very satisfactory house for these two.

5. Using watercolors or chalk, create the mood brought about by the hurricane. Choose your colors and strokes carefully to represent the great danger that is potentially present.

6. With a partner, improvise a talk show on which Phillip is a guest after his operation back in Willemstad. In addition to questions you and your partner prearrange, allow questions from the other members of your class.
7. Prepare a chart showing the differences in values between Phillip and Timothy. The following list will help you begin.

	Phillip	Timothy
education	________	________
family	________	________
work	________	________
courage	________	________
racial understanding	________	________
knowledge of nature	________	________
love	________	________

Discuss how these values changed or remained the same during the island ordeal.

SELECTED TEACHING RESOURCES

Media Aids

Cassettes (2)

The Cay. Perfection Learning Corporation and Sundance.

Internet

Smith, Katy. *The Cay*. Available: http://www.eduplace.com/tview/tviews/khan70.html (Accessed March 10, 2000).
A practical site with additional ideas from teachers for activities related to this book.

Printed Resources

Teaching Aids

The Cay. LIFT series, Novel Ideas Classic series, and Novel Ideas Plus series. Sundance.

The Cay. Novel Unit Guide, Novel Units Student Packet, and Perma-Guide. Perma-Bound.

The Cay. Novel-Ties. Learning Links.

The Cay. Reading Beyond the Basal Plus series and Portals to Reading series. Perfection Learning Corporation.

Tests

The Cay. Essay, objective, and alternative assessment versions. Perfection Learning Corporation.

The Goats

Brock Cole

New York: Farrar, Straus & Giroux, 1987

Available in paperback from Farrar, Straus & Giroux.

SUMMARY

At a summer camp, Howie and Laura are labeled "the goats," kids who are different from everybody else. When they are stripped and marooned on an island by their fellow campers, they make it ashore, determined to leave the camp. For two days they survive on luck, some help from a group of black kids at a camp for inner-city teens, and their own developing inner strength. Together Howie and Laura build a trusting relationship of affection and abiding care previously absent in their lives. When they decide to leave the woods and reunite with Laura's mom, they have come to understand the importance of people taking care of each other through difficult times.

APPRAISAL

The Goats, a poignant story of the power of care and commitment, received more critical acclaim than any other young adult novel published in 1987, including mention on six lists of the "best books of the year." As a perceptive examination of the loneliness of adolescents and of their capacity for cruelty, concern, and love, the novel offers many opportunities for students in grades seven through nine to think, talk, and write about matters important to them. Some adults may find the book mildly objectionable because of its muted treatment of awakening sexuality and its occasional controversial language, but the strengths of the novel and its potential in the classroom far outweigh any problems it may present. *The Goats* seems best suited for grades seven through nine.

THEMES

the importance of caring, outsiders, innocence, growing up, friendship

LITERARY CONCEPTS

characterization, plot, setting, irony, symbolism (e.g., the cave, the museum display, the woods), figurative language

RELATED READING

Other novels about outsiders that students might compare with *The Goats* include *Slake's Limbo* by Felice Holman, *Bless the Beasts and Children* by Glendon Swarthout, *The Moves Make the Man* by Bruce Brooks, and *The Outsiders* by S. E. Hinton. Another book about camp experiences is *Slot Machine* by Chris Lynch (about a sports camp).

READING PROBLEMS AND OPPORTUNITIES

Although *The Goats* is not a difficult novel for students in middle school or junior high who are reading on or above grade level, it does present opportunities for vocabulary enrichment. Words that might be studied include (numbers refer to pages):

askew (p. 4),
vulnerable (5, 176),
sidled (11, 50, 83, 143),
menacing (13),
conciliatory (16),
skittered (24),
archaeologists (28, 109),
excavating (28, 67),
serrated (30),
despicable (36, 109, 110),
hypocrites (36),
bland (38, 59),
indignant (40, 177),
careening (47),
meander (50),
incoherent (59),
irrational (61),
reproachfully (62),
affronted (62),
ludicrous (63),
unsanctioned (64),
judgmental (65),
smirked (66),
constrict (66),
eluded (67),
segregated (72),
scandalized (80),
etiquette (92),
voluminous (93),
relevant (102),
pilfering (103),
klutzy (104),
reproof (108),
intuition (112),
compelling (112),
jittery (120),
facade (122),
chaste (130),
desolate (137),
undulations (168), and
intricate (173).

INITIATING ACTIVITIES

1. Write about a time when you felt alienated from your peers or when you were part of a group that alienated someone else. In either case, what do you think caused the group to isolate the individual? Write about how it felt to be the victim or part of the group. Why do groups sometimes feel compelled to treat outsiders this way? Discuss this in class.
2. Class discussion: Comment on camps you have attended. What kinds of camps were they? What kinds of kids attended? For how long? How did they react to being away from home for long periods? Did the kids tend to be similar to each other, or did the camp have all different kinds of children? How were homesick or "different" kids treated by the staff? By other kids? Was camp for you a happy experience? Why or why not?
3. For each of the following statements, indicate whether you *Strongly agree*, *Agree*, *Disagree*, or *Strongly disagree*:
    a. Children who do not get along well with other children should not be sent to camp by their parents.
    b. Children are crueler to each other than adults are to children.
    c. Parents send their children to camp to gain personal freedom for themselves more than to benefit the kids.

d. Stealing from others is never justified.

e. The older people get, the less they really care about others.

(*Note to teacher:* Have students keep these statements and their opinions for discussion as they read the novel.)

DISCUSSION QUESTIONS

1. *The Island:* How does Howie feel about himself facing the predicament of being left on the island? How does he see himself as different from boys like Bryce and Arnold Metcalf? As he talks with Laura, what is his main concern? Why does he want them "to disappear completely"? Does the conversation between Margo and Max add anything to our knowledge about Howie and Laura? As the chapter ends, what can you conclude about how Howie and Laura differ from the other children at the camp?

2. *The Cottage:* "We're just little kids, he thought. . . ." How does Howie act like a child sometimes? "The centerfold was floating like some kind of angel gone bad." Why do you think the author makes this particular comparison? Why do Laura's long eyelashes and curled lips seem very remarkable to Howie? " 'I'm socially retarded for my age,' she said with a certain dignity." What does this comment suggest about Laura (and Howie) and about their parents? Why does she say it "with a certain dignity"? What might Laura mean when she says that perhaps the cut-up people in the museum display didn't have any family? Why do you think Howie seems so concerned about paying for the things they've used? Comment on the teenagers at the public boat launch: With what are they apparently concerned? Is Howie's final remark genuine or sarcastic?

3. *The Municipal Beach:* Based on the telephone conversation, how would you describe Laura's mother? After Laura and Howie change into new clothes and are walking down the road, why are they so excited, "careening off one another through the patches of shadow and sun"?

4. *The Bus:* As Howie and Laura ride along on the bus, what does he think about? Why does he seem so taken with the idea of their living alone in the woods? How does Maddy feel about Laura? About herself? What *would* it have been like if Wells had called first (see p. 60 in the book)? As Mr. Wells, Miss Haskell, and Maddy discuss the problem in his office, what impression do you get of Mr. Wells? Of the camp? Is Maddy being fair in her threat to sue? To what extent are camps responsible for preventing traditions or incidents like this?

5. *The Dining Hall:* Why do you think Calvin and Tiwanda decide to help Howie and Laura? "His voice was soft and dark, like a bruise." Why do you think the author uses this simile to describe Pardoe? What is Pardoe like? Why do you think the author has included him in the story?

6. *The Cabins:* How does Howie feel about himself after kicking Pardoe? Was he in any way justified in doing this? Why or why not? At this point in the story, has Howie changed at all? Explain. What does Calvin mean by the word "bandit?" Do you agree with him? "It was as if it had all happened to some other, littler kid." Has Laura changed at all? Explain. Why does she feel sorry for her earlier self, "that little kid?" Why does she have to think a minute about her name? What do you think Tiwanda means when she says, "Don't I know, don't I know?" How do the kids at this camp seem different from those at the other camp? What meaning might the dream of the cave have for Howie? Why do you

think he thinks Calvin's father might be the sliced-up man in the museum? "But he knew now that there were people like that." What does Howie mean by this? What might he mean by "they wouldn't be able to stop?" "He wanted to tell her how important she was." Why is Laura important to Howie?

7. *Ahlburg:* How does the sheriff react to Laura's disappearance? What is Maddy's state of mind at this point? Why does she find the phrase "a little fox with glasses" comforting? After she listens to Laura's call, why does she feel that her daughter's making them worry "seemed, finally, fair"?

8. *The Starlight Motel:* As Laura approaches the motel, Howie finds the woods where he sits hidden "all very absorbing." Why? What appeal do the woods seem to have for him? Given Laura's behavior early in the story, how can one explain her confidence and spunk? Why does she seem pleasant and alarming to Howie and why does he like it? Why do you think Howie feels they may be leaving something in the room? In what ways do Howie and Laura seem innocent and childlike? In what ways more like adults? In light of everything else in the story, why is it appropriate that Howie's parents are archeologists?

9. *The Restaurant:* How do Howie and Laura react to the *Benji* movie? Does the movie in any way reflect their own situation? Explain. Why does Howie remember the day in Greece so fondly? As he thinks about telling Laura his secret, what might "they weren't coming back" mean? At the restaurant, "he couldn't understand what he was grinning about." Why is he so happy at this moment? Why does the electric eye in the bathroom bother and then reassure him? What does Laura mean by "it [the old woman's head] was dirty and grubby in there"? Why is Laura so upset by her? How do they escape—and why is Howie's method appropriate?

10. *The Highway:* Why does the image of Laura covered with white flowers make Howie feel lightheaded again? Why do you think the author chose to make the deputy a goat farmer? What does the deputy think about Howie and Laura? In this situation, do you think he reacts the way most adults would? Discuss.

11. *The Woods:* What does Maddy mean by her question, "Why are we driving them away?" Does the question have a larger meaning? What does she mean by "casually inflicted hurts"? Who has hurt whom? What does Howie mean when he tells the old man that he does not have far to go? Why do you think Laura signed her name "Shadow" on the IOU note? Why does the old man prefer the IOU note to the money? As they hide in the woods, why does Laura seem more content than Howie? What has she come to realize? Of what is she afraid? How does she feel about her newfound ability to hurt people? Why does Howie think that things will never work out for them, that "it's against the law"? Why does he tell Laura that he doesn't need her? And why does she react so strongly? "He was sitting on top of her, holding her hands back over her head, but she had won." What does this mean? At the end of the book, why is he "very sure that everything was going to be all right?" What does Laura's "Hold on, hold on" suggest? How have Laura and Howie changed during the course of the book? Throughout the story, why do you think the author refers to the characters as "the boy" and "the girl" instead of using their names?

WRITING ACTIVITIES

1. Write a letter that Howie might have written to his parents from the motel. Explain the situation as you think he might have, given what you know about him and his parents.
2. Write a brief profile of Pardoe in which you speculate about what might have caused him to appear "hurt bad deep down inside." Base your inferences as much as possible on how he acts, what he says, and what others say about him.
3. At the end of the book, write a letter that Laura might send to Tiwanda explaining all that has happened since they last saw each other.
4. In your school or public library, find a reference work that lists summer camps and their addresses. (The information might also be available on the Internet.) Write a letter to a camp asking for dates, ages, costs, etc. Also, ask the following question: What does the camp do to help children adjust to living away from home for the first time? Mail the letter, and later report to the class any response that you receive.
5. Write a diamante poem that begins with the word *outside* and ends with the word *inside* and that reflects the novel in some way (see Appendix A).
6. In the final chapter, Maddy thinks about "casually inflicted hurts." Write in your journal about a time recently when you were hurt by someone who probably did not intend it. How did you react? Is it worse to be intentionally or unintentionally hurt by someone else?
7. Write the text for a brochure for the camp that Mr. Wells might have created to send to parents of prospective campers. (*Note to teacher*: When students have completed this, have them exchange brochures and then write a critique of the one they've received from the point of view of Howie and Laura.)
8. Laura and Howie frequently talk about paying people back for things they have taken or borrowed. Compose an IOU note that Laura might have written to the one person in the novel that you think she is most indebted to.
9. Write a one- to two-page persuasive paper arguing that Howie is or is not a moral person. Support your thesis by referring to specific examples of his behavior in the book.

OTHER ACTIVITIES

1. Role play a meeting that takes place three days after the book ends in which the following people discuss the events of the previous week and possible outcomes: Maddy, Margo, Mr. Wells, the sheriff, and Miss Gallagher, who should conduct the meeting.
2. Create a "split-screen" collage of pictures, printed words and phrases, found objects, and the like that reflects on one side your thoughts about Howie and Laura (or perhaps Maddy) at the beginning of the book and on the other your thoughts about them (or her) at the end.
3. Using poster paper, draw a map of the setting as you visualize it from details in the book. In part, use the chapter titles as places to include: The Island (along with the camp), the Cottage, the Municipal Beach, The Starlight Motel, The Restaurant, and others.

4. Pretend that after the book ends Laura and Howie are separated and do not see each other for several months. Christmas arrives, and each wants to send the other a gift that will represent in some way the experiences they shared and the knowledge they gained. Create an art object of some kind that would serve as the gift that either of them might send to the other.
5. Using an art medium of your choice that facilitates the expression of an idea (perhaps a wire sculpture, a mobile, or even finger-paint), create an abstract representation of Outsiders Versus Insiders.

SELECTED TEACHING RESOURCES

Printed Materials

Teaching Aids

The Goats. LIFT series. Sundance.

The Goats. Novel-Ties. Learning Links.

The Pearl

John Steinbeck
New York: Viking Press, 1947
Available in paperback from Penguin.

SUMMARY

When their baby Coyotito is bitten by a scorpion and the town's wealthy doctor refuses to give medical aid, Kino, a poor pearl fisherman, and his wife Juana pray that they will find the Pearl of the World. They succeed, and there follows a series of fateful events generated by greed and pride: attempts to cheat Kino of his pearl, the destruction of his boat and house, and other acts of violence. Fearful and desperate to get full value for his find, Kino kills a man, and he and his family flee into the desert. There they suffer the ultimate tragedy—their baby's death—after which they return in despair to the village and fling the tainted pearl into the sea.

APPRAISAL

Based upon a legend that Steinbeck heard in lower California, *The Pearl* is a brief, simple parable about good and evil, rich and poor, hope and despair. Although some critics consider it a melodrama, insubstantial in comparison with his earlier novels, the book provides a highly teachable introduction to the Nobel Laureate for students in grades seven through nine.

THEMES

pride, greed, good versus evil, materialism, fate, social class, knowledge versus ignorance, values

LITERARY CONCEPTS

parable, symbol, setting, point of view, naturalism, characterization, plot, foreshadowing

RELATED READING

Students who appreciate the simplicity of *The Pearl* may also respond to *The Old Man and the Sea* by Ernest Hemingway. These novels (which, incidentally, have Hispanic protagonists) concern the effect that fate often has on the lives of simple, uneducated, proud people. Other novels by Steinbeck to consider are *The Red Pony*, *Of Mice and Men*, and *Tortilla Flat*.

READING PROBLEMS AND OPPORTUNITIES

Because it is a parable, *The Pearl* is written in a very simple style. For middle or junior high school students, it poses no serious reading problems. A few words that might be taught, if they are not known, are the following (chapter numbers are in parentheses):

avarice (1),
appraise (1, 4),
indigent (1),
estuary (2, 3, 4, 5),
illusion (2, 6),
deftly (2, 3),
subside (2, 3),
recede (2, 4, 5, 6),
patron (2, 3),
incandescent (2, 3),
judicious (3),
furtive (3),
contemptuous (4),
exhilaration (5, 6),
cleft (6), and
malignant (6).

INITIATING ACTIVITIES

1. With your classmates, discuss the following questions: To what extent is it possible in this country for very poor people to move out of poverty? For the children of such people once they have grown up? What works against them? What does such upward mobility require of the people themselves? What does it require that is beyond their control? To what extent, if any, should private or governmental agencies assist them?
2. Imagine that you have won $100,000 tax-free on a television game show. List several (at least five) ways you would use the money. Be honest. When you have finished, rank all of the items according to importance. Then write the word *Me* by any items that affect mostly yourself, the word *Others* by those affecting other people, and *Less* by those affecting people less fortunate than you. Keep the list for future reference.
3. Read the parables in chapter 13 of the Book of Matthew. Discuss with your teacher and other students the purpose and style of parables.

DISCUSSION QUESTIONS

1. *Chapter 1:* How does Kino feel about his family? Does he seem rich or poor to you? Why does he seem so contented? When the baby is stung, why do the neighbors say the doctor will not come? Why does the whole neighborhood join the procession? Why do the beggars? What is meant by "rage and terror went together"? Why do you think the servant refuses to speak to Kino in the old language? Why does the doctor refuse to help? The doctor is clearly greedy. In what other ways does he seem unlikable? Why do the people feel shamed?
2. *Chapter 2:* Why do Kino and Juana set out to search for a pearl? Why do they insist on a doctor? One needs a boat to guarantee a supply of food. Why does one need to find a pearl? "It is not good to want a thing too much." Do you think Kino and Juana want the pearl too much? Discuss. Why do you think the people feel "you must be very tactful with God or the gods"? Why do you think that songs are so important to the people?
3. *Chapter 3:* How do the various townspeople react to the news? In what way has Kino become their enemy? Describe the brief pattern of Kino's wishes and dreams. Why does he seem hesitant at first? Why does he especially want Coyotito to go to school? Is Kino greedy? How do the neighbors react to Kino's find? To his dreams? Why does Kino begin to hear the music of evil when the priest arrives? "A plan is a real thing, and things

projected are experienced." What does this mean? Why does Kino feel he must make "a hard skin for himself against the world"? Is the doctor concerned? Is he intelligent? Why does Kino let him in? Why does Steinbeck describe the doctor nibbling chocolate and sweet cake? In less than one day, how has Kino changed?

4. *Chapter 4:* What do Kino's neighbors say they would do with the pearl? Do you think they would actually do it? Why or why not? To what extent has Juana's reaction to the pearl differed from Kino's? Kino set his hat carefully. Is he confident as he sets out to sell the pearl? Why or why not? Why does the Father preach the sermon about "the castle of the Universe" every year? Describe the first buyer. How do you know that he is greatly impressed by the pearl? Why is the magnifying glass of the third buyer an effective device? What larger meanings might it imply about the pearl? Why is Kino so reluctant to go to the capital? Do you think his fears are justified? What is his brother's fear? Why does Kino refuse to throw the pearl away? Is his reason the same as it was earlier?

5. *Chapter 5:* How has the pearl changed Kino? How does Juana feel toward him? What does the phrase "I am a man" mean to her? Is this what being a man means to you? Discuss. Why does Juana say, "Here is your pearl"? Why does the hole in the canoe seem worse than anything else to Kino? Why does he feel he must hide from the neighbors? Would the neighbors turn him in? Why or why not? Why is the blessing "Go with God" like death to Kino?

6. *Chapter 6:* What is the "ancient thing . . . some animal thing" that stirs in Kino? In what ways do the chances of Kino and Juana escaping the trackers seem slim? Why is the death of Coyotito particularly tragic? What part does luck play in the whole tracking episode? In the entire book? What might Steinbeck be saying about luck or fate? When Kino and Juana return to town, why do they walk side by side? What do you think they hope to achieve by throwing the pearl away? What could you predict for them? Why do you think this story "has been told so often" in the town? Do you think it is told mostly by Kino's people? Or by everyone? What or who is most responsible for the tragedy: Kino's pride, his greed, the doctor, the community itself, or fate? Why do you think Steinbeck occasionally included passages like these: "Kino watched with the detachment of God while a dusty ant frantically tried to escape the sand trap an ant lion had dug for him (chapter 1); and "Out in the estuary a tight woven school of small fishes glittered and broke water to escape a school of great fishes that drove in to eat them" (chapter 3)?

WRITING ACTIVITIES

1. Pretend that the end of chapter 6 continues with the following:

   > "Kino and Juana then turned toward the crowd, which had observed the incident without comment. There was a commotion at the rear of the crowd, which then stirred forward like a wave toward a point in front, from which emerged the doctor, the priest, and the local constable. The doctor pointed at Kino and Juana."

   From this point, write a new ending of one or two pages for the novel.

2. Write an original two- or three-page parable that illustrates the point that you think Steinbeck is emphasizing in the novel.

3. Do some research on pearls. How rare are they? How large do they get? What determines their value? Are they found only in oysters? Are they "mined" by individual fishermen? If not, how are they obtained? Your report should be at least three pages long.

4. The novel often refers to songs that are important to Kino and his people, but the words are never mentioned. Write some appropriate lyrics for one of the following:

   a. the Song of the Family

   b. the Song of Evil

   c. the Song of the Enemy

   d. the Song of the Undersea

5. Write two brief sets of lyrics for the Song of the Pearl That Might Be: one as Kino would have written it before he finds the pearl; the other after he throws it away.

6. Write a diamante poem using the contrasting words *good* and *evil* reflecting the events, characters, or ideas in the novel. Or, write a cinquain beginning with the word *greed* or *pride* that also alludes to the novel in some way. (See Appendix A.)

7. "It is not good to want a thing too much." Write about a time in your life when you wanted something very, very much and came to realize the truth of this quotation.

8. Kino clearly believes that education (i.e., knowledge) is the only real means of escaping poverty. Today, many of our country's poor seem to climb out of poverty by means other than education. Write a two- to three-page paper agreeing or disagreeing with the argument that education is essential for the poor.

9. List the different ways in which Kino plans to use the money gained from selling his pearl. Then code them as you coded your own in "Initiating Activity" 2. Finally, write a two- to three-page paper comparing your own plans to Kino's.

OTHER ACTIVITIES

1. Kino frequently feels the need to remind himself, "I am a man." Design a collage around this statement as you perceive it. Your collage should answer the question "What is a man?" (*Note to teacher*: This assignment could be altered, if desired, to "What is a woman?" or "What makes up personal strength?" although the original seems more in keeping with the novel's intent and emphasis.)

2. Role play a scene involving the following characters: Kino, the priest, and the first dealer—plus a character who is not in the book: an honest appraiser who favors giving Kino fair value for his pearl but lacks money. Imagine that Coyotito was not killed and that Kino returns to the village with Juana and the baby after having shot the trackers.

3. The four beggars in front of the church knew everything in town. They were students of the expressions of young women who went into confession, and they saw them as they came out and read the nature of sin. They knew every little scandal and some very big crimes. Obviously the beggars are perceptive and wise. Enact a trial of the characters in the novel to determine responsibility for the death of Coyotito—with the beggars as four judges.

4. Make a "shape book" in the form of a circle. With paint or crayon, color the cover so that it looks like a pearl. Illustrate the pages within the book with drawings or pictures that represent Kino's dreams after he finds the Pearl of the World (see chapter 3). Illustrate the last page in a way that reflects his shattered dreams.
5. Make a drawing or model of the Castle of the Universe as it is described in chapter 4. Your work should reflect the real purpose of the castle, not the purpose communicated by the Father to his people.

SELECTED TEACHING RESOURCES

Media Aids

Cassette

The Pearl. Unabridged. Penguin Highbridge Audio.

Cassettes (2)

The Pearl. Unabridged. Recorded Books.

CD-ROM

The Pearl and The Red Pony. 1996. Windows and Macintosh versions. Penguin Electronics and Perma-Bound.

Internet

Smith, Jennifer. 1998. *Center for Steinbeck Studies*. ©1998. Available: http://www.sjsu.edu/depts/steinbec/srchome.html (Accessed March 10, 2000).

A useful website featuring a bibliography, a Steinbeck chronology, a map and pictures of Steinbeck settings, photographs of the author, his Nobel acceptance speech, and a selection on Steinbeck in the schools.

A + LS/Media Weaver, High School Novels Bundle. *The Pearl*. Available: http://www.amered.com/curr/mwprl.html (Accessed March 10, 2000).

This site contains a variety of writing activities for students.

Video

The Pearl. 77 min., b & w. Perma-Bound and Sundance.

Printed Materials

Articles

Karsten, Ernest E. "Thematic Structure in *The Pearl*." *English Journal* 54 (January 1965): 1–7.

Nagle, John M. "A View of Literature Too Often Neglected." *English Journal* 58 (March 1969): 399–407.

Scoville, Samuel. "The *Weltanschauung* of Steinbeck and Hemingway." *English Journal* 56 (January 1967): 60–63, 66.

Book

Workman, Brooke. *Writing Seminars in the Content Area: In Search of Hemingway, Salinger, and Steinbeck*. Champaign-Urbana, IL: National Council of Teachers of English, 1983.

Teaching Aids

The Pearl. Contemporary Classics series and Portals to Literature series. Perfection Learning Corporation.

The Pearl. Literature Unit Plans. Teacher's Pet Publications.

The Pearl. Novel/Drama Curriculum Units. The Center for Learning.

The Pearl. Novel-Ties. Learning Links.

The Pearl. Novel Unit Guide, Novel Units Student Packet, and Perma-Guide. Perma-Bound

The Pearl. REACT series, Novel Ideas Classic series, and Novel Ideas Plus series. Sundance.

Tests

The Pearl. Essay, objective, and alternative assessment versions. Perfection Learning Corporation.

Nothing but the Truth

Avi

New York: Orchard Books, 1991

Available in paperback from Avon Books.

SUMMARY

Philip Malloy looks forward to joining the track team; however, his whole life changes when he has a conflict with his English and homeroom teacher, Margaret Narwin. During homeroom, Philip tries to act cool by humming along with the national anthem, an action that school rules forbid. His behavior becomes a source of great interest when he is suspended from school. Told through a series of memos, interviews, diary entries, and conversations, the story unfolds as the issue garners national interest. The media take his side, and eventually the school administration must temporarily remove Miss Narwin. Philip, who appears as a hero to his parents and the outside world, is not happy with the furor he has caused and eventually changes to a private school.

APPRAISAL

Avi, a highly acclaimed author of young adult books, has written books that received the Newbery Honor Award, the Horn Book-Boston Globe Award, the Golden Kite Award, and the Lopez Memorial Foundation Award. Further, his works have been honored by Editor's Choice, *Booklist*, YASD Best Books for Young Adults, Best Books for Teens, New York Public Library, and Best of the Year, *The School Library Journal*. Avi's focus on issues of interest to teens and his unique style have made him popular among children and adolescents (grades seven through nine).

THEMES

truth, friendship, parent/child relationships, student/teacher relationships, appearance and reality, the influence of media

LITERARY CONCEPTS

documentary style, character development and motivation, point of view, plot, satire

RELATED READING

Students who enjoy Avi's writing may also enjoy some of his other highly recommended novels, such as *The True Confessions of Charlotte Doyle, Romeo and Juliet-Together (and Alive!) at Last*, and *The Windcatcher.* A grimmer portrayal of the conflicts between students and faculty can be found in *The Chocolate War* by Robert Cormier and *Killing Mr. Griffin* by Lois Duncan.

READING PROBLEMS AND OPPORTUNITIES

The use of conversations, memos, and diaries makes the vocabulary in this book fairly simple. The following words might be used for study (chapter numbers appear in parentheses):

carpe diem (2),
facilitate (3),
theoretical (5),
concepts (5),
passive (6),
electorate (6),
bedlam (10),
vigilant (10),
infractions (10, 13),
counterproductive (12),
ultraliberals (15),
animosity (15), and
misconstrues (16).

INITIATING ACTIVITIES

1. With your classmates, discuss the meaning of *patriotic*. Make a list of actions that would be considered patriotic and a list of those that would not be considered patriotic. Keep this list for discussion after you have finished reading the book.
2. Collect at least five definitions of *truth*. Share these with your classmates and then discuss the meaning of *truth*. Is *truth* different for each individual? Should there be one and only one definition of *truth*? Continue these discussions as you read *Nothing but the Truth.*

DISCUSSION QUESTIONS

1. *Introductory Memo:* How does this procedure compare to the one used at your school? Which events could, in your opinion, be eliminated? Why?
2. *Chapter 1:* Compare and contrast the way Philip Mallory feels about Miss Narwin with the way she feels about him. In what ways does he judge her? In what ways does she judge him? Which of them uses the best evidence for his or her decisions?
3. *Chapter 2:* What is Mr. Lunser's attitude toward the opening of the school day? Do you enjoy his remarks or find him annoying? Why? What is Philip's attitude toward school?
4. *Chapter 3:* Chapter 3 begins with a memo from the principal to Philip. In what other formats (dialogue, diary, report) could this information have been presented? Why is the memo format effective? How does Allison respond to Philip's story?
5. *Chapter 4:* Based on Philip's answer to question 4 of the exam, do you think that Miss Narwin's grade is fair? Why or why not? How would you have responded to Philip's answer?
6. *Chapters 5 and 6:* How are the memos in chapters 5 and 6 related? What types of persuasive techniques do the authors use in making their pleas?
7. *Chapter 7:* How does Philip's interaction with Narwin and his father reported in his diary illustrate the generation gap? How could these misunderstandings be resolved?

8. *Chapter 8:* What is the irony in Dr. Doane's statement, "You can always count on me"? Do you feel it is fair that Philip cannot try out for this track team because of his grades? Why or why not?
9. *Chapter 9:* What reason does Philip give his father for not trying out for the track team? How does this inhibit good communication between father and son? How well do Philip's parents understand him?
10. *Chapter 10:* Why does Philip hum during the national anthem? How else might Miss Narwin have responded to Philip's answer? What effects would such a response draw from Philip? How does Philip modify the "Star-Spangled Banner" story for his own purposes?
11. *Chapter 11:* Why does Philip persist in his singing? Is the assistant principal effective in handling the problem with Philip? Why or why not? What parallels exist between the events in Mr. Malloy's job and Philip's school?
12. *Chapter 12:* Why isn't it possible for Dr. Palleni and Philip to come to a resolution to the problem? Why does Philip refuse to apologize? What do the memos show about the assistant principal's understanding of Philip's problems? Why does Mr. Malloy take Philip's problem to Ted Griffin?
13. *Chapter 13:* What generalizations can you draw about a reporter's job from the conversations Jennifer Stewart has with school officials?
14. *Chapter 14:* Identify at least three inaccuracies in the article "Suspended for Patriotism." How is it possible that these occurred? Why do some people hope the whole issue will go away? Why are some people pleased about the story?
15. *Chapter 15:* How well do the responses on the radio talk show reflect the reality of the situation? Is this typical of talk shows? Why or why not? How and why do the following people differ in their accounts of Philip's actions: Miss Narwin, Ken Barchet, Cynthia Gambia, and Allison Doresett? How have Miss Narwin's feelings changed from the time she first dealt with Philip to the time that she learned of the article in the Florida paper?
16. *Chapter 16:* Why does support shift away from Miss Narwin? Separate the real reasons from the apparent reasons. Explain how Miss Narwin's words were taken out of context and used against her. Do you agree with Coach Jameson's advice? Why or why not? How are both Miss Narwin and Philip losers?
17. *Chapter 17:* Why is Miss Narwin considering resignation?
18. *Chapter 18:* Why doesn't Miss Narwin's story get told?
19. *Chapter 19:* What is the irony in Philip's final statement in the book?

WRITING ACTIVITIES

1. Do you agree that there "has to be better stuff to read for ninth graders somewhere"? Make a list of five books you would recommend for students at your grade level. Compare your list to the list of books you are required to read. Explain why you chose your books and why they are or are not better for young people to read. Share your lists and explanations with other students in your class.
2. Make a list of the things that matter to Philip, including such items as achievement in school, success in sports, popularity with girls, and relationship with parents. Try to include at least ten items. With two or three other students, discuss and rank the items you

listed from what mattered most to Philip to what mattered least. Now each of you take a copy of the list and rearrange the order to reflect your own values. Write a comparison and contrast paper about how you and Philip are alike and different.

3. Write a description (with an illustration, if you like) of a place "Where children are educated, not just taught." After you have read your description to your classmates, discuss how this ideal educational facility compares to the school that Philip attends and the one that you attend.

4. Write a note to Philip commenting on his suggestions for ways to impress and aggravate your teachers. You may add your own suggestions or modify some of Philip's ideas. Explain to Philip why you think his ideas were good or not so good.

5. Before reading this book, you discussed patriotic acts. After reading this book, how do you feel about Philip's behavior? Was it an act of patriotism, an act of defiance, or something else? Once you have decided how you would classify his actions, write a paragraph to explain and support your choice.

6. Mr. Malloy describes the role of the school board in this way: "Keeps the schools in line." Check out the role of your own school board. Over what areas do they have jurisdiction? In what areas do they have absolutely no say? How are board members chosen? What qualifications do they have to have? Write a description of your school board, with the first line beginning, "The role of the school board is. . . ." Share your views with your teacher and your principal.

7. "Everyone is famous for fifteen minutes." This prophesy was true for Philip Malloy. Let your imagination take flight and write a brief account of what your own "fifteen minutes of fame" would be like. How is it like Philip's and how is it different?

OTHER ACTIVITIES

1. Interview your parents and others in their age group about the books they were required to read when they were your age. Collect and tally the information from others in your class. Prepare a poster that illustrates how similar or different those sets of required books are.

2. Throughout the novel, different characters saw the same event and reported it in different ways. Prepare a large chart of at least three events and the different ways individuals perceived these events. For example, explore how Miss Narwin, Philip, Philip's parents, and Philip's coach perceived Philip's grade in English. Once you have listed the events and how different people saw and explained them, try to arrive at a consensus about where the truth lies.

3. In this novel, there is disagreement about how school funds should be used. Should money be taken from extracurricular activities and used strictly for academics? Find out about your school budget and prepare a pie graph illustrating where the money goes. Prepare a presentation for your class members in which you argue in support of the budget or in favor of changes.

4. Reenact the radio talk show and then continue to improvise additional comments that might have been made. Try responding with reason and logic. During a second improvisation, allow some participants to respond with off-the-wall statements and inflammatory language. Then discuss how you felt in each case. Classify the responses on the talk show in the book as logical or illogical.

5. Dr. Seymour says, "It doesn't matter if it's true or not true. It's what people are saying that's important." With three classmates, debate this statement, using not only examples from the novel but also current events. Ask your classmates to vote on the winners of the debate.

SELECTED TEACHING RESOURCES

Media Aids

Internet

All About My Books. Available: http://www.avi-writer.com/books.html (Accessed March 10, 2000).
Links providing additional information about Avi's work.

Questions & Answers About Avi. Available: http://www.avi-writer.com/QandA.html (Accessed March 10, 2000).
An interesting site for aspiring young writers.

Printed Resources

Article

Elleman, Barbara. "Book Strategies: *Nothing but the Truth: A Documentary Novel* by Avi." *Book Links* 1 (January 1992): 60–61.

Play

Nothing but the Truth: A Play. Ronn Smith. New York: Avon, 1997.
A dramatic version of the novel.

Teaching Aids

Nothing but the Truth. Novel Aids. Sundance.

Nothing but the Truth. Novel Unit Guide. Perma-Bound.

Nothing but the Truth. Novel-Ties. Learning Links.

The Contender

Robert Lipsyte
New York: Harper & Row, 1967
Available in paperback from HarperTrophy.

SUMMARY

Alfred Brooks is a seventeen-year-old dropout living with his Aunt Pearl and her three daughters in Harlem. Confused by forces pulling him in different directions, he dreams of fulfillment through boxing and begins a strenuous training program at a local gym. With the help of his flinty but compassionate manager, Mr. Donatelli, Alfred wins his first two fights. After he battles his third opponent to a draw, he loses his fourth and final match, but he learns the importance of courage in boxing and in any of life's other battles where one aspires to become "a contender."

APPRAISAL

Written by a former sports editor for the *New York Times*, *The Contender* is one of the most popular young adult novels of the last thirty years. It won the 1967 Children's Book Award of the Child Study Association of America and also recognition as an American Library Association Notable Children's Book for the same year. Of the novel, one reviewer has written, "Lipsyte is most convincing in his unfolding of the inner transformation of a boy gone slack into a boxer gradually responding to different and compelling rhythms." *The Contender* is most often used with students in grades seven through ten.

THEMES

courage in the face of adversity, growing up, identity, friendship, decisions

LITERARY CONCEPTS

point of view, interior monologue, characterization, plot, symbol, dialect

RELATED READING

In addition to Lipsyte's sequel *The Brave* (which portrays Alfred Brooks as an adult and a cop who himself becomes a mentor), other books about young people striving for excellence in athletics (boxing in particular) include *Shadow Boxer* by Chris Lynch, *The Harder They Fall* by

Budd Schulberg, and *In the Ring: A Treasury of Boxing Stories* edited by Martin Harry Greenberg. *Wrestling Sturbridge* by Rich Wallace is about the related sport. More generally, students may enjoy books by and about the tennis player Arthur Ashe, such as *Days of Grace: A Memoir* by Arthur Ashe and *Arthur Ashe: Portrait in Motion* by Frank Deford, as well as novels about friendships like *The Planet of Junior Brown* by Virginia Hamilton and *The Moves Make the Man* by Bruce Brooks.

READING PROBLEMS AND OPPORTUNITIES

According to one readability formula, *The Contender* is written on a sixth-grade level. Thus the book should not be particularly difficult for most secondary school students. A few words that might be used for vocabulary study are (chapters where the terms appear are in parentheses):

swagger (1, 2, 5, 10, 12, 14),	*suave* (4),	*kneaded* (16), and
nationalist (4, 12),	*gaunt* (6),	*pummel* (19).
listless (4),	*mechanically* (10, 14, 18),	

The book has many examples of precise verbs of movement, such as (all in chapter 1):

shuffle,	*shamble*,	*stiffen*, and	*whirl*

as well as:

lope (2),	*slouch* (2),	*lurch* (2),	*trudge* (3),
jostle (7),	*skitter* (9),	*clatter* (10), and	*flail* (14).

INITIATING ACTIVITIES

1. Read "An Encounter to Last an Eternity" in the April 11, 1983, issue of *Sports Illustrated*. Written by Frank Deford, the article tells the story of two young amateur boxers whose match against each other had tragic consequences. (*Note to teacher*: If possible, the article, which can be located on microfilm in most public libraries, should be assigned [or read] to everyone in class and used to stimulate a discussion of the opportunities and problems inherent in boxing.)
2. Try to get a feeling for what life in a crowded urban setting must be like for children and young people. Sources of information include magazine articles, books, and even collections of poems and the Internet. After consulting at least three sources, discuss the subject with your classmates, especially the extent to which such an environment might discourage or alienate those who live there.
3. Write a one- to two-page paper about a time in your life when you were faced with a very important decision that would affect your future. Include in your paper the reasons you had to confront the decision, the factors you had to consider in making it, and the results.

DISCUSSION QUESTIONS

1. *Chapter 1:* What kind of person does Alfred seem to be? How is he different from Major, Hollis, and Sonny? How is he different from James? Why does he refuse to go with them? Why does he go to the cave? What kind of place has the cave been for him and James in

the past? What kind of relationship have they apparently had? Has it changed? If so, how? What kind of setting and mood has the author created for the book so far?

2. *Chapter 2:* How do Aunt Pearl and her daughters seem to feel about Alfred? What details suggest that Aunt Pearl may have difficulty making ends meet? Why does the author include the long description of the television program? When Alfred leaves the apartment, why does he go to Mr. Donatelli's gym? Why do there seem to be so many steps leading up to the gym?

3. *Chapter 3:* According to Mr. Donatelli, how is boxing different from the street? What does he say it takes to be a contender? Why is it important to want to be a contender? Why does he say that quitting before you really try is worse than never starting? Do you agree? Why or why not? How do you think Alfred feels as he leaves?

4. *Chapter 4:* Why does Alfred refuse Harold's plea to join the march? Is it the same reason he had for refusing to join Major, Sonny, and James in chapter 1? Why or why not? What different points of view do Major, Harold, and Alfred represent? What viewpoint is expressed by Reverend Price? What does Alfred's fantasy about the girl on the subway reveal about his character? In what way is Alfred confused? Why does he decide to go into training?

5. *Chapter 5:* How does Alfred feel about Aunt Pearl? In what ways is his day at the store disappointing? How does he let the disappointment affect him?

6. *Chapter 6:* Why does Alfred feel occasional urges to leave the gym? Why doesn't he? What kind of person is Bud Martin? Why does he slap Red? Why is Bud willing to give Red a second chance?

7. *Chapter 7:* What are Alfred's impressions of Madison Square Garden? Why does he feel sure that neither the man at the ticket window nor the one at the door will let them in? What does he learn about Willie Streeter during and after the fight? About Mr. Donatelli? In what ways do Willie and Bill Witherspoon seem different? As he walks home, why does Alfred feel good about his decision to try to become a fighter?

8. *Chapter 8*: Is the reason Alfred refuses Major, Hollis, and Sonny a second time any different from his reason for refusing the first time? Discuss.

9. *Chapter 9:* Compare Alfred's and Aunt Pearl's attitudes toward boxing. How does he try to ease her fears and worries?

10. *Chapter 10:* What does Alfred like about training? What does he dislike? After six weeks, how does he feel? What frequently seems to be in the back of his mind? Why does boxing seem so important to him?

11. *Chapter 11:* Why does Alfred break training by smoking marijuana and drinking wine in the clubhouse?

12. *Chapter 12:* Why do Major and the others involved invite Alfred to the clubhouse and Coney Island? Why does Alfred seem unable to refuse? "If they don't get you one way, they get you another." How does this statement apply to Major's efforts with Alfred? On whom does Alfred blame his troubles? Is he right? Why or why not? According to Mr. Donatelli, why would getting hurt in the ring for the first time tell a person whether or not he were a contender? Alfred asks Mr. Donatelli, "Would you . . . will you tell me then? When you know?" What is implied by his change from *would* to *will*?

13. *Chapter 13:* In what ways is chapter 13 a turning point for Alfred?

14. *Chapter 14:* What role does Henry play in Alfred's efforts to become a boxer? How are they important to each other? Is Alfred's attitude toward Henry changing? If so, how? Are Henry and Alfred alike in any way? If so, how? What are Alfred's impressions of Spoon and his wife? In what ways are Spoon and Donatelli positive influences? Why does Mr. Donatelli tell Henry and Alfred that winning is not enough? The author frequently describes the actions as a series of rapid-fire impressions in Alfred's mind: "Pop-pop, get in there and fight, black boy, pop-pop, you slave." Do you think this kind of description is effective? Why or why not?

15. *Chapter 15:* How is Aunt Pearl a comfort to Alfred? Why do you think "it didn't even taste sweet, the winning"?

16. *Chapter 16:* As he often has before in the novel, Alfred seems confused after his second fight. What contributes to his confusion? How do Donatelli and Bud feel about him after the fight?

17. *Chapter 17:* What seems uppermost in Uncle Wilson's mind? How do he and Jeff disagree? Why has Alfred's attitude toward Jeff changed? Why has Alfred decided to go back to school?

18. *Chapter 18:* Why does Mr. Donatelli want Alfred to quit? Why isn't he sure he'd like Alfred to have the killer instinct? What does he feel Alfred has accomplished? What does Alfred mean when he says, "So I can know, too"?

19. *Chapter 19:* Why is Alfred so nervous? Who has been most helpful to Alfred in his efforts to become a fighter? As he waits, in what ways does he think and talk of helping people in the future? Do you think Mr. Donatelli was wrong to let Alfred fight Elston Hubbard? Why or why not? At the end, what does Alfred know?

20. *Chapter 20:* In trying to convince James to come with him, what experience in the cave does Alfred remind him of? Do you think this helps? Why or why not? More than anything else, what has Alfred learned from boxing? As the novel ends, how strong do you think his determination to *be somebody* is? What future do you predict for him? For James? Do you think the ending is realistic? Why or why not?

WRITING ACTIVITIES

1. Amateur boxing matches are only briefly covered in most newspapers, if at all. Write four brief sports reports on Alfred's fights. Keep in mind the importance of being objective.

2. Write a three- or four-page report on one of the following topics:

    a. a boxer in recent times whose achievements in the sport enabled him to escape from urban poverty

    b. drug rehabilitation clinics like the one mentioned by Bill Witherspoon in chapter 19

    c. skills and tactics in boxing

3. You are a sports publicist hired to develop a promotional campaign for the new young lightweight, Alfred Brooks, after his first two fights. Write a press release that would inform the public about Alfred's background, statistics, training, style, and experience. Use the novel for your information.

4. In chapter 9, Aunt Pearl sums up the complaints that many people have about boxing: "Full of gangsters, and people get hurt bad." Write a defense of boxing as a sport in which you respond to Aunt Pearl's arguments by referring to characters and events in the novel.
5. In chapter 3, Alfred tells Mr. Donatelli that he wants to be somebody. Write a one- to two-page paper explaining what it means, in your opinion, to be somebody.
6. Write a comparison paper of two friendships in the novel: Alfred's friendship with James and Henry's friendship with Alfred. Focus at least partly on the degree to which each of the two friendships is balanced, with both individuals contributing something.
7. You are Alfred. A few weeks after your final fight, you apply for a part-time job as an assistant in a city summer recreation program. The job application form requires that you list your strengths and weaknesses. Write what you would include.
8. Using the same style employed by the author to describe action in the ring (interior monologue), write a version of Alfred's final fight in which he wins.
9. When Alfred tells Aunt Pearl about winning his first fight, she says, "It didn't even taste sweet, the winning, did it, honey?" Write about a time when you worked extremely hard to achieve something that you thought you really wanted only to be disappointed when you got it.
10. Throughout the book, Mr. Donatelli gives Alfred many instructions about boxing (e.g., "Snap that jab out."). Compile as many of these as you can into a booklet entitled "Some Rules for Self-Defense." Include page references from the novel.

OTHER ACTIVITIES

1. The description of Alfred's fight with Elston Hubbard in chapter 19 is vivid and violent. Read the description several times. Then, using oils, acrylics, or even fingerpaint, try to represent Alfred's feelings and perceptions abstractly. Choose the colors and make the strokes and patterns that seem most appropriate.
2. Role play a conversation involving Mr. Donatelli, Bud, Martin, Spoon, and Henry that takes place after Alfred's second fight. Keep the following sentence in mind: "They stared at each other for a long time before Bud shook his head, and Donatelli shrugged."
3. Design a certificate that Mr. Donatelli might award to any fighter who, like Alfred, successfully completes the training program he requires for becoming a contender.
4. Draw an editorial cartoon expressing one of the following arguments:
   a. Boxing provides one possible road out of the urban ghetto.
   b. Boxing fans are attracted to the sport almost solely by the violence and blood.
   c. Urban ghettos are breeding grounds for crime.
5. Role play the scene that will take place after the novel ends, when Herbert Davis, the boy who pulled a knife on Spoon at school (chapter 19), visits Alfred and Henry at the gym.

SELECTED TEACHING RESOURCES

Media Aids

Internet

All You've Ever Wanted to Know [About Boxing]. Available: http://www.amateur-boxing.com/faq.htm (Accessed March 10, 2000).

A list of questions and answers about "the sweet science," including general information, the history of boxing, becoming a boxer or an official, the scoring system, and differences between amateur and professional boxing.

Printed Materials

Articles

Bachner, Saul. "Three Junior Novels on the Black Experience." *Journal of Reading* 24 (May 1981): 692–695.

Lipsyte, Robert. "Facets: YA Authors Talk About Their Writing." *English Journal* 76 (March 1987): 16.
Features *The Contender*.

Scales, Pat. "Book Strategies: *The Contender* and *The Brave* by Robert Lipsyte." *Book Links* 2 (November 1992): 38–40.

Simmons, John. "Lipsyte's *Contender*: Another Look at the Junior Novel." *Elementary English* 49 (January 1972): 116–119.

Teaching Aids

The Contender. Contemporary Classics series. Perfection Learning Corporation.

The Contender. Literature Unit Plans. Teacher's Pet Publications.

The Contender. Novel Ideas Plus. Sundance.

The Contender. Novel Unit Guide, Novel Units Student Packet, and Perma-Guide. Perma-Bound.

The Contender. Novel-Ties. Learning Links.

Tests

The Contender. Essay, objective, and alternative assessment versions. Perfection Learning Corporation.

The Miracle Worker

William Gibson
New York: Atheneum, 1960
Play: Available in paperback from Bantam.

SUMMARY

As an infant, Helen Keller contracts an illness that leaves her blind, deaf, and mute—and by the time she is six, wild and despotic. When her devoted and desperate parents hire a governess, Annie Sullivan, the headstrong young Irishwoman immediately sets out to teach and discipline Helen, only to realize that the child's greatest enemy is the love and pity of her parents. Annie requests—and is reluctantly given—two weeks of total control and isolation with Helen in a small garden house. During that time she succeeds in conveying to the small child the rudiments of self-discipline but fails to teach her the one thing she desperately needs: language. Annie requests more time, but the Kellers resist, grateful already for the miraculous progress that has been made. When Helen returns to the family, she reverts to her unruly behavior by emptying a water pitcher at the dinner table. Annie wrenches her away from her parents to refill the pitcher at the water pump. And suddenly the miracle occurs. With water rushing over her hands, Helen makes the crucial connection between thing and word—and between learner and teacher—to open up new worlds.

APPRAISAL

The Miracle Worker is appreciated by a wide range of students, who respond to the well-known, inspiring story of Helen Keller and Annie Sullivan and to the intensity with which William Gibson has dramatized it. The fierce struggle for dominance between the two protagonists, the subordinate conflict between father and adolescent son, the fascinating combination of profound disability and profound intelligence: All of these elements contribute to the play's appeal. It can be taught almost anywhere in the secondary school, but it is most commonly taught in grades eight through ten.

THEMES

courage and perseverance, love and commitment, enlightenment, renewal and growth

LITERARY CONCEPTS

conflict, staging and lighting, symbol, dialogue, characterization, flashback

RELATED READING

Some students may want to read Helen Keller's autobiography, *The Story of My Life*. Other books about people who have overcome physical handicaps include *Mine for Keeps* by Jean Little (about cerebral palsy), *Listen for the Fig Tree* by Sharon Bell Mathis (about blindness), and *Follow My Leader* by James Garfield (about blindness).

READING PROBLEMS AND OPPORTUNITIES

Like all plays, of course, *The Miracle Worker* is meant to be staged and viewed by an audience. Perhaps more than most, its effect is achieved largely through stage directions, many of which allude to sophisticated lighting instructions, or, more important, through action that is pantomimed or carried along through intense physical struggle. The latter refers, of course, to the battles of will between Helen and Annie, battles that need to be seen for one to appreciate their ferocity. Still, when read, the play can be intense and powerful, especially if the teacher clarifies confusing stage directions as needed and helps students to visualize the action.

The Miracle Worker contains numerous words that may be unfamiliar to students, especially adverbs that often specify for the actors a certain attitude or expression to be conveyed. The following list could be used for vocabulary study (the numbers in parentheses indicate the acts in which the words appear):

indulge, indulgent (1, 3),
vitality (1),
crescendo (1),
unkempt (1, 2),
indolent (1),
blandly (1, 2, 3),
facetiously (1),
impudence (1),
placating (1),
affliction (1),
morosely (1),
inarticulate (1, 2, 3),
obstinate (1, 2),
reproachfully (1),
irately (1, 2),
resolutely (1, 2),
wry (1, 2, 3),
imperious (1, 3),
curtly (1, 2),
incensed (1),
deftly (1, 2),
disheveled (1),
avert (1, 3),
asperity (I),
oblivious (1, 3),
proffers (2),
impassively (2, 3),
temperance (2),
resolve (2, 3),
impaired (2),
indignant (2, 3),
ominous (2),
deferential (2),
evenly (2),
nonplussed (2),
feigned, feint (2),
presumes (2),
hireling (2),
unavailing (2),
compunction (2),
writhe (2),
interminably (2, 3),
plaintively (2),
impertinent (2),
primer (2),
almshouse (2),
witheringly (2, 3),
wary (2),
recoils (2),
careens (2),
paroxysm (2),
incarnate (2),
intractably (2),
diminutive (2),
diminished (3),
haggard (3),
wistful (3),
defer (3),
dutiful (3),
forlorn (3),
ruefully (3),
bountiful (3),
aversion (3),
interpose (3),
consummately (3),
prevail (3),
transfixed (3),
possessed (3),
feverishly (3),
reserve (3), and
deprivation (3).

INITIATING ACTIVITIES

1. At home or at school, try an experiment in which you blindfold yourself (and, if possible, safely stop up your ears) for ten minutes. Try to imagine how it would be to live under such circumstances. Think about how it would be if you were suddenly struck blind and deaf, and then how it would be if you were blind and deaf from infancy. What would be the differences? Which would be worse? Why? Write about your thoughts and feelings on this subject in a page or two.
2. In a scene toward the end of *The Miracle Worker*, one of the characters tells another who is teasing her, "James, now you're pulling my lower extremity." What word did she choose not to use? Why? Discuss with your classmates why a word like *leg* was once considered improper in mixed company and why even today many words remain taboo in certain situations. Discuss especially the source of these taboos: The failure of many people to understand the relationship between a word and that which the word represents.
3. Read the poem "Mutterings over the Crib of a Deaf Child" by James Wright. (The poem may be found in *Some Haystacks Don't Even Have Any Needle*, edited by Stephen Dunning et al. [New York: Scott Foresman, 1969].) Write a brief explication of the poem in which you answer the following questions: How many people are speaking over the crib? Who are they? Who is asking the questions? Who tries to answer them? Is either satisfied with any of the answers? Explain. What does the speaker mean in the last three lines? Who suffers more, the deaf child who cannot hear or the parent who knows what the child cannot hear? Discuss.

DISCUSSION QUESTIONS

Act 1

1. Why does the doctor think the baby will live? What is in her favor? Even when Keller knows Helen cannot hear, why does he continue to shout her name?
2. How does the playwright indicate the passage of time on the stage? As they play around the water pump, why does Helen try to feel Percy's mouth and then her own? Why does she become angry?
3. How do the different family members react to Helen? In particular, how does Kate deal with her? What seems to be Keller's attitude? Why do you think he seems so resigned? Why is James sarcastic? How is Kate different from them? Do you think she loves Helen more than Keller does? Why or why not?
4. What is Helen like? Is she fragile or rough? Curious or withdrawn? Does she show any signs of being intelligent? Does her intelligence make her easier or more difficult to manage? Why? What does Kate mean when she says, "Every day she slips further away"? Why do you think Keller changes his mind and agrees to write to the man in Baltimore?
5. Why do you think the playwright allows the image of Kate and Helen to remain lit until the next scene, with Annie and Anagnos, is well under way? In his "last time to counsel" Annie, describe Anagnos: Is he kind? Critical? Hopeful? From his comments, what must her life at the school and before have been like? What kind of person does she seem to be? Why do you suppose she thinks she will never love anyone again? Do you think she loves anyone now? Why or why not? What characteristics does she have that may enable her to

work with Helen? As she prepares to leave, why is she reminded of an incident in the past? In this scene involving Annie at her school, what are some ways in which the playwright has used lighting to create different effects?

6. Why does Kate insist upon going to meet the train? Do you think the adults are too lenient with Helen? Why or why not? Would this be the natural thing to do? Why is Keller "awkward with her"? Does he love her? Why does he seem to have trouble getting along with James?

7. Is Kate pessimistic about Annie's chances of succeeding with Helen? Is Annie? Are the three advantages she mentions really advantages? Why or why not? Describe their first meeting and their acceptance of each other. What do they like about each other?

8. How does Annie approach Helen? From their first meeting, what seems to be Annie's primary purpose? Why is she pleased? What does the fight between the two suggest about them? What does James's amused inaction in response to Helen's plight reveal about him? At the end of Act 1, how does Annie feel about her situation? Her challenge? Helen? What do you think is Annie's greatest strength? What may be her greatest problem?

Act 2

9. How does Annie seem to feel about her chances of teaching Helen language? How does she convince Kate that the effort may be worthwhile? What does Annie consider the crucial requirement if she—and Helen—are to succeed? (Why do you think the playwright directs "a shaft of sunlight" onto the water pump as Annie says the word "obedience"?)

10. What possible relation does the conversation between Keller and James about Grant at Vicksburg have to the rest of the play? James makes the connection clear with a remark to Annie. What is the remark? What attitude toward James does Keller have, as revealed in their discussion? Why do you think he feels compelled to assume such a superior attitude?

11. How do Annie and the Kellers disagree over how Helen should be handled? With whom do you agree? Why? Annie says, "It's less trouble to feel sorry for her than to teach her anything better, isn't it?" Is this an unfair assessment of the Kellers' point of view? Why or why not?

12. What does the elemental struggle between Annie and Helen reveal about each of them? In what ways does it show Helen to be perceptive? Cunning? Is Annie too harsh with Helen? Why or why not? When Annie comes outside and speaks, why does the fact that Helen folded her napkin seem to affect Kate more than anything else? Why does she weep?

13. What do the different voices from Annie's past seem to say to her? What do they imply about her own past? To what do her experiences seem to have committed her? Why do you think she starts to pack her suitcase? Has she given up? What is there that suggests she has not?

14. How do the Kellers differ in their attitudes toward Annie? How does Keller deal with her? Why is he so ambivalent? Why does he finally consent? Is Keller weak? Why or why not? What does Annie mean when she says, "Whatever her body needs is a— primer, to teach her out of"? Why does she mention her experiences in the almshouse? What does she mean by "No, I have no conditions, Captain Keller"? And what does she mean by "A siege

is a siege"? If not for love or money—why has Annie decided to stay? What does the brief conversation between Annie and James reveal about each of them? Is James afraid? Of what? What does he mean by "Or will you teach me?"

15. Back home, how perceptive is James's remark about Keller's preference for Annie over him? What does Keller admire about Annie? Regret about James? What does James want from his father that he does not receive? Why doesn't he receive it?

16. Why does Annie say. "No! No pity, I won't have it. On either of us"? What element of human nature does she take advantage of to reestablish contact, so to speak, with Helen? What effect does Annie's song seem to have on each person who appears to detect it?

Act 3

17. As the act opens, how much time has elapsed? Why does Kate think it has been interminable? What does Keller mean when he says, "You'll learn we don't just keep our children safe. They keep us safe"? Does he feel safe with either Helen or James? Why or why not? Who has been the greater disappointment to him? Why? How has he been a failure? What advice does Kate give James? Is it good advice? Do you think he will follow it? Is James any different now from the way he was at the beginning of the play? Explain. Why do you think the playwright juxtaposed the two scenes, of the family and Annie? Discuss. From the very beginning of the act, what changes are apparent in Helen? Despite these, why does Annie feel inadequate?

18. As Annie tries to express some measure of optimism to Kate about Helen's learning language, why is her comparison of words to wings appropriate? What is it, exactly, that Helen has not learned? Is the insistence by her parents that she be allowed to return to them selfish? Do they need Helen more than she needs them? Discuss. Keller asks Annie, "What is it to you?" What is the answer to that question? Is Annie being selfish? If so, how? Why does she deny the importance of affection? When a moment later she bends in compassionate frustration to kiss Helen, why does the child instantly pause, "her hands off the dog, her head slightly averted"? Do you agree with Annie that words are the key to all understanding? Discuss.

19. Annie remembers telling Mr. Anagnos, "I think God must owe me a resurrection." What did she mean by that, and what does she now mean by, "And I owe God one"? What is she trying to forget? What does Annie mean when she tells Keller, "I wanted to teach her yes"? Why does her emotion take her by surprise, and why does she laugh through it?

20. Comment on James's blessing. Is it appropriate? Why or why not? As the family and Annie sit around the dinner table in disagreement, what two conflicts are apparent? Discuss how they are resolved. Why does Kate surrender Helen to Annie? And why does Keller surrender, in effect, to James? How has James grown?

21. At that moment at the water pump, what influences might have contributed to Helen's making the miraculous connection between thing and word? Why does she become so frantic? Is it possible for us to appreciate her excitement? Why not? Why does she turn from her parents to Annie? Then, why does she take the keys to Annie? What has been unlocked? In this powerful scene, how has Kate changed and grown? How has Annie grown? What has she lost and gained? What has the family gained?

22. In looking back at the play, why is the variation of lighting an appropriate technique for *The Miracle Worker*? How does it relate to one of the play's themes?

WRITING ACTIVITIES

1. Write the letter that Keller reluctantly agrees to send to Dr. Chisholm in Baltimore in Act 1. As you compose it, keep in mind his feelings toward Kate and Helen as well as his attitude toward sending such a letter.
2. Using reference books, magazine articles, and/or the Internet, conduct research on how the blind and deaf are taught to cope with their handicaps today, a century after Annie Sullivan began her work with Helen Keller. If possible, find material on programs for children who have both disabilities. Write a report on your findings.
3. Write a diary that Annie might have kept during the two weeks in the garden house. Include an entry for each day.
4. Write an editorial that Keller might have written for his newspaper on the day after the play ends. The topic should concern some conclusion he has reached as a result of the events of the last two weeks.
5. Write a cinquain in which the first word (line 1) is "Annie" and the final word (line 5) is "Teacher."
6. If possible, interview a blind student in your school or your community. Write a report that includes the student's answers to the following questions, among others: How long have you been blind? What caused your blindness? What equipment and programs have been helpful to you? What are your biggest problems? Are there any tasks or activities that you can perform better than people who have sight? What are they? How do other people respond to you? If you could, what changes would you make in their response?
7. Soon after she arrives, Annie concludes that the Kellers' love for Helen has become a barrier, in a way, to her growth and education. Write about a time in your life when you feel your parents—in a way—loved you too much.
8. During the two weeks in the garden house, Helen learns three verbs and eighteen nouns, including "key" and "water." On the day she returns, of course, water is the first word she understands. Would you have predicted water would be one of the more likely words with which she would make the first crucial connection? Why or why not? Compile a list of twenty-five words that you think Helen would have been most likely to understand, including brief reasons for each.
9. As two persons of approximately the same age dealing with their separate problems in the play, Annie and James invite comparison. Write a brief paper comparing and contrasting the two characters, partly in terms of their relationship with Keller.
10. Write another ending for the play: Annie succeeds in getting Helen to fill the water pitcher, but the miracle of language does not occur and they return to the house. What happens next? Your ending should include at least twenty exchanges of dialogue, with each character making at least one contribution.

OTHER ACTIVITIES

1. At the end of the two weeks at the garden house, Annie and the Kellers (at least Mr. Keller) seem to have two different ideas about what she and Helen can accomplish. Design two collages that communicate the word "teacher," one from Annie's perspective and the other from Keller's.

2. Imagine that Annie returns to Boston briefly soon after the play ends. With another student, role-play a conversation she has with Mr. Anagnos in which he asks her the following questions (among others to be improvised):
    a. Did you overcome your stubbornness, Annie? Tell me about it.
    b. How were you finally able to forget about Tewksbury?
    c. What have you learned about yourself?
3. Present an oral report to the class on one of the following topics:
    a. sign language for the deaf, or finger language for the deaf and blind
    b. almshouses for the poor and the handicapped in the nineteenth century
    c. Helen Keller's life and accomplishments as an adult
    d. Annie Sullivan's life and career after the play ends
4. In an effort to appreciate Helen's joy and love at the end of the play and the extent to which she has changed, create—while blindfolded—an artistic representation (using clay, finger paint, collage, or some other appropriate medium) of what she knows and feels.
5. The unique relationship between Annie Sullivan and Helen Keller and their achievements as teacher and student provide one of the most inspiring stories in American history. Design a commemorative stamp that would honor these two women.

SELECTED TEACHING RESOURCES

Media Aids

Internet

MotivationalQuotes.Com presents Helen Keller. Available: http://www.motivationalquotes.com/People/keller.shtml (Accessed March 10, 2000).
A diverse site that includes quotations, links to online resources, and related books.

Videos

The Miracle Worker. 107 min., b & w. Anne Bancroft/Patty Duke version. Perma-Bound, 1962.

The Miracle Worker. 98 min., color. Patty Duke Astin/Melissa Gilbert version. Guidance Associates, 1979.

Tragedy to Triumph: An Adventure with Helen Keller. 40 min., color. Grace Products, 1995.
A fictionalized dramatization of Helen Keller's effect upon a boy who is prejudiced against the blind.

Printed Resources

Article

Smith, J. Lea. "Literature Alive: Connecting to Story Through the Arts." *Reading Horizons* 37 (November/December 1996): 102–115.

Teaching Aids

The Miracle Worker. Contemporary Classics series. Perfection Learning Corporation.

The Miracle Worker. Novel/Drama Curriculum Units. The Center for Learning.

The Miracle Worker. Novel-Ties. Learning Links.

The Miracle Worker. Novel Unit Guide and Novel Units Student Packet. Perma-Bound.

Tests

The Miracle Worker. Essay, objective, and alternative assessment versions. Perfection Learning Corporation.

The Moves Make the Man

Bruce Brooks

New York: Harper & Row, 1984

Available in paperback from Harper Trophy.

SUMMARY

Jerome Foxworthy is a thirteen-year-old boy who becomes the first black student in an all-white school in Wilmington, North Carolina. There he befriends an athletically gifted, but emotionally troubled, white boy named Bix. Jerome teaches Bix to play basketball, which the latter quickly masters—except for the moves (fakes) that Jerome considers essential. Bix sees himself as a purist, and for him moves are lies. When he challenges his stepfather to a game, however—and later when he visits his mentally ill mother in a hospital—he is forced to use the deceptions he has disdained. When the visit goes awry, Bix makes his final (and to Jerome, his best) move: He runs away, leaving his friend confused but hopeful.

APPRAISAL

The Moves Make the Man won recognition as a Newbery Honor Book for 1985 as well as listings among the American Library Association's Notable Books and the ALA's Best Books for Young Adults. As the story of a friendship between a black boy and a white youth, set amid the backdrop of sports, the novel has gained a wide readership among young adults, especially boys. Words like *nigger* and *jigaboo* (as well as common obscenities) are scattered throughout the book, most of them spoken by the narrator himself, who is black. The book makes light fun of racial stereotypes (e.g., the reference by the narrator to "White Man's Nonsense"), but it does so in an overall context of members of different races coming to understand each other. It is most appropriate for grades eight through ten.

THEMES

friendship, deception and trust, prejudice, self-image, family, emotional illness

LITERARY CONCEPTS

characterization, stereotypes, plot (flashback), point of view, dialect (slang), symbolism, setting, onomatopoeia (chapter 8)

RELATED READING

Although it is more appropriate for younger readers, *Maniac Magee* by Jerry Spinelli also concerns identity, trust, and racial prejudice. Other young adult books about sports are numerous: *Supercharged: Or How a Good Kid Becomes BAAAD and Saves His Basketball Team* by Bruce Bassoff, *Orp Goes for the Hoop* by Suzy Kline, *Wrestling Sturbridge* by Rich Wallace, *Tangerine* by Edward Bloor, *Pretty Good for a Girl* by Leslie Heywood, the numerous books by Chris Crutcher, and *Ultimate Sports: Short Stories by Outstanding Writers for Young Adults*, edited by Donald Gallo. Students who prefer nonfiction may want to read *Those Who Love the Game* by Glenn Rivers, the professional basketball player, and Bruce Brooks.

READING PROBLEMS AND OPPORTUNITIES

The Moves Make the Man is narrated by a bright, colorful thirteen-year-old boy whose language is characterized by what he himself calls jive talk. The book offers numerous opportunities for vocabulary enrichment, some of them coming from the voice of Jerome's brother Maurice, who enjoys using the language of pop psychology. Among the words many eighth and ninth graders may not know are the following (page numbers are included in parentheses):

endeavor (12),
debut (15),
statistics (16),
averted (16, 32, 123),
fret (16, 159, 218),
ambled (27),
righteous (31),
smirked (32),
intruding (43),
humiliating (47),
integrated (49, 52, 262),
ratio (49),
accelerating, accelerated (50, 55, 61),
principle (53),
agitate (53),
spinster (58),
catastrophe (58),
damsels (59),
lingo (60),
precise (61, 62),
appendages (61),
hostility (62),
denotes (66),
corporeal (66),
deceit, deceive, deception (67, 70, 144, 185, 213),
avenged (67, 185),
servitude (67, 185),
smug (68),
peeved (68),
sarcastic (68),
jaunty (70, 93),
initiated (73),
betrayed (80, 110),
melodrama (88),
perverting (92),
theories (92),
livened (100),
hunkered (100),
inclination (106),
anonymous (110),
orientations (123),
syndrome (125),
deprivation, deprive (126, 144, 230),
dismal (140),
impeached (144),
perceptive (144),
material (144),
skeptical (159),
bland (169),
legitimate (180),
havoc (186),
gyrate (187),
tactic (202),
riled (202, 208),
gloat (209),
prevail (211),
deflected (212),
forlorn (213),
insecurity, insecure (218 ff.),
orthodox (230, 232),
aggression (230),
neurosis (230),
flaunt (231),
notorious (232),
fruitless (232),
socializing (235),
pertain (262),
orderly (262), and
momentum (267).

INITIATING ACTIVITIES

1. Read to the class a poem about basketball, such as "Shooting Baskets at Dusk" by Michael McFee or "Makin' Jump Shots" by Michael S. Harper (which is available in *American Sports Poems* by R. R. Knudson and May Swenson). Both poems are about the allure of basketball even when someone is playing alone. Have the students discuss the nature and appeal of basketball and other sports. Try to get them to be specific, perhaps by modeling (i.e., giving reasons why you like a certain sport or activity).
2. Have students create a split-screen collage that conveys for them the meaning of friendship. They can use pictures, clipped-out words from magazines and newspapers, real objects—anything that can be glued to a piece of paper. Condition: The collage should take up only one-half of the sheet and be saved for completion later.

DISCUSSION QUESTIONS

First Part

1. *Chapter 1:* What do we learn about the narrator of the story in the brief introductory chapter? About Bix? Do you think that Bix and the narrator were good friends, or just acquaintances? Is the story being told or written right after it happened or later?
2. *Chapter 2:* Why do you think Bix was so taken by the phrase "spin light"? Jerome read the repeated phrase in Bix's notebook "until it meant all these different things to me." What are some things it might mean? What detail in this chapter gives you an idea of when the story takes place? What in the chapter tells us something about the depth of the boys' friendship?
3. *Chapters 3 and 4:* Why does Jerome prefer basketball to baseball? How does he feel about his brother Maurice? About the two different baseball teams? Do you think Jerome is prejudiced? Why or why not?
4. *Chapter 5:* What about the shortstop impresses Jerome in particular? "I felt sorry for him, which made me like him even more." Have you ever had this kind of complicated feeling toward someone? Why does Jerome feel sorry for Bix? For Bix's mother? Why do you think Bix's mother behaves the way she does? What more do we learn about Jerome in this chapter?
5. *Chapters 6 and 7:* Why do you think the author includes chapter 6? What does the truck driver mean by "That's the secret of life"? Why does Jerome become angry? Could there be reasons for his anger that even he is not aware of? Discuss.

Second Part

6. *Chapters 8 and 9:* What is there about the basketball court in the woods that Jerome likes the most? Is Jerome a loner? Why does he enjoy shooting baskets by himself so much? Why does he resent Poke's outlandish shots so much?
7. *Chapter 10:* What does Jerome appreciate about his mother? Would you appreciate her for this as well? How do you feel about Maurice's wanting Jerome to be well balanced? Why does Jerome spend so much time practicing his moves? Why does he imagine Bix as his opponent?

8. *Chapter 11:* Why does Jerome not like being picked to integrate the schools? Why is his mother unhappy with this decision? How do they accept it? At this point in the book, how would you describe Jerome? Is he cocky, or just confident? Do you think he will have any problems at Chestnut? Why or why not? Do you like Jerome?

9. *Chapters 12 and 13:* Compare Jerome's views toward his French and communications classes. What does he dislike most about Mr. Egglestobbs? How would you describe the interaction between Jerome and the coach? Is the coach a racist? Are the boys? Is Jerome rude? Why does Vic leave the floor? How do the boys in general seem to feel about what has happened?

10. *Chapters 14, 15, and 16:* React to Jerome's comments about friends early in chapter 14. Do you agree with them? What does the idea of the elevator race tell us about Momma? What does her accident reveal about the boys? How do you feel about the school counselor? About Jerome's reaction to her? On the basis of the comments made in the home ec class, what can we infer about Braxton?

11. *Chapter 17:* What does Jerome mean by "having my onlyness broken"? What more do we learn about Bix in this chapter (at least, about Jerome's perception of him)? What do you think Jerome might be referring to at the very end of the chapter?

12. *Chapter 18:* Why is Jerome dismayed over the Mock-Apple Pie? How do you account for Bix's sudden change of personality when he too questions it? What of significance happens in chapter 18?

13. *Chapter 19:* Why do you think Bix seems so anxious as Mr. Spearman tastes the pie? Why do you think he is so upset by "us tricking him and him tricking us back and tricks and lies"?

Third Part

14. *Chapter 20:* "I drew my worry from knowing how fragile all the ways of being intelligent are." What are some different ways of being intelligent? Does Jerome have all of these? Does anyone? Why does Jerome cry when he tells about Bix? Why is his mother upset when she learns the boys have not been doing some of the things they enjoy?

15. *Chapter 21:* Why does Jerome enjoy practicing his passing skills? What does the incident with the railroad man show? Why does Jerome's mother want him to return the lantern? Do you agree with her or with Jerome and Maurice?

16. *Chapter 22:* What does Jerome now carry with him to practice in the dark? How might this have more than just a literal meaning? Why is he uncomfortable at first with the lantern's light? As Jerome approaches the court, what do you think the numbers that he hears signify? How does Jerome react to Bix at first? Why? Why does he fall down laughing? Jerome says, "It's only a lie if you expect somebody to believe you." Do you agree with this? Why or why not? Why do you think Bix is so upset by lies? Why is he out there playing alone? How does Jerome react to Bix's lantern-spinning? Why? As he leaves, what does Jerome mean by saying he was "full of something I knew and something I did not"? What do we as readers know—and not know—about Bix? What do you think he meant by his journal entry "I WILL PLAY MY GAME BENEATH THE SPIN LIGHT"?

Last Part

17. *Chapter 23:* At the start of the lessons, do you think Jerome is a good teacher? Why or why not? Is Bix a good learner? Why or why not? Why do they not need to talk? Why do you think Bix is so distrustful of talk? What is becoming the nature of their friendship? For Jerome, what exactly are "moves," and why does Bix not have—or even want—them? Do you think the two boys have reached an impasse in their friendship? How might it be resolved?

18. *Chapter 24:* What does Jerome miss about Bix? Why does he feel such a need to practice deceit (his moves)? What does he mean by "I had never been mysterious to me before"? How has *Foxworthy* become a symbolic name? How does Jerome react when he sees Bix again after two months? Why has Bix returned? Why does he need Jerome? Why does Jerome know he'll show up at the game tomorrow night? Why does he think that he will be unable to help Bix?

19. *Chapter 25:* What is Jerome's early reaction to Bix's stepfather? As Bix and his stepfather argue about the game, do you sense anything more about their relationship? If so, what? In the game, why is Bix so ineffective? At the end, why does he begin to sulk? What do you think the stepfather means by saying, "He's the all-time champ at being too good for ugly business"? What is the "ugly business" Bix has experienced? How do you feel about the story the stepfather tells about Bix and his mother? Do you think it is true? Why or why not? Why does Bix suddenly decide to use fakes against his stepfather? How does Jerome feel about Bix as he watches? Why is it fabulous? Why is it sad? What does Jerome mean by "the moves make the man"? What does Jerome mean when he says, "But I was in the dark too"? If Bix is emotionally disturbed, what would you say disturbs him the most?

20. *Chapter 26:* Why do you think Jerome is so fascinated by Bix? Why do he and his mother plan to have Bix over for dinner? Why does Bix try to speak "jive talk," and why does Jerome resent it? At dinner, why does Bix become a different person? How does Jerome react, and why? Why is he so bothered by Bix's pie? Why is Momma's reaction "sad"? Afterwards, why is Bix so dejected? What does he mean when he tells Jerome, "Which is why I'm such a good buddy for you, isn't it?" At this point, what would you say each of them is giving to their friendship? Taking from it? What does Jerome mean by "maybe I needed to draw a new map"? What might be the "few new things" he is sure of as the chapter comes to a close?

21. *Chapter 27:* Why does Bix brings his baseball glove? Why might the author have included this part about Bix "doing his glove"? How does Jerome feel about it? Why does he see both hope and the absence of hope? In what ways does the stop at Jeb's prove to be disastrous? Later, at the hospital, what does the orderly mean by, "We are half crazy as it is, ALL the time. That's HEALTHY"? In the room where they find Bix's mother, why does Bix throw himself upon the woman in the next bed? Even as he hears a change in his own mother's voice, why does he kiss Hazel and say "Good-bye, Mother"? And then, why does he leave the room? In what ways is he, especially to Jerome, gone? Why does Jerome hurt? In the end, has Bix faked out his mother, or himself—or someone or something else? Why does Jerome consider it "the best thing Bix had tried to do since I knew him"?

22. *Chapter 28:* How does Jerome feel about Bix's running away? Why does he refuse to cooperate with Bix's stepfather? Why is Jerome so confused about "what I had given Bix and where it was likely to get him"? What *had* he given Bix? Why do you think Bix sends

Jerome the blank postcard? How does Jerome react to it? What does he mean by the last sentence, and how does the sentence help to convey a major theme in the book?

WRITING ACTIVITIES

1. In chapters 2 and 27, much is made of the proper care of baseball gloves. Write an expository paper on how to take care of another piece of sports equipment, such as a tennis racquet, basketball shoes, a rifle or fishing rod, ice skates or in-line skates, or skis.
2. Jerome much prefers basketball over baseball. Write a comparison-contrast paper on two sports: two that you like or two that you have opposing feelings about. Good possibilities are football and soccer, baseball versus football, tennis versus golf, hunting and fishing, or any number of others.
3. In part, *The Moves Make the Man* is about a young black teenager from Wilmington, North Carolina, in the process of refining his basketball skills. In a way, the book reminds the reader of another young basketball player from the same town who went on to become perhaps the greatest player of all time. Read about Michael Jordan as a young adolescent (you can probably find a biography in the library), and then write a paper comparing him with Jerome.
4. As the book shows, basketball has its own vocabulary, including many words that even fans may not understand. Write a basketball dictionary that defines the following terms mentioned in the book (and any others you wish to add): *stutter step, crossover, low post, lay-up, hanging spin move, jump hook, double pump, running hook shot, fadeaway, lean, finger roll, baseline,* and *pump fake.*
5. Bix invents the game of bounceball as an inventive way to occupy himself when he is alone. Write a paper about a game that you created that you can play by yourself or with other people.
6. Write a missing-persons description of Bix, the kind that you sometimes see on milk cartons. Try to suggest where one might find him in a city like Washington.
7. Among other things, *The Moves Make the Man* is a book about friendship. In chapters 11 and 14 especially, Jerome comments on the nature of friends. With these comments as starting points, write a paper defining friendship. *Or,* write a list poem with each self-contained line providing a specific example: "Friendship is letting your bud borrow your knockout new sweater for a date."
8. In some ways, Bix might be said to be emotionally disturbed. Using at least three sources, write a paper on the common types of emotional (or behavioral) disorders. Try to determine which of these Bix's behavior most resembles. Make specific references to the novel.
9. Throughout the book, Jerome seems to have his own unique brand of slang expressions, such as "stack a z or two" (take a nap) and "we flew on the pie" (we got busy with the pie). Compile a dictionary of a dozen or more examples of these that you find especially colorful. Title your dictionary "Jerome Jive" and share it with your classmates.
10. For Jerome, "the prettiest little concrete half-court basketball court in town" (chapter 8) is a very special place, almost sacred in its appeal. Write about a special place of yours, somewhere you like to get away to for relaxation and perhaps solitude. It could be your room, somewhere outdoors, even the inside of a car.

11. Write a message that Bix might have written to Jerome, but didn't, on the blank postcard sent from Washington (chapter 28).

OTHER ACTIVITIES

1. Draw diagrams of some of the more common moves or plays in basketball. These might include the pick and roll, zone defense, man-to-man defense, the "four-corners" offense, trapping defense, full-court press, and others. Present these to the class and explain which ones you think Jerome might have preferred.
2. Design a Little League T-shirt that might have been appropriate for the Beefy's Lunch team described in chapter 4. In the book, "the team uniforms are just maroon shirts with gold writing . . . [with] a cartoon of Beefy." You can use this design or create one of your own with a different logo.
3. Make a Mock-Apple Pie (chapter 18) or another dish mentioned in the book (e.g., Mexican Meat Loaf or Vegetable Curry, both mentioned in chapter 20). The ingredients for the pie are provided, but you'll need to find directions elsewhere. The Internet would be a good place to look.
4. Design a collage (or create a finger painting) that represents, in abstract form, either the idea of spin light or the concept of "moves" as it is presented in the book
5. In an effort to inform classmates who may not be aware of them, pantomime some of the basketball moves mentioned throughout the book (see "Writing Activity" 4 above). You may need one or two other students to work with you.
6. Complete the other half of the split-screen collage on friendship referred to in "Initiating Activity" 1. If your view of friendship has changed in any way, it should be reflected in this second version.

SELECTED TEACHING RESOURCES

Media Aids

Internet

FiestaNet Communications. 1995–1999. *The Basketball Highway*. Available: http://www.bbhighway.com. (Accessed March 10, 2000).

Includes play diagrams, book reviews, an "Ask the Coach" page, and links to countless other websites of interest to students who love basketball as much as Jerome does.

Printed Materials

Teaching Aids

The Moves Make the Man. Novel Unit Guide. Perma-Bound.

The Outsiders

S. E. Hinton
New York: Viking Press, 1967
Available in paperback from Dell.

SUMMARY

Since the death of his parents in an auto accident, Ponyboy Curtis has lived with his brothers Sodapop and Darrel. Ponyboy is more sensitive and intellectual than the other greasers in his gang, which includes Dally Winston, a tough, mean hood; Two-Bit Matthews, the wise-cracker; and Johnny Cade, the gang's pet, who has been ignored by his parents. The principal enemy of the greasers are the Socs, the wealthy beer drinkers who spend much of their time at parties. When Ponyboy and Johnny make the mistake of befriending two of the Socs' girlfriends, they are jumped by a gang of Socs, one of whom is killed by Johnny. Ponyboy and Johnny are then sent by Dally to hide out in an abandoned church. When Dally comes to visit them, however, a fire breaks out in the church, and Johnny and Dally are injured as the two of them try to rescue some children from the flames. Dally recovers in time to fight in a rumble between the rival gangs, but Johnny dies from his injuries. The news of Johnny's death sends Dally over the edge. He robs a store and is killed by the police. Afterwards, Ponyboy struggles with a serious illness and the emotional trauma of the death of his two friends. Finally, in an attempt to understand what has happened to him, he begins an essay for his English teacher that recounts his experiences.

APPRAISAL

One of the most popular young adult novels ever written, *The Outsiders* has continued to attract an extremely wide readership among adolescents since it was first published in 1967. In it, teenagers find many of the ingredients that for them spell success in fiction: romance, excitement, pathos, and characters that exhibit vulnerability beneath an outer toughness. Written by Hinton when she was seventeen years old, the book contains none of the taboo elements such as profanity and explicit sex that abound in later young adult novels. Despite this, it manages to portray realistically the struggles and emotional responses of lower-class adolescent males. One recent survey identifies this book as the favorite young adult novel among secondary school English teachers, who use the novel in grades eight through ten.

THEMES

loyalty, peer relationships, poverty, love, sacrifice, search for self, socioeconomic conflict

LITERARY CONCEPTS

plot, flashback, foreshadowing, characterization, stereotype, symbol, point of view, allusion, theme

RELATED READING

Students who like *The Outsiders* will probably want to continue with Hinton's subsequent works: *That Was Then, This Is Now; Rumble-Fish; Tex; Taming the Star Runner*. Two other young adult novels about gangs, both by Frank Bonham, are *Cool Cat* and the well-known *Durango Street.*

READING PROBLEMS AND OPPORTUNITIES

Written by an adolescent for adolescents, *The Outsiders* poses very few reading difficulties. The only two worth mentioning are these: an abundance of characters, particularly major characters with similar names (Darry, Dally, etc.) and the occasional use of slang that may be unfamiliar (see "Writing Activity" 7). Opportunities for vocabulary development are minimal, but the following words may warrant discussion (chapter numbers are given in parentheses):

unfathomable (1), *nonchalantly* (2), *stricken* (2), *aloofness* (3), *eluded* (5), *wistfully* (5), *contemptuously* (7), *doggedly* (8), and *grimacing* (9).

INITIATING ACTIVITIES

1. Identify the cliques that exist in your school. Give each group a name based on its principal concern. Decide how these groups feel about each other. Do they talk to each other, socialize with each other, or share common interests? Do members of one group hate members of another? Compare the groups you have identified with those your classmates have listed. Discuss why the different groups exist and why they feel the way they do about each other.

2. Read the statements below and discuss them with members of your class. In one or two sentences, write down your feelings about the statements. After you have read *The Outsiders*, read your sentences again to see if you have changed your mind about any of them. Discuss your responses with others in your class.

    a. Friends are more important than parents.

    b. It's fun to steal things if you don't get caught.

    c. The attitudes toward life you can learn on the street are the most important ones you will learn.

    d. A person's appearance is a good indication of what kind of person is underneath.

    e. If your parents are wealthy, you will probably have a good, happy life.

    f. It is better to look at the world in fresh, new ways—the ways that children see things.

DISCUSSION QUESTIONS

1. *Chapter 1:* Why did Ponyboy go to the movies alone? What does this reveal about his relationship with the gang? Why does it make him the appropriate narrator? Compare and contrast Sodapop and Darry. How does Ponyboy feel about each of them? Why does he feel he must lie to himself about Darry? What person do you know who pretends not to care about someone he or she is close to? Why does he or she do that?

2. *Chapter 2:* Why does Dally take orders from Johnny? How was Johnny affected by his encounter with the Socs?

3. *Chapter 3:* How does Cherry explain the difference between the greasers and the Socs? Why does she feel that she could fall in love with Dally Winston? Why does Darry hit Ponyboy? Why does Ponyboy react by running away? What emotions cause Darry and Ponyboy to act the way they do?

4. *Chapter 4:* What causes the fight between the Socs and Ponyboy and Johnny? What is the immediate cause? What are some deeper underlying causes? Why do Ponyboy and Johnny go to Dally for help? Why don't they go to Darry, Sodapop, or Two-Bit or to Johnny's parents? Which sentences in this chapter give you a clue that the church will play an important part in the story?

5. *Chapter 5:* Why do Ponyboy and Johnny decide to cut their hair? Why is it difficult for them to do this? Why does Johnny compare Dally to the Southern gentleman in *Gone With the Wind*? Do you believe that Dally is gallant? Why or why not? What do you think the line "Nothing gold can stay" means? Why does Cherry become a spy for the greasers?

6. *Chapter 6:* How do you know that Johnny really cares about his parents? Why does he decide to turn himself in? Do you think this is a wise decision? Why or why not? What values cause Johnny, Ponyboy, and Dally to go into the burning church? Do you think it was realistic for them to do this? Why or why not?

7. *Chapter 7:* What kind of atmosphere exists in the Curtis house? What is a hero? Do Dally, Ponyboy, and Johnny fit your definition? If not, what qualities are they lacking? Do you think Randy is a coward for not going to the fight? Why or why not?

8. *Chapter 8:* What does Ponyboy mean when he says, "Darry and me, we're okay now"? What has Ponyboy learned from living on the streets for so many years? What has he not learned? Why does Johnny want to see his mother? What does Ponyboy mean when he says, "The only reason Darry couldn't be a Soc was us"? Why couldn't Cherry go to visit Johnny in the hospital?

9. *Chapter 9:* Why doesn't Darry think Ponyboy should go to the rumble? Why does he give in and let him go? Ponyboy figures out the reasons why each member of the gang is going to fight: for fun, for hatred, for pride, and for conformity. What activities do you participate in for any of these reasons? Why are the others friends at one time and then enemies at another? Which two characters fully realize the uselessness of fighting? Why don't the others figure this out?

10. *Chapter 10:* Ponyboy wonders: "Dally is tougher than I am. Why can I take it when Dally can't?" Explain why. Why does Dally Winston want to be dead? Cite incidents in the book that state or imply the close relationship that existed between Dally and Johnny. Why does Ponyboy worry about the fact that he had not asked for Dally when he was sick? What does this reveal about the change in their relationship?

11. *Chapter 11:* Why does Ponyboy refuse to admit that Johnny killed Bob?
12. *Chapter 12:* How does Ponyboy react to the trauma he has experienced? What new understandings do Darry, Sodapop, and Ponyboy come to? How will they get along in the future? What effect does Johnny's note have on Ponyboy? What makes Ponyboy decide to write the essay that later becomes this book? How does writing about an experience sometimes help the writer understand what has happened? How does it help you?

WRITING ACTIVITIES

1. Prepare a story that might have appeared in the newspaper after Bob's death. Reread the sections in the book about this event so that you can include only the information that would have been available at the time.
2. When Ponyboy is brought to the hospital after the fire, he, Darry, and Sodapop are interviewed by reporters. Reconstruct this interview, including the questions the reporters might have asked and the answers the Curtis boys might have given.
3. Throughout the novel, Ponyboy learns to understand Darry. Write an essay in which you trace the growth of this understanding. Cite particular incidents and bits of dialogue that indicate Ponyboy's maturity in seeing what his brother was like.
4. Write a thank-you note that the parents of one of the children in the fire might have written to Ponyboy.
5. Choose one of the following statements: "People are more alike than different" or "People are more different than alike." Write a paper in which you support your choice by citing examples from *The Outsiders*.
6. Some of the characters in this story are well-rounded; that is, they are pictured as having both good and not-so-good qualities. Others are merely stereotypes with only one aspect of their personalities depicted. Prepare a chart and place the names of the characters under either well-rounded or stereotyped headings. Then, in a separate column list the various characteristics of each character's personality. Characters to include are Dally Winston, Mrs. Cade, Darry Curtis, Tim Shepard, Mrs. Curtis, Mr. Syme (the English teacher), Johnny Cade, Two-Bit Matthews, Randy, and Ponyboy.
7. Slang terms are used throughout the book, many of which have become outdated since the book was published. Prepare a questionnaire using the words below and survey at least ten of your classmates to find out if they know or use these words. Then write a report on your findings (chapter numbers in parentheses indicate the chapter where the words first appear).

tough (1),
cool (1),
hacked off (1),
laid off me (1),
shut your trap (2),
hood (2),
booze (2),
no sweat (2),
you dig okay (2),
rumble (3),
like it or lump it (3),
kiddo (3),
a' woofin' (4),
weed (4),
pansy (5),
fuzz (5),
cancer stick (5),
a heater (5),
beefed (6)
JD's (6),
holler uncle (7),
rep (7),
juiced up (8),
play chicken (8),
bopper (9),
savvy (9),
fake-out (9), and
sonofagun (12).

8. Cherry says to Ponyboy, "Things are rough all over." In a paragraph, explain the irony in that statement as it applies to the Socs. In a second paragraph, explain whether or not the statement applies to you. Discuss why it does or does not apply.

OTHER ACTIVITIES

1. Design a T-shirt for the greasers. Keep in mind the values of the gang and try to represent these in your design.
2. With some of your classmates, act out the scenes that reveal how the relationship of Darry, Ponyboy, and Sodapop changed. These might include the scene in chapter 3 where Darry hits Ponyboy, the scene in chapter 6 in the hospital, and the scene in chapter 12 when Sodapop runs to the park, as well as other scenes you think are important.
3. Draw a caricature of one of the following characters: Two-Bit Matthews, Cherry Valance, Johnny Cade, Dally Winston, or Mrs. Cade. Remember that a caricature exaggerates one or two prominent features of a person.
4. Using whatever medium you wish (perhaps oils or even finger paint for a bold, striking effect), draw the rumble. Try to capture the intensity of the scene through your use of line and color.
5. Enact the scenes between Ponyboy and Cherry. Use facial expressions and gestures to show the empathy that exists between these two characters even though they come from two different worlds.
6. Prepare a collage to represent the split that existed between the greasers and the Socs. Find magazine pictures, bits of material and print, and other objects that represent the two groups. Arrange these to indicate clearly that the two groups were enemies.

SELECTED TEACHING RESOURCES

Media Aids

Cassette (4)

The Outsiders. Unabridged. Listening Library, Perfection Learning Corporation, Perma-Bound, and Sundance.

Internet

A + LS/Media Weaver, Intermediate Novel Bundle. *The Outsiders*. Available: http://www.amered.com/curr/mwout.html (Accessed March 10, 2000).

Varied activities and reading responses to help students develop an understanding of the novel.

Kerby, Mona. *The Author Corner*. Available: http://www.carr.lib.md.US/mae/hint-bks.htm (Accessed March 10, 2000).

A good starting point with links to S. E. Hinton's books and other websites.

Video

The Outsiders. 91 min., color. Perma-Bound and Sundance, 1983.

Printed Resources

Articles

Mills. Randall K. "The Novels of S. E. Hinton: Springboard to Personal Growth for Adolescents." *Adolescence* 22 (Fall 1987): 641–646.

Rosch, Sue-Ann. "Outsiders Read and Write." *English Journal* 75 (January 1986): 42–45.

Seay, Ellen A. "Opulence to Decadence: *The Outsiders* and *Less Than Zero*." *English Journal* 76 (October 1987): 69–72.

VanderStaay, Steven L. "Doing Theory: Words About Words About *The Outsiders*." *English Journal* 81 (November 1992): 57–61.

Book

Daly, Jay. *Presenting S. E. Hinton*. Updated Version. Boston: Twayne Publishers, 1989.

Teaching Aids

The Outsiders. Contemporary Classics series and Portals to Literature series. Perfection Learning Corporation.

The Outsiders. Literature Unit Plans. Teacher's Pet Publications.

The Outsiders. Novel/Drama Curriculum Units. The Center for Learning.

The Outsiders. Novel-Ties. Learning Links.

The Outsiders. Novel Ideas Classics series and Novel Ideas Plus series. Sundance.

The Outsiders. Novel Unit Guide, Novel Units Student Packet, and Perma-Guide. Perma-Bound.

Tests

The Outsiders. Essay, objective, and alternative assessment versions. Perfection Learning Corporation.

Great Expectations

Charles Dickens
New York: Buccaneer Books, 1976
Available in paperback from several publishing companies.

SUMMARY

Having aided an escaped convict, a young boy named Philip Pirrip (Pip for short) feels guilty for his actions when the felon is recaptured. Shortly thereafter, Pip is taken to the home of Miss Havisham, a wealthy woman who has secluded herself following an unhappy romance and who nurses a hatred toward men. Pip is made to feel inferior in these surroundings, but he falls in love with a haughty girl named Estella and attends school. Still, he remains poor and eventually is apprenticed to his brother-in-law, a blacksmith named Joe Gargery.

Mr. Jaggers, a London lawyer, then visits Pip to inform him of great good fortune: Pip is to be made into a gentleman by an unknown benefactor. Pip assumes it's Miss Havisham because the lawyer is her solicitor. Pip then moves to London to live with Mr. Herbert Pocket and begins his tutelage under Mr. Pocket's father Matthew with two other students, the surly Bentley Drummle and Startop. When Estella returns from a trip abroad, Pip's love for her continues to grow.

After helping his friend Herbert find a place in a business firm, Pip's fortunes decline when his benefactor reveals himself to be Abel Magwitch, the convict Pip had befriended years ago. Having been deported for life, Magwitch has risked his life to visit his prodigy. In response, Pip and Herbert work to help the fugitive escape, and Pip begins to realize that he has forgotten old and faithful friends like Joe Gargery in his efforts to become a gentleman. He also realizes that Estella is not to be his when she marries the dolt Drummle.

A valiant attempt by Pip, Herbert, and Startop to help Magwitch board a ship is foiled by the old man's long-time enemy, the evil Compeyson. Although the latter is killed, Magwitch is recaptured and dies in prison with the compassionate Pip at his side. Now deeply in debt, Pip falls ill, but he is nursed back to health by the loving Joe, who also settles Pip's debts. Afterwards, Pip returns to his boyhood home, arriving on the wedding day of Joe and a kind woman named Biddy, whom Pip had hopes of marrying. Pip then leaves England to join Herbert in business in the East. After eleven years, he returns and once again meets the lovely Estella, now a widow, and their relationship resumes.

APPRAISAL

Many critics consider *Great Expectations* one of Charles Dickens's greatest works, if not his greatest. It includes all of the elements for which he is famous: the humor, the adventure, the carefully drawn minor characters, and the twists and surprises of plot. The novel represents a significant achievement in unity, symbolism, and insight into the nature of mankind.

It should be noted, perhaps, that some critics consider the ending of the novel flawed, pointing to the fact that Dickens rewrote it, bringing Pip and Estella together only upon the insistence of Bulwer-Lytton, the English author. Still, the tale has delighted countless generations of readers and continues as a classic in the high school English curriculum, where it is most often taught in the ninth and tenth grades.

THEMES

pride, revenge, friendship, success, appearance versus reality, loyalty, the individual versus society

LITERARY CONCEPTS

characterization, plot and subplot, satire, symbolism, irony, point of view, deus ex machina, serial novel

RELATED READING

Students attracted to Dickens may also want to read *David Copperfield*, *Oliver Twist*, *A Tale of Two Cities*, and *Hard Times*, his most approachable novels. Another book that traces the growth of an individual from childhood well into adulthood is the English classic *Tom Jones* by Henry Fielding.

READING PROBLEMS AND OPPORTUNITIES

Great Expectations is not easy reading for most young people. Dickens's prose is sometimes lofty and flowery, and it is often peppered with archaic phrases and esoteric terms. It also includes, at times, a variety of dialects in the dialogue of the characters. While this serves well to delineate the characters, it can also frustrate the young reader, who must often scrutinize passages to unravel their meaning. As one might expect, the novel is replete with words that will be unfamiliar to most high school students. Many of these are defined in context; others (e.g., *farinaceous, myrmidons, exordium*) are so obscure as to be easily overlooked. Hundreds of others remain, however, all of them useful for vocabulary study. They include the following (chapter numbers in parentheses indicate the chapter where the words first appear):

ravenously, eluded (1);
connubial, trenchant, apothecary, elixir, interlocutor (2);
ague, imprecation, fetter (3);
vicarious, goads (4);
execrating, parley (5);
exonerated (6);
erudition, perspicuity, sagaciously, conciliatory, ablutions (7);
disputations (8);
ignominiously, reticence, rumination (9);
felicitous, derision, refractory, discomfiture, cogitation (10);
superciliously, inexplicable, inefficacy, sanguinary (11),

trepidation (12),
remonstrances, mollified, diabolical, malevolent (13),
morose, unscrupulous, maudlin (15);
aberration, conciliate (16);
stratagem, capricious (17);
subterfuge, placable, expostulatory, valedictory (18);
condescension, affable (19);
mottled (21);
magnanimous, acquiesced, imbued, languor, inveterate (22);
serpentine (23);
niggardly, cupidity, inveigled, exultingly (25);
capacious, inexplicable (26);
incongruity, providentially (27);
lethargic (28);
imperiously (29);
impetuosity, diffidence (30);
contiguous (31);
acetious (32);
superfluous, languidly, conflagration, staid (33);
remunerative, edifying (34);
ostentatiously, obsequious, abject, cogent (35);
apoplectic, injudicious (36);
rubicund (37);
repugnance, reiterate (39);
physiognomy (40);
extenuated, incursion (43);
superseded (44);
despotic (45);
truculent (46);
discursive, commiseration, vivacity (49);
obdurate, abeyance (51);
vacillating (54);
querulous, portentous (55);
proscribed (56);
remonstrate and *vestige* (57).

INITIATING ACTIVITIES

1. Imagine that you suddenly become independently wealthy. How might this change your life? How would your style of living change? How would your relationships with friends and family change? Prepare a list of ten things you would do in your new situation. Then note any problems you fear might arise. As you read *Great Expectations*, compare your list with Pip's actions.
2. With two other students, role play the following situation: In a household the parents are a strong, spiteful mother given to scolding and physically punishing her children and a kind, easygoing father who tries to shield them. What happens when one of the children comes in late and can offer no good explanation for his tardiness? How does each of the parents react to the child and to each other? Compare the results of your dramatization with the scene in chapter 2 of *Great Expectations*.
3. Consider your possible reactions to being held captive by an escaped convict. Discuss such a situation with the other members of your class. Would you give food or medical aid to such a person? Under what conditions? Would you feel any pity or compassion toward the convict? Fear or anger? Is a criminal's behavior ever justified? Is aiding a criminal always a crime?

DISCUSSION QUESTIONS

1. *Chapter 1:* How is Pip able to visualize his father, mother, and brothers? What kinds of objects might you use to help yourself imagine a person if you had never seen the individual or a picture of him or her? How is the convict able to intimidate Pip? What does this reveal about the boy? Why is the marsh setting of the opening scene particularly effective?

2. *Chapter 2:* Explain the relationships between Joe, Mrs. Joe, and Pip.
3. *Chapter 3:* How does Pip's imagination run away with him as he tries to carry his stolen goods to the convict? Is this realistic? Why or why not? Compare his images to those of the convict. Dickens draws a clear analogy between the way the convict eats and the way a dog eats. How is this helpful in emphasizing the plight of the convict?
4. *Chapter 4:* In what ways is Pip made to feel uncomfortable during the Christmas dinner? What can you conclude about the child-rearing practices of the time based on these incidents? How does Dickens build suspense around the discovery of the missing food?
5. *Chapter 5:* How does the sergeant play on Pumblechook's vanity? Can you recall examples from your own experience where flattery was used for a similar purpose? What are Joe's and Pip's attitudes toward the escaped convicts? How would you account for these attitudes? Based on the conversation between the two convicts, what events probably took place prior to their capture? What attitude do the two men have toward each other? Why does Pip's convict confess to stealing the food?
6. *Chapter 6:* What rationalizations does Pip offer for not disclosing his crime to Joe? How does Dickens use Pip's actions to ridicule mankind in general?
7. *Chapter 7:* How does Joe's background help to account for his attitudes toward his wife and Pip? How do Joe's revelations regarding his background change Pip's attitude toward him?
8. *Chapter 8:* How is Satis House similar to Miss Havisham? What is Estella's reaction to Pip and his to her? How does Pip's experience affect his view of himself? Why do you think children in general feel injustice so keenly?
9. *Chapter 9:* How is Joe's wisdom contrasted with Pip's false pride and aspirations? At the end of chapter 9, the author intrudes and asks his reader to pause and consider his own life. Do this.
10. *Chapter 10:* What conditions in the school prevent Pip from getting an education? How is it possible that Mr. Wopsle's great aunt could continue to run her school in such a way? Why does the stranger at the Three Jolly Bargemen trouble Pip?
11. *Chapter 11:* What indication is there that Estella will play an important role in Pip's life? Why do Miss Havisham's relatives come to visit? Is there a difference between the stated reason and the real reason for their visit? Discuss. What differences exist between the fighting skills the pale young man initially appears to have and those he actually displays? Have you known people who similarly put on a good show? Why do they behave this way?
12. *Chapter 12:* Why does Miss Havisham send for Joe? What is Mrs. Joe's reaction? How does she try to disguise her feelings? Is this kind of reaction typical? Why or why not? How does Joe cleverly soothe his wife's hurt feelings? What does this reveal about him? What indications are there that Pip is changing in his feelings toward Joe and toward his aspirations in life?
13. *Chapter 15:* How does Miss Havisham receive Pip's visit? What effect does this have on him?
14. *Chapter 16:* In what way does Pip feel responsible for his sister's injuries? Why doesn't he reveal his secret about the convict? How do the police handle the case of Mrs. Joe's

assault? What is Dickens's purpose in describing their actions? How is Mrs. Joe changed, physically and mentally, after the attack? In what ways is this a blessing? In what ways is it not?

15. *Chapter 17:* Explain the relationships that exist between Biddy and Pip and between Biddy and Orlick.

16. *Chapter 18:* How is Mr. Jaggers able to gain the advantage over Mr. Wopsle during their discussion of the murder? Why does Pip assume that Miss Havisham is responsible for his great expectations?

17. *Chapter 19:* In what is it clear that Biddy understands Joe better than Pip does? Describe the behavior of Trabb and Mr. Pumblechook. Is this typical of the way people behave toward those with money? Why or why not?

18. *Chapter 20:* In what ways is Mr. Jaggers's office a reflection of the man himself? How does Mr. Jaggers treat his clients and prospective clients? What is their attitude toward him?

19. *Chapter 22:* How does Herbert impress Pip in his new quarters? Consider Herbert's tale about Miss Havisham's background. What other courses of action might she have taken?

20. *Chapter 23:* What type of person do you think Dickens is satirizing through the character of Mrs. Pocket? How do you account for Mr. Pocket's responses to his home situation?

21. *Chapter 24:* What quality in Matthew Pocket's teaching inspires Pip to become a diligent student?

22. *Chapter 25*: Compare and contrast Bentley Drummle and Startop. "A man's home is his castle." In what ways is Walworth literally like a castle? In what ways is it symbolically a castle for Wemmick? Compare and contrast Jaggers's house with Wemmick's Walworth. Why does Pip feel more comfortable at Walworth? In general, are physical surroundings the most important factor in determining one's feelings about a place? If not, what is? Why does Jaggers refer to Drummle as Spider? Why does the lawyer seem to take a fancy to him? How does Dickens arouse the reader's curiosity about Molly the housekeeper?

23. *Chapter 27:* In what subtle ways do Joe and Pip make each other uncomfortable? Is Joe wise to refuse Pip's invitation to return for dinner? Why or why not? Joe explains that he is at home at the forge. How is the forge a symbol of Joe's character?

24. *Chapter 28:* What pushes Pip farther and farther away from Joe and his childhood home? What does Pip realize about his actions toward Joe? How does Pip learn about the man who gave him the two one-pound notes? Does this part of the story seem realistic to you? Why or why not?

25. *Chapter 29:* How does Pip continue to delude himself regarding Estella? How has Estella changed? How is she still the same? How do Pip's feelings toward her change?

26. *Chapter 30:* Why does Pip wish to avoid Pumblechook? How does Trabb's boy succeed in humiliating Pip? What other course of action might Pip have taken? Pip and Herbert exchange confidences about their respective romances. Which of these two is more realistic and reasonable in his choice of a sweetheart? Why?

27. *Chapter 31:* In what play is Mr. Wopsle appearing? How is the performance distorted almost beyond recognition? Is Dickens making fun of the actors, the audience, or both?

Discuss. What adjectives does Herbert judiciously choose to describe Mr. Wopsle's portrayal? Suggest two or three similar noncommittal adjectives he might have used.

28. *Chapter 32:* How does Pip's trip to Newgate further impress him regarding his guardian's standing in London? After Pip leaves Newgate, he tries to rid himself of the place in much the same way that Jaggers does when he washes his hands after consulting with his clients. In what ways do people today literally or symbolically avoid the unpleasant?

29. *Chapter 33:* How is Miss Havisham using Pip? Why is it ludicrous for Matthew Pocket to be noted for lectures on the management of servants and children? Recall times in your life when the adage "Do as I say, not as I do" was used with you.

30. *Chapter 34:* In what ways does Pip's method of dealing with his debts prove to be effective? In what ways is it ineffective? Explain the phrase "leaving a Margin." Why is this a dangerous practice?

31. *Chapter 35:* Which aspects of Mrs. Gargery's funeral seem inappropriate to Pip? How might the funeral have been carried out more reasonably?

32. *Chapter 36:* What changes occur in Pip's life when he comes of age? In what ways is he disappointed? Why doesn't Pip accept Wemmick's advice given at the office?

33. *Chapter 37:* Contrast the way Wemmick cares for his Aged P with the way Pip treats Joe. What is Miss Skiffins's station in life? How do you know? Is Pip totally unselfish in setting up Herbert in business? Why or why not?

34. *Chapter 38:* How is Pip's love for Estella ironic? Compare the story of Miss Havisham and Estella to the tale of King Midas and his daughter. Why does Estella show favoritism toward Drummle?

35. *Chapter 39:* How does Pip first react to the returned convict? How does he respond upon learning that the convict was his benefactor? What does this reveal about Pip?

36. *Chapter 40:* Who might the lurker on the stair be? What was Magwitch's purpose in making Pip into a gentleman? How does Mr. Jaggers protect himself when Pip questions him? Why is it necessary for him to do this?

37. *Chapter 41:* How is Herbert able to talk Pip out of doing anything foolish?

38. *Chapter 42:* Discuss Magwitch's background. In what ways can his actions be traced to weaknesses in his character? To the circumstances of his environment? How does his background serve to tie together various threads of the plot?

39. *Chapter 43:* What causes Pip's acts of hostility toward Drummle?

40. *Chapter 44:* Why has Estella decided to marry Drummle?

41. *Chapter 45:* In what ways does Wemmick prove himself to be a true friend to Pip?

42. *Chapter 46:* Why is Mrs. Whimple's house chosen as a hideout for Magwitch (Provis)?

43. *Chapter 47:* Pip avoids the newspapers so that he will not have definite news of Estella's marriage to Drummle. Have you ever practiced this kind of avoidance to protect yourself from information you didn't want to receive? Discuss. How does Pip learn that Compeyson is indeed a threat? How does this revelation serve to recall the opening scenes of the book and tie the plot together?

44. *Chapter 48:* What first leads Pip to suspect that Molly is Estella's real mother?

45. *Chapter 49:* How is Herbert's future at last secured? How do you account for Miss Havisham's sudden change of heart? Why does Pip return to Miss Havisham's room just in time to save her from the fire? Is Pip courageous in saving her? Why or why not?

46. *Chapter 50:* How does Herbert again reveal his kind and gentle nature?

47. *Chapter 51:* Why won't Jaggers admit that Pip has discovered the secret of Estella's parentage? Why does Pip finally decide not to disclose his secrets?

48. *Chapter 52:* Does Pip act wisely in deciding to travel to the sluice-house alone? Why or why not? What possibilities should he have taken into consideration?

49. *Chapter 53:* Why does Orlick hate Pip so? Why does Orlick prolong the murder of his longtime enemy? How does Dickens build suspense in the rescue scene?

50. *Chapter 54:* Why does Magwitch seem so unconcerned about the possibility of his own capture? Does he exhibit complete trust and confidence in Pip and his friends? Is this wise? Why or why not? How is the capture of Magwitch similar to the capture of the two convicts at the beginning of the novel?

51. *Chapter 55:* Why doesn't Pip want Magwitch to know the truth about the money he plans to leave him? Why does Herbert leave his good friend Pip at such a trying time? Is he right or wrong in doing this?

52. *Chapter 56:* How have Pip's feelings toward Magwitch now changed? What do these changes reveal about Pip's character? Do you believe that Magwitch was foolish to return to England? Why or why not?

53. *Chapter 59:* In the original version of the novel, Dickens did not have Pip and Estella meet to renew their old relationship. Do you think this happy ending that he later substituted for the original is more satisfactory? Why or why not?

WRITING ACTIVITIES

1. Pip invents an imaginary picture of Miss Havisham's surroundings and of her behavior. Create your own tale of this strange woman, writing it as a monologue that Pip might have delivered. Your story may be a fantasy, but it must be believable to Mrs. Joe and Uncle Pumblechook.

2. Research the prison system in England in the early nineteenth century. Prepare a written report in which you compare it to the current system in the United States. In your conclusion, judge the merits and weaknesses of each system.

3. Throughout the novel, Dickens uses phrases that are not readily understood today: "Give it mouth" (chapter 1), "punished the Amens tremendously" (chapter 4), "throw your eye over them" (chapter 5), "a gentleman that you would like to hear give it out" (chapter 10), "I don't think it would answer" (chapter 17), "We made up the money this morning" (chapter 20), "I am looking about me" (chapter 22), and others. Using these phrases and others you find in the novel (at least ten), prepare a glossary in which you translate them into twentieth-century American English.

4. Education has changed in many ways since Dickens's time. In a short paper compare and contrast your education with Pip's. Refer to physical setting, materials used, the curriculum studied, and the nature and quality of the teachers.

5. Imitating the style of sensational newspapers like the *National Enquirer*, write a story exposing Estella's background. Create an eye-catching headline and include relevant details from the events presented in the novel.
6. Write a eulogy Pip might have given at Magwitch's funeral.
7. On several occasions Pip rationalizes his behavior to avoid painful situations (e.g., when he does not tell the truth about stealing the food). Examine your own behavior for a week and keep a list of any rationalizations you develop.
8. Like many heroes, Pip undertakes several journeys. In a well-organized essay, explore his journeys and how they lead him to maturity and self-awareness.
9. As a child, Pip often complains of unjust treatment. In a paper of two or three pages, compare an injustice that you suffered as a child with one experienced by Pip.
10. Write a manual entitled "The Young Englishman's Guide to Manners and Morals" from which Pip might have benefited before he arrived in London.

OTHER ACTIVITIES

1. Draw a sketch of Satis House (or a section of it) as it might have appeared on the day of Miss Havisham's wedding and another of the same place twenty years later.
2. You are a television writer-producer. You wish to make *Great Expectations* into a miniseries, but you must first sell your idea to a network. To do this, you need to select one scene from the book that would have wide appeal. Rewrite the scene in the form of a television drama, including the lines to be spoken, sets and props to be used, appropriate music, and even the camera shots. Select noted actors and actresses to play the various roles. If videotape is available, film your scene and present it to the class. If not, present the scene to the class live.
3. Find copies of books on historical costumes at your school or public library. Using the books as sources, choose appropriate clothing for the major characters in the novel and reproduce these costumes in color. Several characters may need more than one outfit.
4. Many of the characters in the fiction of Charles Dickens are memorable, partly because of certain qualities or features that the author has exaggerated. Draw a caricature of one such character from *Great Expectations*.

SELECTED TEACHING RESOURCES

Media Aids

CD-ROM

The Time, Life, and Works of Charles Dickens CD-ROM. Macintosh and Windows versions. CLEARVUE/eav.

Internet

Great Expectations by Charles Dickens. Available: http://www.canisiushs.buffalo.ny.us/expectations (Accessed March 10, 2000).

Videos

Great Expectations. 118 min., b & w. Alec Guinness/Jean Simmons version, directed by David Lean. Learning Corporation of America, 1947.

Great Expectations. 300 min., color. BBC Charles Dickens Collection. Perma-Bound, 1988.

Scenes from Great Expectations. 30 min., color. Coronet MTI, 1990.

The World of Charles Dickens. 15 min. CLEARVUE/eav.

Printed Resources

Articles

Crago, Hugh. "Prior Expectations of *Great Expectations*: How One Child Learned to Read a Classic." *College English* 58 (October 1996): 676–692.

Granata, May. "Pip's Great Expectations and Ours." *English Journal* 54 (September 1965): 525–529.

Simmons, Susan. "Pip—A Love Affair." *English Journal* 58 (March 1969): 426–417.

Books

Bloom, Harold (ed.). *Charles Dickens's* Great Expectations. Bloom's Notes Series. Bloomall, PA: Chelsea House Publications, 1996.

Hornback, Bert G. *Great Expectations: A Novel of Friendship*. Masterwork Studies. New York: Macmillan, 1987.

Teaching Aids

Great Expectations. Insight Series. Sundance.

Great Expectations. Literature Unit Plans. Teacher's Pet Publications.

Great Expectations. Masterprose series. Perfection Learning Corporation.

Great Expectations. Novel/Drama Curriculum Unit. The Center for Learning.

Great Expectations. Novel-Ties. Learning Links.

Great Expectations. Novel Unit Guide, Novel Units Student Packet, and Perma-Guide. Perma-Bound.

Tests

Great Expectations. Essay, objective, and alternative assessment versions. Perfection Learning Corporation.

Fahrenheit 451

Ray Bradbury
New York: Ballantine Books, 1953
Available in paperback from Del Rey (Ballantine).

SUMMARY

At some unspecified future time in an American city, Guy Montag works as a fireman, one of a cadre of professionals whose job is the burning of books to prevent the spread of disturbing ideas. Events and certain people he meets (in particular, a girl named Clarisse, who dares to talk and think for herself, and an elderly intellectual named Faber) cause him to question his work, his unhappiness, and the shallowness of his society. He begins to hide books at home, and inevitably he is caught. Montag escapes, however, by killing his nemesis, Captain Beatty, and the monstrous Mechanical Hound and by taking refuge in a river on the edge of the city. Beyond the river, Montag encounters a group of intellectuals who have assumed the responsibility of saving history's great written works by memorizing them. As the book ends, a foreign bomb destroys the city, and the small group of hopeful dissenters makes its way back to the city.

APPRAISAL

Since its publication in 1953, at the height of the national paranoia that accompanied the McCarthy Senate hearings into "un-American activities," *Fahrenheit 451* has achieved universal recognition as the book that examines, perhaps more successfully than any other, the value of books and free expression in modern society. Like Bradbury's other works, *Fahrenheit 451* is science fiction, a compelling novel that tells a good story while exploring an issue of importance to every person in a democratic society. The book is most often taught in the early years of high school, grades nine or ten.

THEMES

censorship, freedom versus oppression, openness, the role of media in society, the nature and pursuit of happiness, the individual versus the state

LITERARY CONCEPTS

plot, setting, symbol, metaphor and simile, personification, point of view (including stream-of-consciousness narration), irony, allusion

RELATED READING

The two most famous futuristic novels about mind control are *1984* by George Orwell and *Brave New World* by Aldous Huxley. Both are often taught or assigned for outside reading, as is the more recent novel *The Giver* by Lois Lowry. Students interested in the censorship issue might read the young adult novels *The Day They Came to Arrest the Book* by Nat Hentoff and *The Last Safe Place on Earth* by Richard Peck. Or they might prefer such nonfiction works as *50 Ways to Fight Censorship* by Dave Marsh and George Plimpton. A useful reference work is *Banned in the U.S.A.: A Reference Guide to Book Censorship in Schools and Public Libraries* by Herbert N. Foerstel.

READING PROBLEMS AND OPPORTUNITIES

Written from the third-person limited point of view of its protagonist, *Fahrenheit 451* is well within the reading range of most high school students. Still, the book contains numerous words worth teaching or reinforcing (part numbers are included in parentheses):

venomous (One),
stolid (One),
luxuriously (One),
irritable (One),
refracted (One),
imperceptibly (One),
mausoleum (One),
pulverized (One),
impersonal (One),
earnestly (One),
distilled (One, Two),
conjure (One),
olfactory (One),
proboscis (One),
multifaceted (One),
ballistics (One),
trajectory (One, Three),
proclivities (One),
odious (One),
objectivity (One, Three),
ritual (One, Three),
fervor (One),
flourish (One, Three),
condemnation (One),
heresy (One),
abyss (One),
ravenous (One),
centrifuge (One, Two),
cacophony (One),
luminescent, luminous (One, Three),
feigning (One),
nomadic (One),
cower (One),
titillation (One),
noncombustible (One),
melancholy (One),
bestial (One),
rationalizing (One),
suffused (Two),
gibbering (Two, Three),
profusion (Two),
insidious (Two),
contemptible (Two),
ruinous (Two),
verbiage (Two),
rebut (Two),
beatific (Two),
perfunctorily (Two),
phosphorescent (Two, Three),
gobbledygook (Three),
burdensome (Three),
aesthetic (Three),
mannikin (Three),
liquefaction (Three),
blanched (Three),
penance (Three),
instinctively (Three),
plummeting (Three),
exhalations (Three),
grotesque (Three),
oblivion (Three),
seance (Three),
ricochet (Three),
juggernaut (Three),
scapegoat (Three),
avenged (Three),
incite (Three),
incriminate (Three),
pedant (Three),
convolutions (Three),
desolation (Three),
prattled (Three), and
incessantly (Three).

INITIATING ACTIVITIES

1. Look up the word *heresy* (or *heretics*) in a dictionary. Then look up the word in several encyclopedias. Who were some of history's most famous heretics? What was the context of their actions? Whom did they offend? What were the consequences? Do these actions and consequences have anything in common? Discuss these people and these questions with your classmates.
2. *Fahrenheit 451* was published in 1953 at a time when a United States senator named Joseph McCarthy inflamed the American public about his concerns over the alleged presence of communists and communist sympathizers in various organizations and professions in our society. Do some research on Senator McCarthy, on the Senate hearings he sponsored and conducted, on his accusations and the climate of fear they inspired, and on the outcome of his efforts. Report your findings to the class.
3. Before reading the novel, complete this "opinionnaire," providing one of the following responses to each statement: *Strongly Agree*, *Agree*, *Disagree*, or *Strongly Disagree*.
   a. Books can be dangerous.
   b. An open society will make all books available to the public through its libraries.
   c. Television is a greater threat to the public good than books.
   d. The open expression of diverse ideas is essential to a democracy.
   e. Sometimes censorship is necessary.

DISCUSSION QUESTIONS

1. *Part One (The Hearth and the Salamander):* Why do you think Montag enjoys the burning so much? Why is he so intrigued by the girl Clarisse? What is she like? Shy or forthright? Curious or accepting? Thoughtful? Provocative? Dangerous? What seems important to her? To Montag? How would you describe Montag? His uniform features several symbols. What might the salamander and the phoenix imply? Why does he seem to know less about some things than Clarisse does? On the basis of their first conversation, what can we infer about their society? Why do you think Clarisse asks Montag if he is happy? Why is he bothered by her question? What is unusual about Montag's house? What does he seem particularly aware of? What are the implications of his comparing Clarisse's face with that of a clock? How does he perceive her? Why do you think Montag sees himself as unhappy? How would you characterize Mildred's condition? Why do you think she has taken the sleeping pills? What does Montag mean by "There are too many of us"? Why is he so intrigued by Clarisse's house and family? What is suggested by his thoughts as he lies in the bedroom in the moonlight? Why does he say, "I don't know anything anymore"? What are the Seashell ear-thimbles? Is Mildred addicted to them? Why? What does Mildred mean by "The man's *thinking*"? Why do you think she denies having taken the pills? Why is her involvement in the script so interesting to her? Why does she want the fourth wall-TV installed? Why might others think that Clarisse needs a psychiatrist? How is she apparently different? How does she think Montag is different? Do you think he is? Why or why not? Why does he think Clarisse is easy to forgive? Is thinking dangerous? Curiosity? Discuss. Describe the Mechanical Hound. In what ways is it living? In what ways is it dead? Why do you think it has the characteristics of an insect but is identified as a hound? What purpose does it seem to serve? Why do you think it threatens Montag? What more do we learn about Clarisse and about her society? How does she view the

difference between "social" and "antisocial?" Do you agree with her? Do you see any similarities between this society and ours today? Explain. Why does Montag miss Clarisse? Why do you think the author uses the word form "dis-ease"? So far, how is the environment of the book different from our own? Why is the society so opposed to books? Why do you think Montag often thinks of the ventilator grille at home? Why is he so uneasy? At this point, how do you think the other firemen view him? What are the implications of the rule book? What else do we learn about the society during the raid? Why does Montag save a book? Why do you think the books are compared to birds? What are the implications of Beatty's comment that "none of those books agree with each other"? What does the woman mean by "you can't ever have my books"? Why does she light the fire herself? What is the significance of Beatty's recalling the quotation and of Stoneman's missing the turn to the firehouse? Why does Montag feel infected and so upset? Why does Montag want to remember when he met Mildred? What are the implications of her response? Is Mildred obsessed? If so, by what? How would you characterize her relationships with others? Who are the "relatives?" Why does Mildred like their constant talking? Montag says, "We need to be really bothered once in a while." Do you agree with this? Why or why not? Why does Beatty think that Montag needs to know "the history of our profession"? What does he mean by *mass*? What trends does he think have dominated the twentieth century? Does he think they are good or bad? What do you think? Why? Why do you think the word *intellectual* had become a swear word in the society? What does Beatty have to say about education? According to Beatty, what is government's most important role? At the end of this section, do you think he suspects Montag? Why wouldn't the government want people sitting and talking? What do you think will be the results of Montag's decision to read the books he has hidden away? What is he hoping for?

2. *Part Two (The Sieve and the Sand):* Why does Montag consider reading and books so important? Why does Mildred oppose them? Why is his remembered meeting with Faber significant? What is the difference between "*things*" and "the *meaning* of things"? Why does Montag ask Mildred if the White Clown loves her? How does the metaphor of the sieve relate to Montag's situation? How are the subway riders affected by the dentifice message? According to Faber, how have "they" changed the Bible and Christ? What does Faber mean by saying a book has "pores," texture, "*telling detail*"? Why does he compare the fate of Antaeus to their present situation? In what way does Faber feel that leisure is absent from their society? What is the third necessary quality? What is Montag's plan? What does Faber mean by saying that the great plays "are too *aware* of the world"? What does he mean by saying the government wants "people reading only about passionate lips and the fist in the stomach"? What role does war seem to play in the society and in the book? As Montag and Faber talk with each other over the ear devices, why does Faber say, "You're wise already"? What do the women's various remarks in Montag's parlor reveal about them? Why is Montag unable to resist reading poetry to them? Why is Faber so upset? Why is *Dover Beach* an ironic choice? Why does Mrs. Phelps cry? Afterwards, how does Montag feel? How does he see himself changing? Why does Faber comfort Montag? What motivates Faber? Is he a mentor? A conscience? At the firehouse, what does Beatty mean by the quote "Who are a little wise, the best fools be"? How do the other quotes serve his purpose? What is he trying to achieve? Does he succeed? Why is it important to Faber that Montag makes his own decision "as to which way to jump, or fall"? What does he mean by "the terrible tyranny of the majority"? At the end, why do you think Beatty has chosen Montag's house? As a test, or as punishment?

3. *Part Three (Burning Bright):* What does Montag enjoy about burning his own house? When he aims his flame-thrower at Beatty, what does he mean by "We never burned *right*"? Why does Montag call himself a fool? Do you think he really believes that Beatty wanted to die? Do you believe it? Why or why not? What does Montag feel the need to clean up? How does Montag react to the realization that it was children and not the police who almost hit him in the beetle? Are you as surprised as he was? Why or why not? Why does Montag plant books in the house of Mrs. Black? Do you think his actions here are justified? Why or why not? Why is Montag so absorbed with the idea of the "civilian parlor sitters" observing on television his pursuit by the Mechanical Hound? What incident in America in the mid-1990s might this remind us of? What does it suggest about Montag's society, as well as our own? Why is it appropriate that Montag escapes in a river? After Montag's escape, for what purpose does the author describe the setting? Why does Montag think about Millie? Why does he imagine the barn and the hayloft? Why does he envision a glass of milk, an apple, and a pear? Why is he then so overcome by smells? Why is Montag attracted to the fire and the men around it? As he and the men watch the climax of the chase on TV, what is sacrificed besides the "poor fellow" out for a walk? What do you think about the men's approach to maintaining the great works of literature, science, history, and so on? Why do the men think they are safe from the government? Why do they seem something other than enthusiastic to Montag? How do you respond to Granger's argument that everyone must leave the world a little changed by his or her touch? What does he mean by quoting his grandfather, "I hate a Roman named Status Quo"? When the war strikes, why does Montag again think of Mildred? After the terrible concussion, what books does Montag try to remember? What else does he feel he must try to remember? Why? In what way does Granger believe that man differs from the Phoenix? Do you agree? Why or why not? Why does Granger want the men to believe that they are not important? Why does he want to build a mirror factory? What do these survivors believe is important as they walk back toward the city?

WRITING ACTIVITIES

1. In Part Three, as Montag visualizes himself captured by the Mechanical Hound, he wonders "would he have time for a speech" to the citizens. Write that brief speech to the people—in twenty words or less, "a few words, that would sear all their faces and wake them up."

2. The wall-TVs in Montag's society are described as emitting an endless array of meaningless gibberish that mesmerizes Mildred and the others. Write a paper entitled "Television at the Turn of the Century: *Fahrenheit 451* Comes True." Your paper should cite specific examples of American television as a "vast wasteland." *Or,* write a paper in which you rebut the idea that television does more harm than good.

3. Imagine yourself as a member of the group of outsiders responsible for remembering the great books of the past. Compile a list of five works (or parts of works) that you would wish to be responsible for. For each work, write a one-paragraph explanation of why it is important. Compare your list with those of other classmates.

4. Write an epitaph for Clarisse. Make it no longer than a line or two, but try to capture her uniqueness in the society that destroyed her. A possible approach is to consult a book of quotations, such as *Bartlett's Quotations*, for an appropriate line or two from a work of literature.

5. Write a report on the state of censorship in this country in the last five or ten years. For information, consult the Internet (see "Selected Teaching Resources" below for a useful website) or books like *Banned in the U.S.A.* by Herbert N. Foerstel. Try to determine the most commonly challenged titles and the most common reasons cited for efforts to censor them.
6. In reference to Clarisse and her family, Captain Beatty says that "heredity and environment are funny things. You can't rid yourselves of all the odd ducks in just a few years." Throughout history "odd ducks" have often been the ones who accomplish the most. They are often inventive, original, single-minded, and open to new ideas. Write a paper about one of history's accomplished individuals. Just a few examples are Einstein, Van Gogh, Emily Dickinson, Beethoven, and Benjamin Franklin.
7. Write one of the "rhymeless poems" that Montag remembers Faber having spoken (opening of Part Two). A possibility is a cinquain that begins with the word *anger*.
8. *Fahrenheit 451* has several unidentified quotations read from old books, like Beatty's quote about Master Ridley and the one on friendship at the very beginning of Part Two (second paragraph). Using *Bartlett's Quotations*, various concordances, or even the Internet, try to find the sources for some of these. Report your findings to the class.
9. Check out or rent the movie *Wag the Dog*. After viewing it once or twice, write a paper in which you compare the society, government, or media in the movie with "the State" in *Fahrenheit 451*.
10. In Part Three, Granger mentions a book he wrote, *The Fingers in the Glove: The Proper Relationship between the Individual and Society*. Write a one- to two-page explanation of why *The Fingers in the Glove* might be an appropriate title for such a book. Keep in mind some of the ideas Bradbury seems especially interested in conveying in *Fahrenheit 451*.

OTHER ACTIVITIES

1. Design a collage or mobile that reflects the "philosophy" of happiness promoted by the society in the novel as described by Beatty during the history of the firemen that he relates to Montag. *Or,* create a collage or mobile that would represent Montag's or Faber's ideas of happiness.
2. With several other students, act out and record one of Mildred's "family" gatherings. Write a script for it that involves several characters and conveys some of the qualities that make the gatherings seem so appealing to her.
3. Imagine that the firemen, concerned with public relations, have decided to mount a campaign to remind citizens of the important role played by firemen in the society. Design a poster, a bumper sticker, and a thirty-second radio ad that promotes their work and contributions. You might also want to design a website for the firemen.
4. Sketch several possible uniforms for the firemen. Include some of the symbols that are mentioned in the book. Pay particular attention to color and functionality.
5. Stage a class debate based on the following resolution: Books are essential in a democratic society. Half of the class should prepare to argue in favor of the statement; half against.

6. Depending on your interests, try your hand at one of the following:
   a. Using descriptions in the book as guides, especially in Part One, draw a detailed picture of the Mechanical Hound. Try to convey the malignant terror it inspired.
   b. Draw or paint a still life of the glass of milk, apple, and pear mentioned in Part Three.

SELECTED TEACHING RESOURCES

Media Aids

Cassettes (4)

Fahrenheit 451. Unabridged, 5.5 hrs. Recorded Books.

Internet

American Library Association. 1999. *Banned Books Week: Free People Read Freely*. 1999. Available: http://www.ala.org/bbooks/ (Accessed March 10, 2000).

Includes an annotated list of the most challenged books, notable First Amendment cases, quotations, and a resource guide.

Video

Fahrenheit 451. 102 min., b & w. Julie Christie and Oskar Werner version. Perfection Learning Company, Perma-Bound, and Sundance, 1966.

Printed Materials

Article

Gardner, Robert. "A New Fashioned Book Burning." *English Journal* 86 (February 1997): 63–64.

Teaching Aids

Fahrenheit 451. Contemporary Classics series. Perfection Learning Corporation.

Fahrenheit 451. Literature Unit Plans. Teacher's Pet Publications.

Fahrenheit 451. Novel/Drama Curriculum Units. The Center for Learning.

Fahrenheit 451. Novel Ideas Classic series and Novel Ideas Plus series. Sundance.

Fahrenheit 451. Novel Unit Guide, Novel Units Student Packet, and Perma-Guide. Perma-Bound.

Fahrenheit 451. Novel-Ties. Learning Links.

Tests

Fahrenheit 451. Essay, objective, and alternative assessment versions. Perfection Learning Corporation.

Julius Caesar

William Shakespeare
1599
Play: Available in a variety of paperback versions.

SUMMARY

While the people of Rome have a holiday to celebrate Caesar's victory over Pompey, two tribunes, Marullus and Flavius, move about the city, scorning the commoners who are taking part in the festivities. When Caesar and his party enter, a soothsayer approaches and bids him "Beware the ides of March." After Caesar leaves, Cassius begins his appeal to turn Brutus against Caesar, who has three times refused the crown offered to him by Antony. Caesar observes Cassius and explains his distrust of him to Antony. Brutus begins to succumb to Cassius's entreaties and agrees to meet with him again. Cassius and Casca meet, Cinna joins them, and they agree that the ambitious Caesar must be stopped and that Brutus is a key to the success of their plot.

On the eve of the ides of March, a fierce, strange storm rages. Brutus cannot sleep because he must decide whether or not to join the conspirators: Cassius, Casca, Decius, Cinna, Metellus Cimber, and Trebonius. Hidden by their cloaks, the conspirators come to Brutus and lay the final plans for killing Caesar. Portia, Brutus's wife, is distraught, tries to uncover Brutus's secrets, and later sends a servant to check on the happenings at the Capitol. Calpurnia, Caesar's wife, begs her husband to stay at home because of evil omens, but he is moved by the speech of Decius, one of the conspirators, and leaves for the Capitol with the other conspirators. Along the way, Artemidorus waits to hand Caesar a warning letter, but neither this entreaty nor the words of the soothsayer dissuade the mighty ruler from entering the senate-house.

Inside the senate-house, the conspirators crowd around Caesar, ostensibly to plead the cause of Metellus Cimber's brother, but actually to inflict the many stab wounds that kill him. All the senators flee in terror, but Antony sends a servant to ask the conspirators if he can present Caesar's funeral oration. Brutus agrees, but speaks before Antony does to tell the people of his love for Caesar but also of the need to rid Rome of Caesar's tyranny. Antony, more adept at handling the masses, presents an eloquent funeral oration that moves the crowds to seek out and kill the conspirators. In fact, they are so enflamed that they mistakenly kill Cinna the poet, even though he is innocent.

Several months later, Brutus and Cassius have gathered legions of soldiers and are preparing to face Antony, who has combined forces with Octavius and Lepidus. The two conspirators quarrel both in front of their forces and privately, but later resolve their differences and decide to move to Phillipi to face Antony and his forces. The battle does not go well for Brutus and Cassius, and Cassius mistakenly believes that all is lost and ends his own life. Ironically, the cheers Brutus heard were for his victory, but when Brutus discovers Cassius's body, he begs his few followers to hold his sword for him while he kills himself. When Antony arrives and finds Brutus's body, he declares him "the noblest Roman of them all."

APPRAISAL

A strong component of the traditional high school English curriculum, *Julius Caesar* carries a message that remains important for each new generation of students. The excesses of tyranny continue to crop up around the globe but unfortunately never disappear. The responses to these excesses continue to be combat, death, and destruction. Perhaps what history cannot correct, literature can at least illumine. This play is most often taught to ninth and tenth graders.

THEMES

power, betrayal, love of country, friendship, ambition, honor, supernatural forces, courage

LITERARY CONCEPTS

puns, tragedy, character development, blank verse, asides, foreshadowing, irony, metaphor, simile, couplets

RELATED READING

Other historical plays by William Shakespeare, including *Henry IV* (Parts 1 and 2), *Henry V, Richard II,* and *Richard III,* allow the reader to explore the lives of English kings. *Antony and Cleopatra* depicts Antony's later exploits and unveils his weaknesses and follies.

READING PROBLEMS AND OPPORTUNITIES

The reading of Shakespeare's plays poses a variety of problems for young people. First of all, they were not written to be read, but rather to be seen in the theater, so reading becomes a somewhat artificial way of experiencing the play. Second, during the 400 years that have elapsed since the initial performance of these plays, major changes have taken place in the English language, both in vocabulary and syntax. And finally, most students are not familiar with the lives of great Romans and Greeks, so they often do not understand allusions to characters and events that many of Shakespeare's contemporaries had at least heard about.

Most textbooks and paperback versions of Shakespeare's plays provide footnotes to explain the archaic words, phrases, and even allusions. Therefore, the following vocabulary study list includes only words that might be a valuable addition for contemporary vocabulary (act and scene numbers are in parentheses):

tributaries (1:1),
intermit (1:1),
cognitations (1:2),
rout (1:2),
accoutred (1:2),
tempest (1:3),
portentous (1:3),
factious (1:3),
redress (2:1),
visage (2:1),
affability (2:1),
augurers (2:1),
portents (2:2),
ague (2:2),
fray (2:4),

puissant (3:1), *clamours* (3:2), *mantle* (3:2), *vesture* (3:2), *proscription* (4:1, 4:3), *wrangle* (4:2), *chastisement* (4:3), *choler* (4:3), *choleric* (4:3), *apparition* (4:3), *reveller* (5:1), *disconsolate* (5:3), and *envenomed* (5:3).

INITIATING ACTIVITIES

1. Check your library or the Internet for a brief biography of Julius Caesar. What important facts can you find to answer the following questions: When was he born? Who were his ancestors? How was he educated? When and how did he achieve prominence in the Roman government? What titles did he hold? What was his relationship with Pompey? Prepare an oral report for your classmates to help them understand what has happened before the opening of the play.
2. With your classmates, review and list the current key rulers in the world. For each ruler, make two lists: good traits and bad traits. Try to generalize from your lists which traits are essential for a good ruler and which traits must be present for a ruler to be declared bad. Keep the resulting list of traits and review it as you read *Julius Caesar*. It will help you to analyze a number of the characters you will meet.

DISCUSSION QUESTIONS

1. *Act 1, scene 1:* Why do Marullus and Flavius drive the people from the streets? Why do they plan to take the adornments from Caesar's statues?
2. *Act 1, scene 2:* How does Cassius try to turn Brutus against Caesar? Why does Caesar distrust Cassius? Are his reasons justifiable? Why or why not? Why does Caesar refuse the crown three times?
3. *Act 1, scene 3:* What does Casca think the "great storm" means? What does Cassius think it means? Why do the conspirators need to convince Brutus to join them?
4. *Act 2, scene 1:* What is preventing Brutus from sleeping? Why does Brutus say they should not swear an oath? How does Brutus convince the others to spare Antony? Which of Portia's arguments causes Brutus to agree to reveal his secrets to her?
5. *Act 2, scene 2:* How is the scene between Calpurnia and Caesar similar to the scene between Portia and Brutus in Act 2, scene 1? How is it different? Why is Decius able to convince Caesar to go to the Capitol? Are the other conspirators really needed to get Caesar to leave his home? Why or why not?
6. *Act 2, scene 3:* Why is Artemidorus so anxious to get his note to Caesar?
7. *Act 2, scene 4:* Why does Portia send Lucius to the senate-house instead of going herself? What causes Portia to be even more concerned about Brutus?
8. *Act 3, scene 1:* Why doesn't Caesar heed the warnings of Artemidorus and the soothsayer? Why is Caesar unyielding in the case of Publius Cimber? Do the crowds behave as the conspirators had hoped? Why or why not? How do the conspirators attempt to rationalize their murder of Caesar? How do Antony's actions among the conspirators contrast with his words to the body of Caesar? Which actions/words do you think reflect his true feelings?

Why? What does Antony predict for the future of Rome? Why does he tell Octavius to stay away?

9. *Act 3, scene 2:* How does Brutus attempt to win the people over? How successful is he? How does Antony attempt to win the people over? Why is he more successful than Brutus?
10. *Act 3, scene 3:* What is motivating the Plebians who confront Cinna? Why do they kill him even after they find out he is the poet, not the conspirator? What elements of human behavior is Shakespeare depicting in this scene?
11. *Act 4, scene 1:* Why have Antony, Octavius, and Lepidus selected men who must die? What is Antony's opinion of Lepidus's value? Why must Antony and Octavius go to the council soon?
12. *Act 4, scene 2:* How does Brutus know that his relationship with Cassius is not what it once was? What does Brutus advise Cassius to do about airing his griefs? Is this a wise suggestion? Why or why not?
13. *Act 4, scene 3:* Over what do Brutus and Cassius argue? What are the apparent reasons that Brutus verbally attacks Cassius? For what other reasons is Brutus angry and upset? How are Brutus and Cassius able to reconcile their differences? Why does Cassius believe they should wait for Antony's army to advance? Why does Brutus believe they should proceed to the battle and meet the army in Phillipi? Which plan do you think is better? Why? What does Brutus's treatment of his men, who are weary, reveal about his character?
14. *Act 5, scene 1:* How do Octavius and Antony know what Brutus and Cassius plan to do? How do Octavius and Antony view the conspirators at this time? Why does Cassius say that Antony would not be insulting them now if he had had his way? In what ways have the birds flying overhead had an impact on Cassius's feelings about the outcome of the upcoming battle? Under what conditions do Brutus and Cassius bid each other farewell? What outcome to the battle do they anticipate?
15. *Act 5, scene 2:* Why does Brutus send Messala with orders for the legions on the other side?
16. *Act 5, scene 3:* How does Titinius perceive the battle is progressing? What orders does Cassius give to Titinius and Pindarus? What is the danger of mistakes in this plan? How would these dangers be eliminated today? Why is Cassius in such a hurry to end his life? How does Pindarus feel about his role in Cassius's death? What irony is revealed when Titinius returns? How does Messala think that Brutus will receive the news of Cassius's death? Why does Titinius take his own life? To what cause does Brutus attribute these suicides?
17. *Act 5, scene 4:* How does Lucilius trick Antony's soldiers? Why does Antony require kindness for the captured Lucilius?
18. *Act 5, scene 5:* Why does Brutus believe it is time for him to die? How does Brutus view his loss in battle? Why does he think he will have more glory than Octavius and Antony? Why does Brutus kill himself more easily than he killed Caesar? What is Antony's final appraisal of Brutus and his actions? Do you agree? Why or why not?

WRITING ACTIVITIES

1. Using a dictionary of literary terms and/or other reference materials, establish a definition for "tragedy." Prepare an analysis of *Julius Caesar*, explaining which elements of the play fit the definition of tragedy and which do not. Share your analysis with your classmates.

2. Many lines from *Julius Caesar* have become a part of the English language today. Choose one of the following lines and write a side-by-side story: On the right-hand side of the page, prepare a paraphrase of its use in the play *Julius Caesar*, and on the left side write a contemporary story using the same line from *Julius Caesar:*

   He thinks too much: such men are dangerous. (1:2)

   But, for my own part, it was Greek to me. (1:2)

   A dish fit for the Gods. (2:1)

   The heavens themselves blaze forth the death of princes. (2:2)

   But I am constant as the northern star. (3:1)

   This was the most unkindest cut of all. (3:2)

   Ready to give up the ghost. (5:1)

   And say to all the world, "This was a man!" (5:5)

3. Portia and Calpurnia are the only females in the play *Julius Caesar.* Based on their speeches and what others say to and about them, prepare an essay on the role of women in Rome in 44 B.C.E. Use specific examples from the play to illustrate your points.

4. Several recent movies have updated Shakespeare's plays, either by modernizing the language, modernizing the setting, or both. Select a scene from *Julius Caesar* and revise it in a contemporary setting, use contemporary language, or both. If equipment is available, videotape your scene and show it to your classmates.

5. In Act 5, scene 5, Brutus makes his farewell speech and Antony provides a eulogy for Brutus. Prepare similar speeches for Cassius: a farewell to his friends and a eulogy by Antony. How will these differ from those by and for Brutus, based on what you know of Cassius?

6. Research life in Rome in 44 B.C.E. What are the activities that make up a typical day? What are the differences between the lives of the nobles and the lives of the commoners? Write a set of diary entries (at least five) surrounding the assassination of Caesar from a noble's viewpoint and another set from a commoner's viewpoint.

7. Before the battle at Phillipi, Brutus and Cassius meet with Antony and Octavius. Check your history books and prepare a description of the rules of war in Rome in 44 B.C.E. Then write an evaluation of how accurately Shakespeare adhered to historical reality in presenting battle preparations and battle scenes.

OTHER ACTIVITIES

1. In Shakespeare's era, his Globe Theatre was one of the most popular. The history of the Globe Theatre recently added a new chapter when a newly re-created Globe was opened in London. Construct a timeline illustrating the key events in the history of this theater. Place your timeline on the bulletin board or put it on your school's web page.
2. A large part of every audience at Shakespearean plays consisted of the groundlings, commoners who stood in the center of the theater. To appeal to this less educated section of the audience, Shakespeare used comic relief and spectacle. Make a list of these elements in the play *Julius Caesar*. Explain why each one would have audience appeal.
3. Pantomime the murder of Caesar in Act 3, scene 1 while a narrator reads the scene. Repeat the scene in slow motion to get the full effect of the conspirators' movements. Have the various players report about their feelings during their performance.
4. Create an artistic interpretation of the evening of March 14, before the infamous ides of March. Review the descriptions and dialogue in Act 1, scene 3 for details. Use any medium that suits your image of this terrifying night.
5. Research the tombs prepared for important persons in Rome in 44 B.C.E. Design an appropriate tomb for either Caesar or Brutus. Prepare an oral presentation that could be given to sell your design to the people of Rome.

SELECTED TEACHING RESOURCES

Media Aids

Cassettes (2)

Julius Caesar. Perfection Learning Corporation and Sundance.

Internet

What the Electronic Julius Caesar Site Currently Includes. Available: http://www.perseus.tufts.edu/JC/JC.includes.html (Accessed March 10, 2000).

Scholarly site containing several versions of the text, extensive commentary, background information, and student papers.

Julius Caesar Project. Available: http://www.svms.santacruz.k12.ca.us/portal/Julius_Caesar_Project.html (Accessed March 10, 2000).

Compendium of bookmarks for geographic, Shakespearean, and Roman history sites, plus a script of the play.

Videos

Julius Caesar. 120 min., b & w. Marlon Brando version. Guidance Associates, 1953.

Julius Caesar. 117 min., color. Charlton Heston/Jason Robards version. Perma-Bound and Sundance, 1970.

Julius Caesar. 23 min., color. BBC Shakespeare in Rehearsal series. Coronet/MTI, 1989.

Printed Resources

Article

Crapse, Larry. "Julius Caesar." *English Journal* 72 (March 1983): 51–52.

Book

Bloom, Harold, ed. *William Shakespeare's* Julius Caesar. Bloom's Notes series. Bloomall, PA: Chelsea House Publications, 1996.

Abridged Text

Julius Caesar. Shakespeare for Young People series; language unchanged. Learning Links.

Parallel Text

Julius Caesar. Original text and modern language text side-by-side. Perfection Learning Corporation.

Posters

Julius Caesar. Set of four, 17" x 22", color. Sundance.

Teaching Aids

Julius Caesar. Literature Unit Plans. Teacher's Pet Publications.

Julius Caesar. Masterprose series and Latitudes series. Perfection Learning Corporation.

Julius Caesar. Novel/Drama Curriculum Units. The Center for Learning.

Julius Caesar. Novel-Ties. Learning Links.

Julius Caesar. Novel Unit Guide, Novel Units Student Packet, and Perma-Guide. Perma-Bound.

Julius Caesar. REACT series. Sundance.

Tests

Julius Caesar. Essay, objective, and alternative assessment versions. Perfection Learning Corporation.

The Chocolate War

Robert Cormier
New York: Pantheon Books, 1974
Available in paperback from Dell.

SUMMARY

Jerry Renault, a freshman at an all-boys parochial high school, faces enormous physical and emotional challenges. He battles physically on the football field as he tries to make the Trinity team. He faces emotional dilemmas as he tries to adjust to his mother's death and his father's indifference. In addition, he faces the Vigils, the school bullies who try to force him to defy the Trinity officials. At first he acquiesces, but when Archie, the Vigils' leader, and Brother Leon, a corrupt administrator, insist that he take part in a school chocolate sale, Jerry takes a stand by refusing to participate. Finally, he is tricked into a rigged boxing match in which he is beaten senseless while the members of the student body applaud.

APPRAISAL

In recent years, Robert Cormier has been heralded as an outstanding writer of fiction for young adults. In particular, *The Chocolate War* has been praised for its honesty and realism, its uncompromising characterizations, and its devastating ending. Some critics, however, feel the book is too depressing and pessimistic. Cormier counters these comments assertively:

> As long as what I write is true and believable, why should I have to create happy endings? My books are an antidote to the TV view of life, where even in a suspenseful show you know before the last commercial that Starsky and Hutch will get their man. That's phony realism. Life just isn't like that.

In the best tradition of the young adult novel, *The Chocolate War* clearly treats the adolescent reader as an adult capable of responding to the complex social and moral problems that modern man confronts. This book is most appropriate for the eleventh and twelfth grades.

THEMES

the importance of commitment, alienation, injustice, violence, death, corruption in high places, peer pressure, mass psychology

LITERARY CONCEPTS

point of view, symbolism, realism, characterization theme, setting, plot, irony

RELATED READING

Because *The Chocolate War* has been referred to as a combination of *Lord of the Flies* by William Golding and *A Separate Peace*, many students may wish to read these two novels, especially the latter, a contrasting book by John Knowles with a prep school setting. Other works by Robert Cormier with similar outlooks are *I Am the Cheese* and *After the First Death*.

READING PROBLEMS AND OPPORTUNITIES

Cormier's portrayal of violence, fear, and guilt in *The Chocolate War* includes sexual and scatological elements as well as a heavy dose of profanity. But by far the most difficult reading problem for many adolescents will be the brutality, despair, and unmitigated pessimism presented in the book. Students who thrive on happy endings may find this novel a bitter pill to swallow. Opportunities for vocabulary study abound. Possible words include (chapter numbers are in parentheses):

malice (2),
surreptitiously (3),
perusals (3),
languid (3),
incapacitated (3),
audacity (3),
exulted (5),
irrevocable (5),
inscrutable (5),
nemesis (5),
perceptible (7),
pandemonium (11),
tumultuous (11),
adulation (13),
infuriated (21),
disembodied (24),
momentum (24),
precarious (24),
ravenous (26),
insolent (27),
unintimidated (27),
defiance (27),
sabotaging (27),
eluded (27),
vulnerable (28),
meticulous (29),
futility (31),
sanctimoniously (34),
inhibition (35),
momentous (35),
maliciously (36),
ineffectually (37),
catapulting (37), and
exultant (37).

INITIATING ACTIVITIES

1. Read T. S. Eliot's poem "The Love Song of J. Alfred Prufrock." With your classmates, discuss the kind of person Prufrock is and the kind of comments Eliot seems to be making about society and modern man in describing this person. What is Prufrock's problem?
2. A recent criticism of American public schools is that they lack discipline and the efficient enforcement of rules. Pretend that your school principal plans to address this problem by creating an elite cadre of "enforcers" made up of tough, aggressive boys who will help the principal and the staff in the maintenance of discipline at the school. Discuss with your classmates how you would respond to this idea.

DISCUSSION QUESTIONS

1. *Chapter 1:* What agonies does Jerry Renault suffer as he tries to make the football team? What dream drives him on? Read carefully the description of the coach. In what ways do his physical characteristics underscore his personality?

2. *Chapter 2:* What techniques does Archie use in his assignments for the Vigils? Why does he choose Jerry for an assignment? What relationship exists between Jerry and Obie?

3. *Chapter 3:* What does the Hippie mean by saying, "You're missing a lot of things in the world"? Do you agree that people with a middle-class background who live routine lives are missing a lot? Why or why not?

4. *Chapters 4 and 5:* Compare and contrast Archie's encounters with Brother Leon and Goober. How are his approaches similar? How does his appearance belie his true feelings? Why do Brother Leon and Goober fall under Archie's power?

5. *Chapter 6:* How are Brother Leon's games like those of Archie? Who do you feel is more contemptible, Archie or Brother Leon? Why?

6. *Chapter 7:* Is Emile Janza a well-rounded character or a stereotype? Why? Does he have any sympathetic qualities? If so, what are they?

7. *Chapter 8:* What forces influence Goober as he tries to carry out his assignment? Who sends him help? Why?

8. *Chapter 9:* What methods do Jerry and his father use in coping with the death of Jerry's mother? What other methods have you observed people using in similar situations? Discuss the effectiveness of these methods.

9. *Chapters 10 and 11:* The introduction of the chocolate sale and the destruction of Room 19 are presented from Archie's point of view. What are the advantages of using this technique?

10. *Chapter 12:* Explain Jerry's elation at successfully completing a football play. Do you feel this is exaggerated or realistic? Why?

11. *Chapters 13 and 14:* Why does Jerry refuse to sell the chocolates? How does Brother Leon react? In what other ways might Leon have handled the situation? Why do you think he chooses this particular approach? What is the socioeconomic position of Tubbs Casper in relation to his neighbors? Point out specific details to support your conclusion.

12. *Chapters 15 and 16:* How do Archie and Brother Leon manipulate people to get what they want? Why are Emile and Caroni capable of being manipulated? What pleasure or benefits do Archie and Leon exact from those they control? Do you know of individuals like these, who enjoy their control over others? Discuss.

13. *Chapter 17:* At the end of this chapter the author describes the scene: "Cities fell. Earth opened. Planets tilted. Stars plummeted. And the awful silence." What actual occurrence is he describing? What irony is apparent in this description?

14. *Chapters 18 and 19:* What forces are pulling at Jerry regarding his decision not to sell chocolates? Do you think this issue was worth taking such a stand against? Why or why not?

15. *Chapter 20:* How does Archie control Obie? If Obie hates Archie, why does he allow this manipulation to continue?

16. *Chapters 21 and 22:* What effect does Jerry's refusal to cooperate have on the other students at Trinity? Do you think this effect of one person on a group is realistic? Why or why not? Why are the Vigils forced to become involved in Jerry's refusal to sell? What are Brother Leon's reactions to the declining sales? What do these reactions tell you about his personality?
17. *Chapter 23:* Goober says that he is going to quit the football team because of "what they do to us." What does he mean by this statement?
18. *Chapter 24:* In the confrontation between Brother Leon and Archie, each knows more about the other's position than he is willing to reveal. How does this secret information affect their responses to each other?
19. *Chapter 25:* In what ways is the Vigils' meeting more like a performance than an actual club gathering? How are Archie and Carter different? In what ways is each uniquely suited for the position he holds in the Vigils?
20. *Chapter 26:* Why does Jerry hang up on Ellen Barrett? What other kinds of behavior might cause a similar destruction of an illusion for a teenage boy or girl?
21. *Chapter 27:* What does Rollo's defiance of the Vigils symbolize? In what ways does Carter take over the meeting and embarrass Archie? How is Archie able to maintain his position in the group?
22. *Chapter 28:* What physical and psychological tortures do the Vigils employ against Jerry? Which of these do you think is the most effective? Why? Why does Jerry suddenly understand the poster that asks, "Do I dare disturb the universe?"
23. *Chapters 29 and 30:* Although the chocolate sale appears to be going well, how in reality is it being handled? Why do Cochran and Brother Leon choose to ignore what is happening? Why is Goober's attempt at protest never discovered?
24. *Chapters 31 and 32:* How is Janza able to taunt Jerry into a fight? What other insults or accusations will usually start a fight? Why does the author insert the words, "Let it be, let it be" from the Beatles' song?
25. *Chapters 33 and 34:* Why does Archie continue to lead Emile Janza on rather than telling him the truth about the picture directly? In what ways is the freeze technique effective on Jerry? In what ways is it not effective? Is it astounding that all but fifty boxes of the chocolates are sold? Why or why not?
26. *Chapters 35, 36, and 37:* How is Archie able to manipulate Janza, Jerry, and Cochran into agreeing to the raffle? In addition, what techniques does Archie use to enlist the support of the entire student body? Why does Carter have second thoughts about his part in the raffle? What devastating realization comes to Jerry during the fight? Who saves Jerry?
27. *Chapter 38:* How have Jerry's attitudes changed? In the end, does good or evil win out? Do you believe that *The Chocolate War* presents a realistic portrayal of society today? Why or why not?

WRITING ACTIVITIES

1. Write a constitution for the Vigils. Include in this document the purpose of the organization, the rules and regulations, and the officers and their duties.

2. Prepare two notices of the chocolate sale to be posted in the halls of Trinity. One of these should be written as Brother Leon would have composed it; the other as Archie might have written it.
3. Write a character sketch of Brother Leon from one of the following character's point of view: Archie, Cochran, Caroni, or Jerry.
4. Investigate the methods of raising money used by your school. Write an essay in which you describe, compare, and evaluate these methods. Discuss which of the approaches is the most successful and why.
5. Write an argumentative essay based on one of the following statements from *The Chocolate War* (your paper should defend or refute the statement):
    a. "The world was made up of two kinds of people—those who were victims and those who were victimized."
    b. "Life was rotten, there were no heroes really, and you can't trust anybody, not even yourself."
    c. "This is the age of do your own thing."
    d. "People are two things: greedy and cruel."
    e. "Don't dare disturb the universe."
6. Write the speech that Brother Leon might have given to the student assembly after the successful completion of the chocolate sale. As you write, you may need, at times, to disregard the reality of the situation. Place yourself in Brother Leon's position and describe events to suit your own purpose.
7. *The Chocolate War* grew out of an actual incident experienced by the author's son at a private school for boys. Although nothing happened to the boy, Cormier speculated on what could have happened in a similar situation. Recall a similar experience of your own, particularly one in which you chose to defy tradition. Consider what might have happened in the situation and write a story about this imagined series of events.
8. Write a how-to paper on dealing with bullies. Choose an audience—elementary school, junior high school, or high school students—and gear your suggestions to students of that age. Review the tactics used by the Vigils before you start to write.
9. Students and teachers in different schools have different ways of granting acceptance and distinction to other students. (For example, see the methods used by the football coach in chapter 1.) Write a paper in which you explain the ways in which students are granted acceptance and distinction at your school. Compare and contrast these methods with those used at Trinity.

OTHER ACTIVITIES

1. The last paragraph in chapter 2 is an early example of the religious symbolism used throughout the book. By means of a charcoal drawing, mobile, collage, or any other medium of your choice, prepare a visual representation of this scene.
2. Design a T-shirt to be worn by members of the Vigils. The design should include a logo that is appropriate for the organization with a lettering style that suits the Vigils' character. This may be prepared using a computer or be drawn free hand.

3. Draw a pair of contrasting posters—one to promote the chocolate sale and one that Jerry might have produced to oppose it.
4. Improvise a scene in which Jerry and his father attempt to communicate meaningfully. One possibility: Jerry tries to explain to his father why he is refusing to sell chocolates and his father reacts.
5. Act out the scene that might have taken place between Archie and Brother Leon after the conclusion of the book. Keep in mind that these two characters were frank with each other and understood each other's power base. Consider what demands each might have placed on the other.
6. Using posterboard or chart paper, prepare psychological profiles for Archie and Jerry. Draw twelve horizontal lines (see short example below). At the opposite end of each line, write the following pairs of words: *cruel/kind, clever/stupid, insecure/confident, gentle/harsh, brave/cowardly, foolish/wise, strong/weak, dependent/independent, unfair/fair, passionate/indifferent, serious/light, amoral/moral.* Then, on each of the twelve lines make a mark for Archie and a mark for Jerry, indicating where on the line each of them falls—toward one extreme or the other. When you have marked each of the twelve lines, draw two sets of vertical lines that connect the marks for each boy.

cruel -kind

clever -stupid

insecure -confident

SELECTED TEACHING RESOURCES

Media Aids

Cassettes (4)

The Chocolate War. Perma-Bound and Sundance.

Cassettes (5)

The Chocolate War. 6.5 hrs. Recorded Books.

Internet

Robert Cormier. Available: http://www.scrtec.org/track/tracks/t01540.html (Accessed March 10, 2000).
This site provides fourteen links to sites about Cormier and/or *The Chocolate War.*

Videos

The Chocolate War. 103 min., color. Sundance, 1989.

Good Conversation! A Talk with Robert Cormier. 22 min., color. Tim Podell Productions, 1996.

Printed Materials

Articles

March-Penny, Robbie. "From Hardback to Paperback: *The Chocolate War* by Robert Cormier." *Children's Literature in Education* 9 (Summer 1978): 78–84.

McLeod, Anne Scott. "Robert Cormier and the Adolescent Novel." *Children's Literature in Education* 12 (Summer 1981): 74–81.

Susina, Jan. "*The Chocolate War* and 'The Sweet Science'." *Children's Literature in Education* 22 (September 1991): 169–177.

Sutton, Roger. " 'Kind of a Funny Dichotomy': A Conversation with Robert Cormier." *School Library Journal* 37 (June 1991): 28–33.

Teaching Aids

The Chocolate War. Contemporary Classics series. Perfection Learning Corporation.

The Chocolate War. Novel Idea Plus series. Sundance.

The Chocolate War. Novel Unit Guide, Novel Unit Student Packet, and Perma-Guide. Perma-Bound.

The Chocolate War. Novel-Ties. Learning Links.

Tests

The Chocolate War. Essay and objective versions. Perfection Learning Corporation.

The Red Badge of Courage

Stephen Crane
1895
Available in paperback from several publishing companies.

SUMMARY

Amid the boredom of Union Army camp life during the Civil War, Henry Fleming awaits his first battle, wondering if he will run under fire. He soon finds out, fleeing in panic during a brutal attack and then spending several more hours roaming the battlefield at large, observing skirmishes, tagging along with troop remnants, and alternately condemning and justifying his actions to himself. Finally, after receiving a wound from another Union soldier, he rejoins his regiment, its members greeting him as a lost comrade. He then distinguishes himself in battle by fighting with abandon during a furious charge. He is a hero. As his regiment leaves the battlefield, however, Henry is a different person, with feelings of guilt that linger and a deeper, more complex understanding of war and himself.

APPRAISAL

This short American classic of the Civil War has been called an observation of "the nervous system under fire." Written in 1894, it provides an intense, impressionistic account of a young soldier's reactions to war with all its noise and confusion, its tedium and pain, its savagery, and its ironies. Crane wrote the novel with no battlefield experience, a fact that students may find hard to believe given its convincing ring of truth. The book seems most appropriate for grades nine through eleven.

THEMES

courage, fear, initiation, war, the importance of self-awareness, change

LITERARY CONCEPTS

irony, symbol, characterization, imagery, conflict, figurative language, impressionism

RELATED READING

Perhaps the most famous other war novel is *All Quiet on the Western Front* by Erich Marie Remarque, which takes place during World War I. More recent novels about the Civil War are *Killer Angels* by Michael Shaara (a book about Gettysburg that won the Pulitzer prize), *Gods and Generals* by Jeff Shaara, and *Cold Mountain* by Charles Frazier. Two well-known young adult novels about the war are *Across Five Aprils* by Irene Hunt and *Rifles for Watie* by Harold Keith.

READING PROBLEMS AND OPPORTUNITIES

Partly because it is a short novel with short chapters, *The Red Badge of Courage* is very teachable. It does include many words that will be unfamiliar to high school students, but most of them can be understood in context. A large number of them reflect the desperate, violent nature of the novel; as such, they could perhaps be grouped and taught as "Words of Tension and Trauma." Among many others, they include the following (chapter numbers are in parentheses):

clamor (1, 2, 5, 6, 11, 12, 13, 17, 22, 23),
altercation (1, 12, 16, 18),
ominous (2, 6, 12, 19, 23),
deride, derision (2, 7, 11, 15, 16, 17),
din (3, 4, 5, 8, 11, 12, 16, 22, 24),
formidable (3, 6, 11, 22, 23),
insolent (3, 11, 14, 16, 17),
reproach (5, 9, 21, 22, 24),
imprecations (5, 11, 19),
impotent (5, 17, 20, 21),
annihilate (6, 7, 17),
lurid (8, 11, 12, 19),
writhe (9, 12, 17, 19, 23),
lurch (9, 12, 19, 23), and
indifferent (11, 13, 14, 18).

INITIATING ACTIVITIES

1. Write a two- or three-page paper on a time in your life when you were required to be brave, to show courage. In preparation for the paper, discuss with other students the following questions and others: What is courage? Are there different kinds of courage? If so, what are they? Can a person be both fearful and courageous? If so, how? Are courageous people more (or less) intelligent than those who are not brave?
2. The actual setting of *The Red Badge of Courage* is the Battle of Chancellorsville, which took place in northern Virginia on May 1–2, 1863. Read about this conflict: its location, preliminaries, developments, outcome, and significance. Two excellent sources are *The American Picture History of the Civil War* (New York: American Heritage Publishing, 1960) and *The Civil War: An Illustrated History* (New York: Knopf, 1990).
3. Research the terms of army rank (*private, corporal, sergeant,* etc.), unit (*brigade, regiment, company,* etc.), and nineteenth-century weaponry (*musketry, artillery,* etc.). Report on them to the class.

DISCUSSION QUESTIONS

1. *Chapter 1:* As he contemplates his baptism under fire, how does the youthful private feel about battles? How has his experience disappointed him so far? What is his main concern? Why does he feel "compelled to give serious attention to it"? The three main characters introduced in this chapter are described as tall, loud, and youthful. Apply two more adjectives to each of them.
2. *Chapter 2:* Why does the youth wish to find another self-doubter? Why does he feel "vast pity for himself"? Besides his own self-doubts, what seems to bother him the most?
3. *Chapter 3:* What does the youth mean by a "blue demonstration"? Why does he dislike it? As the youth looks at the dead man, what does he mean by "the Question"? How does the tall soldier seem different from the youth and the loud private? Why does the youth feel misunderstood? What might have been Crane's reason for not having named his characters up to this point?
4. *Chapter 4:* How do the officers react to their retreating troops? How is their response ironic?
5. *Chapter 5:* Why doesn't the youth run during the first attack? Is his reaction an example of courage? Why or why not? Which of his senses seems most affected by the battle? Why do you think Crane used the simile, "The men dropped here and there like bundles"? At the end of the chapter, in what ways does the youth seem surprised?
6. *Chapter 6:* Describe the youth's thoughts and feelings as he runs. Why does he seem so critical and sensitive?
7. *Chapter 7:* The youth tries to convince himself that in running he has done the proper thing. Has he? Is discretion often or ever "the better part of valor"? Is the coward sometimes wise? Discuss. Why is the youth bitter? Has he indeed run because of his "superior perceptions"? Why does the opening in the woods seem like a chapel to him? What point might Crane have been making about what the youth feels he must do?
8. *Chapter 8:* How does the youth begin to perceive his own efforts in the war? Why does he seem so insistent upon viewing the ongoing battle? What is the tattered man like? Why is he resented?
9. *Chapter 9:* Why does the youth wish for "a red badge of courage"? Is this self-pity or something else? What has become his primary concern? Why is Jim Conklin's death so traumatic for the youth and the tattered man? Chapter 9 is filled with ironies. Explain some of them.
10. *Chapter 10:* Why does the youth leave the tattered man? "He now thought that he wished he was dead." Does he feel worse about leaving the tattered man or about the possibility of his being discovered to be a coward?
11. *Chapter 11:* Why does the youth envy the forward-going column? Is he overly concerned with heroism? In what ways does he imagine that defeat of the army would be to his advantage? Why does he finally reject the idea?
12. *Chapter 12:* What is particularly ironic about the youth's wound?
13. *Chapter 13:* How does Henry explain his absence? "He gave a long sigh, . . . and in a moment was like his comrades." How is Henry like his comrades? How is he different?

14. *Chapter 14:* How has Wilson changed? Why? Why does Henry say, "So?" at the end of the chapter?

15. *Chapter 15:* How does Henry show himself to be little and vindictive? "He had performed his mistakes in the dark." What does this mean? Why does he begin to feel more self-confident and virtuous? Is he virtuous and generous? Why or why not?

16. *Chapter 16:* How do Henry's moods change? Why do they change?

17. *Chapter 17:* How does Henry's response in this skirmish differ from earlier responses? Here, are his actions courageous? Are acts of courage always acts of total self-absorption? "And he was now what he called a hero." What does Henry call a hero? Is he heroic? If so, in what way or ways? What do you call a hero? Who are some examples of heroes in contemporary life?

18. *Chapter 18:* In paragraph 11 ("Looking down an aisle of the grove . . ."), what point might the author be making?

19. *Chapter 19:* During the charge, why does Henry feel that everything is bold and vivid and clear? Why does the charge seem incomprehensible to the men? Why is Henry suddenly so attracted to the flag?

20. *Chapter 20:* What motivates Henry most during the charge? Is disregard for personal safety because of wounded pride an example of courage? Discuss.

21. *Chapter 21:* Why is the praise they get from the colonel and lieutenant so important to Henry and Wilson? Are the two soldiers unusually susceptible to flattery? Discuss.

22. *Chapters 22 and 23:* Why do you think the soldiers "sprang forward in eager leaps" this time? Does courage demand a certain recklessness? Henry "himself felt the daring spirit of a savage religion-mad." What does this mean?

23. *Chapter 24:* "They could see changes going on amongst the troops." It has been suggested that change is the main theme of the novel. Explain this in terms of the troops, the battle itself, and the characters, especially Henry. How has he, in particular, changed or grown during the novel? What is ironic about the regiment's movement in the final chapter? How does Henry feel about his overall battle experience? What disturbs him? Why is he so guilt-stricken by the memory of the tattered man? "He found that he could look back upon the brass and bombast of his earlier gospels and see them truly." What does this mean? At the end, "he was a man." Was he? In what ways has he been courageous? Is he still lacking courage in any way? If so, how? How does he regard war? How do you think Crane regards it?

WRITING ACTIVITIES

1. Stephen Crane wrote *The Red Badge of Courage* without ever having witnessed battle scenes. Try to write an account of some event that you have never observed (e.g., a bull-fight, a hockey match, an earthquake, a tornado). Like Crane, try to make your description as realistic as possible. What are your problems with such a task? How can you deal with them?

2. You are Henry Fleming. Write three letters to your mother: one written at the end of chapter 1, another after you have rejoined your regiment, and a final one at the end of the novel. Communicate fully to her your impressions and concerns.

3. The novel is written in third-person limited point of view with the narrator revealing the thoughts and feelings of only one character, Henry Fleming. Write a description of Henry's experience with the tattered man from the latter's point of view.
4. Write a three- or four-page report on the Battle of Chancellorsville. (See "Initiating Activity" 2 for possible sources.) Describe the various assaults and the results, but also try to determine where in the actual battle Henry Fleming's involvement might have occurred as determined by Crane's description of setting and troop movements. (*Note to teacher:* This activity assumes that "Initiating Activity" 2 was not used.)
5. In chapter 11, the youth argues with himself over the possibility of returning to battle. Write a dialogue between the youth and his conscience over whether or not to desert altogether and return home. Include at least ten exchanges of dialogue.
6. In all his writings Crane took pains to describe scenes and events accurately, particularly through the use of colors. (In the novel, see chapter 3, paragraph 1, and chapter 18, paragraph 8.) Write a description of an outdoor setting you're familiar with in which you try to use colors precisely and vividly.
7. Pretend that Henry Fleming is killed in the final charge in chapter 23. Write an obituary that might appear in his hometown newspaper or a eulogy that a fellow soldier might write.
8. General William T. Sherman, who achieved great fame in the same war, said that "war is hell." The poet Dryden wrote, "War . . . is toil and trouble/ Honor but an empty bubble." What might Henry Fleming have said about war perhaps five or ten years later? Write at least a page of his thoughts on the subject.
9. Stephen Crane worked frequently as a reporter for newspapers during his short, incandescent life. If he had chosen to express his views about war in an editorial, what might he have said about the subject? Write a 300-word editorial about war as Crane might have written it.

OTHER ACTIVITIES

1. During the novel the 304th Regiment from New York overcomes a bad, perhaps unjustified reputation and achieves a certain measure of self-respect. Design a banner for the regiment that reflects its accomplishments as revealed in the book.
2. Prepare an oral reading of several of Crane's poems about war. Record them on a cassette with an appropriate musical background, perhaps marches or antiwar songs of the 1960s.
3. Role play a conversation between Henry Fleming and the tattered man that might occur if the two met shortly after the book ends. Keep in mind their differences in personality, the emotional experience they briefly shared, and the feelings Henry has at the end of the book.
4. Design a collage on one of the following topics:
   a. courage as you see it reflected in today's society
   b. war as you think Crane viewed it
5. Design a poster that the youth might have created before his own involvement in the war to get others to enlist in the Union cause. Base your perception of his attitude toward the

war largely on chapter 1. Then design a second poster, one Henry might have produced at the end of the novel. How would the two posters differ?

6. Draw a coat of arms for the Fleming family based on the values, concerns, and achievements of Henry Fleming as they are reflected in the novel.
7. It has been suggested that the photographs of Matthew Brady exerted a major influence upon the writing of this book. Report to the class on Brady's pioneering work during the Civil War. Suggest how Crane might have been influenced.
8. Crane's fascination with color derived partly from his interest in the Impressionist paintings of the period, especially those of Monet. Select a scene from the book in which colors are vividly used (example: chapter 18, paragraph 8) and paint it in oils or watercolors.

SELECTED TEACHING RESOURCES

Media Aids

Cassettes (2)

The Red Badge of Courage. Richard Crenna version. Perma-Bound.

Cassettes (3)

The Red Badge of Courage. 4.5 hrs. Recorded Books.

Filmstrip & Cassette/Record

The Red Badge of Courage. Thomas S. Klise Co. An interpretation.

Internet

Jewett, Leah Wood. *The United States Civil War Center*. Available: http://www.cwc.lsu.edu (Accessed March 10, 2000).

Includes information on battles and battlefields, flags, uniforms, governments, weapons, artillery, diaries and letters, cemeteries, forts, prisons, maps, reenactments, and much more. One of many useful websites on the Civil War.

Maynard, Michele. 1997. *Stephen Crane: Man, Myth, & Legend*. 1997. Available: http://www.cwrl.utexas.edu/~mmaynard/Crane/crane.html. (Accessed March 10, 2000).

Includes a brief biography; sound clips; lists of themes, issues, and literary techniques; photographs, related links, and a bibliography.

Videos

The Red Badge of Courage. 70 min., b & w. Perma-Bound and Sundance.

The classic Audie Murphy version.

The Vision of Stephen Crane. Color. Guidance Associates.

Describes the author as a literary pioneer; includes excerpts from *The Red Badge of Courage*, the movie.

Printed Materials

Articles

Crapse, Larry. "Developing Stimulating Activities on *The Red Badge of Courage*." *Exercise Exchange* 25 (Spring 1981): 26–31.

LaRocca, Charles. "Stephen Crane's Inspiration." *American Heritage* 42 (May/June 1991): 108–109.
Argues that the Battle of Chancellorsville inspired the novel.

Phillips, Leay. "First Impressions: Introducing Monet to Megadeth." *English Journal* 78 (March 1989): 31–33.

Books

Gibson, Donald B. *The Red Badge of Courage: Redefining the Hero*. Boston: Twayne, 1988.

Peck, David. *Novels of Initiation: A Guidebook for Teaching Literature to Adolescents*. New York: Teachers College Press, 1989.
Includes a chapter on *The Red Badge of Courage*.

Teaching Aids

The Red Badge of Courage. Insight series. Sundance.

The Red Badge of Courage. Literature Unit Plans. Teacher's Pet Publications.

The Red Badge of Courage. Masterprose series. Perfection Learning Corporation.

The Red Badge of Courage. Novel/Drama Curriculum Units. The Center for Learning.

The Red Badge of Courage. Novel-Ties. Learning Links.

The Red Badge of Courage. Novel Unit Guide, Novel Units Student Packet, and Perma-Guide. Perma-Bound.

Tests

The Red Badge of Courage. Essay and objective versions. Perfection Learning Company.

Fences

August Wilson

New York: Plume, 1986

Available in paperback from Penguin.

SUMMARY

Troy Maxson is a middle-aged black man who works as a garbage collector in an unnamed American city in 1957 (apparently Pittsburgh). He lives with his wife Rose and teenage son Cory in a ramshackle house on the edge of poverty. With his close friend Bono, Troy engages in male bantering that reveals a deep-seated rage at his lot in life. He resents his two sons (the grown Lyons because he is always asking for money; Cory because he wants to play football instead of working at the A & P). Eventually Troy drives Cory away after a violent fight and alienates even Rose by fathering a child with another woman. In the final scene, eight years later, everyone returns for the funeral of Troy, whom they have come to see as a tragic, very human figure.

APPRAISAL

Fences is a tough, funny, powerful play most appropriate for the upper grades of high school, perhaps grades ten and eleven. *Fences* explores the feelings of regret, responsibility, and rage. The language of the play is occasionally profane and vulgar, with more than a few sexual references. It is also characterized by a relaxed, teasing use of the word *nigger*. Teachers and students who find the language offensive will need to view the dialogue in its larger context: a drama by an acclaimed African-American playwright about the long-term effects of racism upon the lives of ordinary people. *Fences* won the Pulitzer prize for drama in 1987.

THEMES

anger (especially self-hatred), barriers ("fences"), the effects of racism, freedom versus responsibility, family, friendship

LITERARY CONCEPTS

characterization, comedy versus tragedy, symbol, irony, juxtaposition, personification

RELATED READING

The most obvious comparable play about urban African-Americans struggling to overcome prejudice and reach middle-class respectability in mid-century America is *A Raisin in the Sun* by Lorraine Hansberry. Other plays by August Wilson with similar concerns include *Ma Rainey's Black Bottom*, *The Piano Lesson*, *Joe Turner's Come and Gone*, *Two Trains Running*, and *Seven Guitars*. *The Invisible Man* by Ralph Ellison and works by James Baldwin, such as *Go Tell It on the Mountain*, may also be of interest to students.

READING PROBLEMS AND OPPORTUNITIES

Like all plays, *Fences* is almost entirely dialogue. The characters are intelligent but poorly educated, so there are comparatively few opportunities in the play for vocabulary enrichment. Most of them occur in background commentary or stage directions. They include the following (numbers indicate pages where the terms appear):

congruence (xv),
dubious (xv),
receptacle (xv),
destitute (xvii),
tenacious (xvii),
devoured (xvii),
guile (xvii),
vengeful (xvii),
flourishing (xviii),
turbulent (xviii),
provocative (xviii),
sensibilities (1),
emulate (1),
ritual (1, 5, 13, 101),
profound (1),
illuminating (5),
integral (5),
vigilant, vigilance (11, 12, 77),
scrutiny (13),
methodical (40),
seniority (42),
uncompromising (57),
reluctantly (58),
consume (77),
indelicateness (78),
taunt (88, 89),
trauma (101), and
atavistic (101).

INITIATING ACTIVITIES

1. The subject of "deadbeat dads" is frequently in the news. The term refers, of course, to men who abandon their families and withhold support for their children. Discuss this issue with your classmates. What might contribute to a father's taking such action? Is such behavior in any way defensible? Should we even try to understand it? To what extent do events like the Million Man March and organizations like the Promise Keepers offer hope in dealing with this problem?
2. The fact that racism in America is perceived to remain a problem is shown by President Clinton's efforts to address it during the second term of his presidency. Using magazine articles and books as resources (examples: *Race Matters* by Cornel West and *The Color Line: Legacy for the Twenty-First Century* by John Hope Franklin), try to find out more about the long-term effects of racism, especially upon its victims. Discuss these effects with the rest of the class.

DISCUSSION QUESTIONS

1. *Act 1, scene 1:* What immediate impression of Troy Maxson do we get? What has been troubling him to the point of his raising a question about it? What does this suggest about him? How would you characterize the relationship between Troy and Bono? Between Troy and Rose? Describe the nature of the interaction between Troy and Rose. Is there

fondness between them? Anger? How do they disagree about Bella's store—and what does this say about them? Whom would you agree with on this matter? What do we learn about Troy's past? How do the three characters view his background in baseball? Why is Troy opposed to the idea of Cory being recruited to play football in college? Why is Troy so unimpressed with the argument that times have changed for blacks? When Lyons arrives, does the atmosphere change? If so, how? What does the incident involving "the devil" suggest about the relationship between blacks and whites as Troy sees it? What is the basic conflict between Troy and Lyons? With whom do you most sympathize at this point? Why? How do you feel about Lyons's statement that he needs something to "make me feel like I belong in the world"?

2. *Act 1, scene 2:* How do Troy and Rose differ over "the numbers"? Why is Troy unimpressed with Pope? How does Troy feel about Gabriel? Does he pity him? Envy him? What is ironic about Gabriel's impairment? What more have we learned about Troy by the end of this brief scene? He claims not to be worried about his meeting with the Commissioner on Friday. What does seem to bother him? When he says to Rose, "Now see if you can understand that!" what does he mean?

3. *Act 1, scene 3:* Again we see a relationship between Troy and a son—this time Cory. How would you describe it? Is it different from Troy's relationship with Lyons? How are they similar? Again, baseball comes up. What is baseball a symbol of for Troy? For Cory? Why does Cory feel his father doesn't like him? On the basis of what we know, do you agree with Cory? Why or why not? Why is Troy so hostile to the idea of liking or needing to be liked? Why is he so reluctant to praise his son? Does Troy's anger surprise you? Why or why not? What is its source?

4. *Act 1, scene 4:* What mood is Troy in at the beginning of the scene? How do we know? Why does he like the song about Blue? What happened at the meeting with the Commissioner—and afterwards? Why doesn't Troy accept the payback money from Lyons? How do Troy and Rose see Gabriel's move to Miss Pearl's differently? Do you think Troy would interfere with Gabriel's sense of freedom? Why or why not? What does Bono mean by "searching out the New Land"? Explain Troy's feelings toward his father. What effect do you think his father's brutal beating of Troy had on Troy (besides making him run away)? What did he mean by, "And right there the world suddenly got big" and by, "the place where I could feel him kicking in my blood"? How does Troy's story about running away affect Lyons? Why does Lyons want Troy to hear him play? Does Troy's refusal suggest that he is like his father? When Cory tells Troy, "You just scared I'm gonna be better than you," is he right? What does Troy mean when he tells Cory, "See . . . you swung at the ball and didn't hit it"? Do you think Troy feels trapped? Why or why not? Do you feel sympathy for him? Why or why not?

5. *Act 2, scene 1:* Why is Bono concerned about Troy's relationship with Alberta? What comparison does Bono make? How does the fence begin to function in the play? What function or purpose would you say Gabriel has in the play? Is he important? How important is Rose? When Troy confesses to Rose, what dramatic effect does the juxtaposed dialogue between Troy and Rose and between Troy and Gabriel have on us as "viewers"? What does Rose mean by "my whole family is half"? How does this extend the meaning of the play? How do you feel about Troy's explanation? About his saying he has forgotten about himself? Do you agree that this is his problem? How do you feel about Rose's response? Do you agree that Troy takes "and don't even know nobody's giving"? After the fight, does Troy's comment mean that he wants Cory to "strike out"? What does he want for Cory?

6. *Act 2, scene 2:* What appears to be the nature of Troy's and Rose's relationship now? Has he become completely irresponsible? Why is she upset with him with regard to Gabriel? Why does Troy want to fight Mr. Death? What would defeating Mr. Death do for him? Why does he want to build the fence "around what belongs to me"? What does he want?

7. *Act 2, scene 3:* Does Troy expect too much of Rose? Too little of himself? Too much of himself? How do you feel about Rose's response at the end of the scene? Is she being fair?

8. *Act 2, scene 4:* This scene, which begins on a hopeful note, ends in violence and rage. What triggers the fight? Who is responsible? Early in the scene, why does Cory practice swinging the bat? At the end, why does Troy also assume a stance? Why do you think the song about the dog Blue becomes such a frequent refrain for Troy?

9. *Act 2, scene 5:* How do you think Cory feels about being a Marine? How have the lives of Cory and Lyons changed in eight years? Of the two, who is more like Troy? Does either have a hopeful future? What might one make, if anything, of the manner of Troy's death? Is Cory justified in wanting to avoid his father's funeral? Discuss this, as well as Rose's response. Do you agree with Rose that Cory is just like Troy? Why or why not? How has Rose come to view Troy? How have you come to view him? Is he a tragic figure, with a tragic flaw? Discuss. What is the dramatic significance of Cory and Raynell singing Troy's song about Blue together at the end? What is the significance of Gabriel's appearance, especially his "eerie and life-giving" dance? What does he—and through him, the playwright—mean by his final declaration?

WRITING ACTIVITIES

1. Write a personal essay on "What Makes Me Feel Like I Belong in the World." You may want to open the paper by referring to Lyons as a character in the play and explaining briefly why he seemed to feel the way he did and how it affected him.

2. In large measure, *Fences* is a play about barriers, in particular those erected by racism in this country. The play opens in 1957, when these obstacles were still all but insurmountable, and ends in 1965, when the civil rights movement was beginning to produce hopeful changes. Conduct some research on this eight-year span in America. Find out what changes took place, especially through social protest and legal efforts, to provide people like Cory with more opportunities than his father had. Write a two- to three-page paper on what you learn. (If you wish, broaden your scope to 1950–1970.)

3. We never really know what happens to the Maxson family between scenes 4 and 5 in Act 2. Write a brief summary of the family's history in that span in which you answer some of the following (and other) questions: Where does Cory go when he first leaves home? Does Troy continue to work as a truck driver? Do he and Bono continue their ritual conversations? Does Troy refrain from relationships with other women? Does Rose focus her life totally on Raynell? How do Lyons's problems with the law begin?

4. Much in this play revolves around the ritualistic Friday after-work talk sessions between Troy and Bono. Write a paper about your family's rituals (or those of individual family members), meaningful activities that occur at steady and frequent intervals. Try to express why they are important. (Possible examples: a Wednesday night family pizza-and-problem-solving meeting, Dad's monthly breakfast in bed for Mom, the Sunday night video, etc.)

5. In Act 1, scene 4, Troy refers to "the walking blues" (page 51). Using the song about the dog Blue as a guide, write some lyrics for this song that convey the message it was meant to express.
6. Read the poem "The Whipping" by Robert Hayden. (The poem can be found in *Sound and Sense: An Introduction to Poetry*, 8th edition, by Laurence Perrine and Thomas R. Arp [Harcourt, 1992], as well as in many anthologies.) Then write a paper in which you discuss the similarities you see between the poem and the play. Focus in particular on Troy's relationship with both his father and his son Cory.
7. Numerous books have been written in recent years about anger and how to control it, among them *Anger: How to Live With and Without It* by Albert Ellis and *Anger: The Misunderstood Emotion* by Carol Tavris. Look over one or two of these books (or perhaps magazine articles). Then write a self-help paper of suggestions that you think might be helpful for people like Troy Maxson.
8. Write a eulogy for Troy that Bono might have read at the funeral. The eulogy should emphasize Troy's strengths, but not ignore his weaknesses altogether.

OTHER ACTIVITIES

1. Like all plays, *Fences* needs to be seen. The performances of actors, for example, who portray the vitality and anger of Troy and the tolerance and understanding of Rose need to be witnessed. A particular scene that would benefit from enactment is the final one, Gabriel's triumphant dance. Read this scene over several times and prepare a pantomime of it for the class.
2. On two occasions, *Fences* features a juxtaposition of, in effect, three people engaging in two conversations simultaneously: in Act 1, scene 4 (Rose, Cory, and Cory's friend Jesse on the telephone) and, more powerfully, in Act 2, scene 1 (Troy, Rose, and Gabriel). With two other students, write a scripted scene in which you depict a similar three-way conversation in which one of the dialogues is momentous and the other trivial. Then act out the scene.
3. Create a collage that conveys one of the following:
   a. Troy's rage
   b. "You got to take the crooked with the straight."
   c. Gabriel's performance that ends the play
   d. fences
4. The play includes several references to music, including gospel (Rose's song at the beginning of Act 1, scene 2) and the blues. Using the library or perhaps the Internet as sources, try to find a recording of one of the following to play to the class: a spiritual that you think expresses Rose's view of life or a blues song that conveys Troy's view. If you cannot find a recording, share a copy of the lyrics.
5. Interview some people in your community whom you consider thoughtful and fair-minded. Possibilities might include a minister or two, perhaps a city official, your school principal and one or two teachers, or a respected businessperson. If possible, try to include men and women and people from different races. The topic: racism in your community. Do they think racism is present? To what extent? Where is it most likely to show up? Has it changed in the last ten, twenty, or thirty years? Report the results to the class.

SELECTED TEACHING RESOURCES

Media Aids

Internet

Hewston, Curtis. 1995-1998. *The Blue Highway*. 1995–1999. Available: http://www.thebluehighway.com/tbh.html. (Accessed March 10, 2000).

A beautiful, comprehensive website that tells you all you want to know about the blues; provides history, biographies, radio program listings, news, photos, sound clips, catalogs, a map, and more.

Videos

August Wilson. 22 min.; color. Films for the Humanities & Sciences, 1994.

Features *Fences* and other plays.

In Black and White: August Wilson. 22 min.; color and b & w. California Newsreel, 1992.

Printed Materials

Criticism

Elkins, Marilyn, ed. *August Wilson: A Casebook*. New York: Garland, 1994.

A Lesson Before Dying

Ernest J. Gaines
New York: Alfred A. Knopf, 1993
Available in paperback from Vintage.

SUMMARY

In Louisiana in the late 1940s, a young black man named Jefferson has been sentenced to die for his alleged involvement in the murder of a grocery store owner during a botched robbery. Jefferson's ancient, weary godmother, Miss Emma, asks a young schoolteacher named Grant Wiggins to visit Jefferson and "make him a man" before he dies. With a great reluctance born out of his own despair over living in such an oppressive environment and his lack of faith, Wiggins begins the task of trying to reach the prisoner and teach him self-respect. Over many weeks, he meets with Jefferson, but only after the setting of the execution date do the two of them begin to truly communicate. By the end, each has learned much from the other about maintaining dignity and courage in the face of great hardship and anguish.

APPRAISAL

Like many of the author's earlier books (e.g., *The Autobiography of Miss Jane Pittman* and *A Gathering of Old Men*), *A Lesson Before Dying* has received high praise for its strong characterization, its evocative description of a time and place, and its great sense of dignity and conscience. The book won the National Book Critics Circle Award as the best work of fiction of 1993 and was featured on *The Radio Reader*. In 1997 *A Lesson Before Dying* was chosen for discussion on *The Oprah Winfrey Show*. The book is an excellent contemporary novel for teaching in high school (especially grades ten and eleven). If the sex scene in chapter 14 is offensive, it can be glossed over; and those upset by racial epithets can be urged to consider them in context and reminded that the book's author, one of our finest writers, is African-American himself.

THEMES

human dignity, racial prejudice, responsibility and commitment, resistance, justice, faith, courage

LITERARY CONCEPTS

characterization, plot, conflict, point of view, irony, stereotypes, setting, symbolism

RELATED READING

Dead Man Walking: An Eyewitness Account of the Death Penalty in the United States by Sister Helen Prejean and *The Green Mile* by Stephen King (both of which were made into notable films) provide excellent parallel reading. In addition, any work of fiction or nonfiction that explores racial prejudice, especially in the South during the same time period as this novel or even later, would be useful. These include *To Kill a Mockingbird* by Harper Lee, *A Time to Kill* by John Grisham, and the other novels of Ernest J. Gaines.

READING PROBLEMS AND OPPORTUNITIES

The novel is narrated in the first person by the protagonist, Grant Wiggins, a young African-American school teacher in Louisiana. As such, it is a story told directly and simply with neither clutter nor pretension. (Only chapter 29 is problematic: it comprises Jefferson's diary in black dialect and may need to be read aloud by a teacher who is well prepared.) Words for vocabulary study among tenth or eleventh graders could include the following (page numbers are given in parentheses):

immobile (3),
credit (4),
gaping (5),
conspiracy (7),
bystander (7),
modicum (7),
implore (7),
illegible (11),
ante-bellum (17, 251),
flaunt (28),
tyrant (38),
petrified (38),
averted (39),
stealth (41),
innate (41),
cynicism, cynical (43, 84, 221),
pervaded (43), *agitated* (44),
humiliate (46, 79),
aggravate, aggravation (49, 81, 134, 157),
stifling, stifled (52),
humanitarianism (56),
grudgingly (61),
relented (61),
residue (71),
patronizing (82),
emphatically (88),
chaos (88),
universality (90),
inquisitor (99),
gravity (100),
theological (100),
rustic (104, 105, 106),
pastoral (104, 116),
ashen (107),
contemplating (114),
caste (115),
vexing (129),
precedent (133),
inflection (138),
mulatto (145, 195–98),
inclement (146, 147),
afflicted (146),
beseeching (146),
ascending (148),
snickered (149),
potential (191),
scapegoat (191),
justification (192),
emancipation (198),
guillotine (201),
tranquil (252), and
transformation (254).

Geographical regionalisms that may need to be taught in advance include *quarter*, *parish*, *Creole*, and *bayou*.

INITIATING ACTIVITIES

1. Have students in small groups write a group list poem in which each line begins with the phrase "Dignity is . . ." and concludes with a concrete example. Model the process by offering an example: "Dignity is keeping your cool when someone accuses you of something you didn't do." "Dignity is the statue of Abraham Lincoln in the Lincoln Memorial." The activity could be preceded by a discussion of several questions: "Is dignity reserved

for just older people? How can a child be dignified? Does dignity come within a person? Or can dignity be conferred upon someone by another? Is it possible for an animal to be dignified? What enables one person to show more dignity than another? (*Note to teacher:* Students may prefer to work with the word *respect.*)

2. Have students read and discuss James Joyce's short story "Ivy Day in the Committee Room," which is discussed briefly, but significantly, in chapter 12 of this novel.

DISCUSSION QUESTIONS

1. *Chapter 1:* What do you think is meant by the first sentence in the book? Who are the people described by the narrator, and what are their attitudes? What is happening? Why do you think the godmother seems so impassive? What is the only thing that moves her? Who is the narrator? Does he seem to be telling the story shortly—or many years—after it happened? Is it his voice that narrates the story of what happened the night of the killings? If not, whose? As readers, do we believe the boy Jefferson? Why? How do you feel about the argument presented by Jefferson's defense lawyer? Do you think the attorney believes his own argument, or is it just a tactic? Why is it so deeply offensive to the aunt and godmother? Is it also offensive to the narrator? Why or why not? Looking back at this chapter, where is there evidence of racism?

2. *Chapter 2:* Why doesn't the narrator (Grant) want to see Miss Emma? What is his attitude toward her and his aunt? Is he afraid of them? Angry with them? Does he respect them? Why is Miss Emma so troubled? How do you think she distinguishes between a "hog" and a man? What do you think she wants Grant to do? Does he understand yet what she wants? Do we? How do Miss Emma and Tante Lou differ in their views of the situation? Why do you think Grant is "screaming inside?" Why is he "running in place here"?

3. *Chapter 3:* What is Grant's attitude toward what is being expected of him? Do you feel sympathetic toward him? Why or why not? Why do you think Aunt Emma keeps saying, "He don't have to go"? What do we learn about Grant's aunt, especially about her attitude toward Mr. Pichot's house? What is becoming clear about Grant's status—and about his aunt's expectations of him and hopes for him? In the Pichot kitchen, what subtle differences do we see in the responses of Miss Emma, Grant's aunt, and Grant himself to the two men? Does what Miss Emma wants from Grant become clearer? Explain. What is she asking of Mr. Pichot? Why is she so insistent? How do Mr. Pichot and Grant regard each other? Comment on the nature of respect—and lack of it—that is in the room throughout the conversation.

4. *Chapter 4:* What initial impression do we get of Vivian? How does she differ from Grant? Why does Grant think he wants to leave Bayonne? Why had he left once before and then returned? Is he opposed to meeting with Jefferson? Why? Why does Vivian want him to go to the jail?

5. *Chapter 5:* How does Grant seem to regard his job? How does he describe the school and its surroundings, and how do we come to view them? What does his treatment of the children in the school tell us about him? Is he cruel? Is his behavior in any way justifiable? Understandable? Explain.

6. *Chapter 6:* Why has Inez been crying when Grant arrives? What kind of person does Edna Guidry seem to be? How do the men in the dining room exert indirect control over Grant? Does he exert any control over them? Explain. Why do the four men come into the kitchen

rather than asking Grant to come to them? Why do you think they bring their drinks with them? Explain the dynamics that develop among the five men in the kitchen. To what extent is there understanding? Respect? At the end of the chapter, do you think Grant's attitude toward his assigned task has changed in any way? Discuss.

7. *Chapters 7 and 8:* Why is there such concern over the superintendent's visit? How would you characterize his treatment of the children? Why does Grant hate himself for having drilled the children? Why do you think the author has included chapters 7 and 8? In the latter, how does Grant feel about the two men who deliver the wood? Do we as readers feel any differently toward them? Why does Grant think about Matthew Antoine? Describe their earlier relationship and interaction. For Grant, what does Antoine represent? Why does he have such hatred?

8. *Chapter 9:* What is your first reaction to Jefferson? What do you think he means by "Chicken, dirt, it don't matter"? Why does Grant think Jefferson's eyes mock him? Why do you think the author depicts the deputy, Paul, as he does? What purpose does he seem to serve in the novel?

9. *Chapter 10:* At this point in the book, how does Grant feel about his aunt and Miss Emma? Does he dislike them? Respect them? How do you feel toward them? How do you feel about Grant? To what extent, if any, are his resentments justified?

10. *Chapter 11:* How are Sheriff Guidry and Paul different? Why do you think Jefferson is more talkative during this visit? Does your view of either him or Grant change any as a result of the visit? Explain.

11. *Chapter 12:* Why does the author include the details about Jackie Robinson and Joe Louis? About Parnell and Joyce and the latter's story? How do these details lead to Grant's thinking about "that cold, depressing cell uptown"? About the boy in the cell in Florida? What does the schoolroom conversation between Grant and Vivian tell you about both? What does she mean by "This is all we have"?

12. *Chapter 13:* What other difference between Grant and the older women becomes evident here? Why does he feel the need to lie? Do you think he is doing the right thing in lying? Why or why not? What does Reverend Ambrose bring to the conversation? Why does he say "deep in you"? Does Grant respect Reverend Ambrose? Do you think Grant is right in thinking that he himself left the church mostly because he did not have time for it? Discuss.

13. *Chapter 14:* Do you think Vivian is honest when she says, "I like it [the house]"? How does Grant feel about it? Why does he say, "Sunday is the saddest day of the week"? Do you agree with Vivian that he believes (i.e. that he has faith)? Why or why not?

14. *Chapter 15:* Why had Vivian's family been so unreceptive toward her marriage? What does this say about the nature of prejudice? Who would you say emerges from the conversation in the aunt's house as the victor—or is *victor* the right word?

15. *Chapter 16:* Why did Jefferson seem to hate Reverend Ambrose? Why did Miss Emma slap him—and then hug him? What does she mean when she says, " 'Cause somebody go'n do something for me 'fore I die"? Do you think Miss Emma and Tante Lou are expecting too much of Grant? Why or why not?

16. *Chapter 17:* Why does Jefferson believe that Grant is vexing him? What does he mean by saying "Manners is for the living"? On the basis of the meeting at the sheriff's house,

what do we learn about Mrs. Guidry? Is she genuinely sympathetic? Are there other reasons that might explain her responses? Discuss.

17. *Chapter 18:* Why do you think Jefferson asks Grant what he wants? At this point, has what Grant wants changed? If so, explain. At the end of the chapter, why does Vivian say, "Something is [changing]"?

18. *Chapter 19:* Why do you think the author includes the detail about Miss Rita Lawrence's contribution of the one gray sheet to the Christmas program? What do the other details of the setting of the Christmas program and the people who are or are not there convey? How would you describe the Christmas program? Is it trite? Sad? Meaningful? Beautiful? Discuss. How is Grant, who is a self-described nonbeliever, affected? Do you think he might be affected in ways he is unaware of? Discuss.

19. *Chapter 20:* Why does Mr. Farrell seem so reluctant? In the room at Henri Pichot's house, why does Mr. Pichot look so worried? In what way does the date for Jefferson's execution bother Grant? Do you think he is justified in his resentment? Why or why not? What does the telephone conversation between the sheriff and the doctor reveal about both of them? At the end of the chapter, is Grant's behavior understandable? Discuss. Cite some examples of irony in the chapter.

20. *Chapter 21:* Why does Vivian seem concerned about Irene? How does Grant explain to Vivian what Miss Emma wants? Does his explanation seem reasonable? Why or why not? What does the explanation say about Grant himself? What does he mean by "in order for me to be what … they want me to be, I must run as the others have done in the past"?

21. *Chapter 22:* How do you account for the slight change in Jefferson's responses? Why does Grant read so much into Thelma's comment, "Here," when she gives him the money? Do you think it is possible to read so much into a single word? Later, why is he so insistent that the radio he buys be new? What evidence of prejudice do you see in this chapter?

22. *Chapter 23:* Why do you think the radio becomes so important to Jefferson? Is it merely a source of entertainment for him, or is it more than that? What more do we learn in this chapter about the differences between what Grant and the older people want for or from Jefferson? After his visit with Jefferson, why is Grant so elated?

23. *Chapter 24:* Here and throughout the novel, how do some of the white men try to maintain their control over blacks? During her visits, why is it so important for Miss Emma to use a tablecloth? As he and Jefferson walk in the dayroom, why does Grant begin talking about heroes? Why does he not want the others in the room to hear? Do you agree with his definition of a myth? What are other examples of bad myths that some people in our society believe? Are there good myths in our country? During their walk around the dayroom, to what extent is Grant concerned for Jefferson? To what extent for himself? Do you think he is being selfish? Is he being honest? Is he effective? Why does Jefferson cry? Why does Grant? What does Grant mean when he says, "Lowly as I am, I am still part of the whole"?

24. *Chapter 25:* What role does the Rainbow Club play in the novel? Is Grant being fair in his feelings about Reverend Ambrose? From his thoughts conveyed to the reader as he sits in the bar listening to the mulattos—and then in the fight—what else do we learn about Grant? It seems clear that he considers the mulattos prejudiced. Is he prejudiced as well? Is this chapter in any way ironic?

25. *Chapter 26:* Why is Grant so anxious to leave Vivian's house? Why does he think he needs her? Again, to what extent do you think Grant is self-centered? Is Vivian's disgust simply about Grant's having chosen to fight—or something more? What does she want? At the end of this chapter, how do you view Grant in terms of character? In what ways is he weak? In what ways strong?

26. *Chapter 27:* Throughout the book, in what ways has Tante Lou tried to maintain some degree of control over Grant? How does he react? How would you summarize Grant's feeling about religion? He says he believes in God; do you think he does? Is Reverend Ambrose right when he says, "You don't even know yourself"? Why does the Reverend think he needs Grant's help? Why does Grant think he owes no one anything? How do the two of them differ in their views of "kneeling" and "standing"? In their views of being "lost"? Of "lying"? What is the nature of the conflict between Grant and the preacher? How do you feel about the two of them?

27. *Chapter 28:* What do Jefferson's erasures suggest? His writings? What seems to impress him about the Easter story concerning Jesus? In this chapter, the conversation about faith that Reverend Ambrose predicted would happen happens. Why does Grant want Jefferson to pray? To believe? Do you think Grant has accepted the preacher's argument in the final chapter? Jefferson says, "Y'all axe a lot, Mr. Wiggins." What are they asking of Jefferson?

28. *Chapter 29 (Jefferson's Diary):* What do we learn about Jefferson through his writings? What thoughts does he wrestle with? Why is Mr. Wiggins unable to give him "a a" so far? What does Grant seem to be holding out for? What do you make of the visit by the three white men? Why do you think the author includes the incident with Bok and the marbles? The concerns expressed by Sheriff Guidry? What kinds of changes are evident in the chapter? When Grant reads the diary, how do you think he will feel, besides sad?

29. *Chapter 30:* Why do you think the author includes such detailed reaction to the approaching event from different perspectives? What do the reactions tell us about the town and its people? Discuss in particular the following: the sheriff's comments to his wife, those of Melvina Jack and Juanita deJean, the bank clerk's remarks, and the conversation between Jefferson and Paul.

30. *Chapter 31:* What occupies Grant's mind as he walks around outside the school? How are his memories of hitting the ragball symbolic? Why does he think "nothing will ever be the same after today"? As he sits beneath the pecan tree, why is he so adamant about not believing? Yet, to what does he feel he is a slave? Why do you think the author ends the book with the conversation between Grant and Paul?

31. *Culminating questions:* To what extent is Grant Wiggins a different person at the end of the book? What has he learned? Is he more, or less, confused? Is he more, or less, hopeful? Does he have faith? If so, in what or whom? What has he taught and to whom? What was "the lesson before dying"?

WRITING ACTIVITIES

1. An older student who admires Grant Wiggins, Irene Cole is often left in charge when he leaves the room. Write a paper written by Irene about Mr. Wiggins as a teacher. Be sure to include what you think she would say about his strengths and weaknesses as a teacher.

2. Try to project where Grant Wiggins will be ten years from the end of the book. Write a paper on what he might be doing based on his experiences and what he has learned. Is he still teaching? Has he remained in Louisiana? Did he marry Vivian? Has he stayed in touch with Paul and others?

3. Imagine that after a few weeks Paul takes Grant up on his offer to speak to the students about Jefferson. Write out the prepared remarks that Paul would give to the class. *Or,* write a diary that Paul might have kept during Jefferson's incarceration. Keep in mind that Paul is a product of the oppressive racial climate that characterized most of the South at mid-century, but also that he symbolizes hope and understanding.

4. Write an epitaph for Jefferson. In the very brief space allotted to you, try to write a phrase or even a verse that would help the people of the community remember him and what he meant to them. *Or,* write a ballad about Jefferson that would convey the same thoughts and feelings in a song.

5. Conduct some research on the sports figures Joe Louis and Jackie Robinson and on what they meant to black Americans in the 1940s. Possible sources include *Joe Louis: A Champ for All America* by Robert Lipsyte, *Jackie Robinson: A Biography* by Arnold Rampersad, and *A Hard Road to Glory* by Arthur Ashe. Write up your findings in a report and read it to the class.

6. It is hard for many of us to imagine how difficult life was for many Americans, especially the poor, as our country emerged from the Great Depression in the late 1930s and 1940s. After recalling some of the details of everyday life in chapter 19 and elsewhere in the book, research what life was like for lower- and even middle-class people in that period. In particular, find ways in which they were resourceful and self-sufficient. Write a paper and present it to the class.

7. Few weeks go by without our hearing some reference to the death penalty in the media. Sometimes, movies like *Dead Man Walking* examine the issue, and now even the appropriateness of the penalty for children is debated. After reading about the controversy and perhaps discussing it in class, write a paper in which you objectively present the pros and cons of capital punishment.

8. Choose a section of Jefferson's diary in chapter 29 and write a transcription into standard English. Consider the two versions and then write a paragraph on what is gained—and what is lost—in your rewritten version.

9. Write a one- to two-page paper that discusses the extent to which you believe *A Lesson Before Dying* is a statement of hope about race relations in America.

10. Imagine yourself as the editor of a progressive newspaper in, say, New Orleans or Baton Rouge during the time of Jefferson's trial. Write an editorial that condemns the way it was handled and its outcome.

11. Today many young people, like Grant, continue (or return) to live at home with their parents or guardians after graduating from high school or even college. Write a paper on the advantages and disadvantages of doing this.

OTHER ACTIVITIES

1. Role play the conversation that takes place among the four women in Tante Lou's house after Grant and Vivian leave, in chapter 15. How do they feel about her, and how are their feelings affected by how they feel about Grant?
2. The narrator, Grant Wiggins, often reads between the lines, as on page 153 when, referring to Mr. Farrell, he says, "He wanted me to read more into what he had said than he had told me." Write and act out a sketch in which the Reverend Ambrose and Grant meet right after the book ends—and Grant tries to conveys his feelings toward the preacher without expressing them directly.
3. Draw the butterfly that Grant sees in chapter 31 in such a way as to convey its possible symbolic meaning.
4. At the end of chapter 2, Grant describes himself as "screaming inside." Using finger paint or oils or even collage, try to represent in an abstract artwork Grant's extreme frustration with his situation.
5. Draw an approximate map of the novel's setting. Include the community—"the quarter"—where Grant Wiggins lives and teaches (the black as well as the white sections: the church/school, Tante Lou's and Miss Emma's houses, Mr. Pichot's, etc.) and thirteen miles away, the town of Bayonne (the courthouse and jail, the Rainbow Club, and other details). For help in drawing the map, reread the first few pages of chapter 4 in particular.
6. Design a split-screen collage of words and phrases, pictures, and found objects. Depict on one side the word *hog* as it is used in the book to describe Jefferson and on the other side the word *man* as you think he has earned the respect conveyed by the word in the time and place of the book.
7. Imagine that Jefferson receives a stay of execution from the governor at the last moment and that, because of a technicality, a motion is made and approved for a retrial. Plan an enactment of the new trial to include testimony from people like Paul Bonin and summarizing statements by the prosecutor and a new defense attorney. Instead of having a jury decision, have students write paragraphs on whether they think Jefferson's conduct leading up to his day of execution would make a difference in the new sentence he receives.

SELECTED TEACHING RESOURCES

Media Aids

Cassettes (2)

A Lesson Before Dying. Abridged, 3 hrs. Time Warner Audiobooks.

Cassettes (6)

A Lesson Before Dying. Unabridged, 9 hrs. Random House Audio and Books on Tape.

Internet

Random House. 1997. *A Lesson Before Dying*. 1997. Available: http://www. randomhouse.com/acmart/lesson.html (Accessed March 10, 2000). A Vintage Books Teaching Guide.

Includes information on the author as well as notes on structure and plot, characterization, setting, themes, imagery, and suggestions for further reading.

Video

A Lesson Before Dying. 101 min., color. Home Box Office Studios.

Printed Resources

Article

Auger, Philip. "A Lesson About Manhood: Appropriating 'the Word' in Ernest Gaines's *A Lesson Before Dying*." *The Southern Literary Journal* 27 (Spring 1995): 74–85.

Book

Lowe, John, ed. *Conversations with Ernest Gaines*. Jackson, MS: University Press of Mississippi, 1995.

Includes several interviews that touch upon the development of *A Lesson Before Dying*.

Things Fall Apart

Chinua Achebe
New York: Doubleday, 1959
Available in paperback from Anchor Books,
a division of Bantam Doubleday Dell Publishing Group.

SUMMARY

Okonkwo, a respected elder and a member of an Ibo clan in Nigeria in the late 1800s, has successfully overcome the stigma of his shiftless father and proudly displays his wealth, consisting of three wives, seven children, and a fine yam crop. However, he has achieved his position at the cost of his humanity: He shows little emotion and controls his family with beatings. To maintain this position and assert his manhood, he even assists in killing a young boy, who has been held in his home for three years in exchange for a crime committed by a member of another village. During a funeral ceremony, Okonkwo's rifle explodes accidentally, killing a young clansman. This act forces Okonkwo and his family to be banished for seven years in his mother's homeland. Although Okonkwo is distraught about this punishment, he fares well and returns in hope of triumphing again in his homeland. Alas, much as changed: The white men have come, the church and schools have been erected, and the white man's law has replaced the clan law. Unable to cope with these changes, Okonkwo leads an attack on the church and burns it down. As a result, he and five of his friends go to jail. As soon as his clansmen raise the required funds for bail, he is set free, but he then proceeds to chop off the head of a messenger. When the District Commissioner finds him to take him to prison, he has already killed himself—a tragic end to a once-great warrior.

APPRAISAL

This novel by Chinua Achebe, who has been called the father of African literature, remains a perennial favorite, selling more than 100,000 copies a year in the United States. A deceptively simple book, it explores the issues of justice, violence, and the oppression of imposed by Christian missionaries and the British Empire. It is most appropriate for grade eleven.

THEMES

cultural differences, justice, male/female relationships, love, parent/child relationships, violence, superstition, gods and religion

LITERARY CONCEPTS

irony, character development, figurative language, symbolism, limited third-person point of view, foreshadowing

RELATED READING

Chinua Achebe has written five additional works of fiction, including *Anthills of the Savannah, Arrow of God, Girls at War and Other Stories, A Man of the People,* and *No Longer at Ease.* Another poignant view of Africa can be found in *Cry, the Beloved Country* by Alan Paton. George Orwell wrote several works that focus on cultural classes, particularly involving members of the British Empire, including the essay "Shooting an Elephant" and the book *Burmese Days.*

READING PROBLEMS AND OPPORTUNITIES

Basically, *Things Fall Apart* is not a difficult book to read; however, it does contain three elements that could be stumbling blocks: (1) the Ibo words and phrases that are defined in the glossary, (2) words describing objects or actions native to Nigeria (these are not covered in the glossary), and (3) general words that warrant study. Words from groups 2 and 3 are listed below (page numbers on which the words or phrases first appear are given in parentheses):

Group 2

harmattan (3),
cowries (4),
kola nut (6),
alligator pepper (6),
machete (17),
calabashes (36),
pottage (43), and
life to you (104).

Group 3

improvident (4),
plaintive (6),
imperious (12),
malevolent (13),
incipient (13),
valediction (32),
harbingers (56),
copiously (56),
coiffure (71),
audacity (76),
voluble (97),
esoteric (120),
callow (147),
miscreant (152),
ostracise (159),
resilient (172),
expedient (178), and
palavers (193).

INITIATING ACTIVITIES

1. Prepare a bookmark that includes the Ibo words and phrases found in the glossary. Begin by listing the words and as much of the definition as you need to understand the meaning of each word. If you need more explanation or an example, include that as well. You might even draw a small illustration. Use this bookmark as you read *Things Fall Apart*; it will save you time (no need to turn to the back of the book and search through) and will help you become familiar with terms used in the book before you start to read.
2. Prepare a chart on Nigeria that includes information on its history, economics (including its major crops), political system, geography, religions, visual arts, and music, as well as

other areas that interest you. You may find information in reference books in your library. The following URL links to a variety of useful sources about Nigeria: http://www.landow./stg.brown.edu/post/nigeria/nigeriaov.html (Accessed March 10, 2000). Save this to refer to as you read *Things Fall Apart.*

DISCUSSION QUESTIONS

Part 1

1. *Chapter 1:* Compare and contrast Okonkwo and his father Unoka. Why is Unoka considered a failure?
2. *Chapter 2:* How does Okonkwo know the gong and town crier signify something is wrong? How is Umuofia able to avoid war? What kind of parent and spouse is Okonkwo? How does Ikemefuna feel about his new home?
3. *Chapter 3:* What is the role of the oracle? Why was Unoka so unsuccessful? Why isn't Okonkwo successful in his first year of farming? What effect do you think this failure will have on his character?
4. *Chapter 4:* How do those in Okonkwo's family feel about Ikemefuna? Why doesn't Okonkwo show his feelings? Why does Okonkwo break the peace week? What lessons does Okonkwo try to teach his sons?
5. *Chapter 5:* Why is Ani the most important goddess? In what ways is she like the central God of other religions? Why is the Feast of the New Yam such a happy time? How do the people celebrate? Why doesn't Okonkwo like feasts? Why does Okonkwo beat and shoot at his second wife? What important information do you glean from this chapter about various members of Okonkwo's family?
6. *Chapter 6:* What are the rules of the wrestling match? How is it like wrestling matches in the United States? How is it different?
7. *Chapter 7:* Why does Okonkwo tell his boys stories of violence and bloodshed? Why does Nwoye prefer his mother's tales? How were the locusts both a curse and a blessing? Why do the elders of Umuofia decide to kill Ikemefuna? Why does Okonkwo participate in the killing even when Ezeudu told him he should have nothing to do with it? What is Nwoye's reaction to the killing?
8. *Chapter 8:* How is Okonkwo able to deal with his feeling for Ikemefuna? Why does he chastise himself? Why hadn't Obierika participated in the killing? Why are the deaths of Ogbuefi Ndulue and Ozoemena unique? How are the customs of finalizing a marriage in Nigeria different from those in the United States? How are they the same?
9. *Chapter 9:* What kind of child is Ezinma? Why is she so special to her mother Ekwelfi? How does Okagbue keep Ezinma from the possibility of death in the future? Why did Ezinma lead him around the village before pointing to the spot under the orange tree? What cure does Okonkwo use for Ezinma? Based on her symptoms, what kind of disease do you think Ezinma has and is the treatment she received a good one? Why or why not?
10. *Chapter 10:* What ceremonies precede the presentation of the case? What do you think is the purpose of these ceremonies? How are both sides of the case presented? Do you agree with the solution presented by Evil Forest? Why or why not?

11. *Chapter 11:* What are the purposes of the stories that the women and children tell each other? Why is Ezinma willing to let her daughter go with the priestess? Why does she decide to follow her? How is the rising of the moon both a blessing and a curse? Why does the author say that "Chielo was not a woman that night"? What does Okonkwo's coming to the cave tell you about his feelings for Ezinma and Ekwefi?

12. *Chapter 12:* Why is the *uri* really a woman's ceremony? What is the significance of the number of pots of palm wine? What elements of this ceremony are similar to a contemporary wedding ceremony in the United States? What elements are different?

13. *Chapter 13:* What elements of Ezeudu's funeral are the most frightening? The most solemn? The most frenetic? Why is Okonkwo banished? Do you think this is a wise and just punishment? Why or why not?

Part 2

14. *Chapter 14:* What is Okonkwo's attitude after he arrives in Mbanta? Why does he believe he will never achieve the greatness he sought? How does Uchendu try to change his attitude by explaining the importance of the motherland and explaining his own losses?

15. *Chapter 15:* Why does Obierika come to visit Okonkwo? What terrible tale does he tell? What future events are suggested by this tale? Why do Uhendu and Okonkwo agree that the members of the Avama clan were fools? Do you agree with them? Why or why not?

16. *Chapter 16:* Why does Obierika go to visit Okonkwo a second time? How do the missionaries overcome the language barrier? Why aren't they completely successful? Why is Nwoye drawn to the missionaries and their messages?

17. *Chapter 17:* Why do the men of the clan consider the missionaries crazy? Why did they allow the missionaries to build their church? Why does Nneka become a convert? How does Okonkwo react to his son's newfound religion? What does he fear will happen?

18. *Chapter 18:* How is Mr. Kiaga able to turn the outcasts into a new strength for his church? Why was the royal python sacred? What action do the elders and rulers take against the Christians for killing the python? In the end, why is no further action needed?

19. *Chapter 19:* Why does Okonkwo feel he must have such a large feast for his mother's people? Why would you agree or disagree with his decision? Why do the old people fear for the future of the clans?

Part 3

20. *Chapter 20:* What has Okonkwo planned for his return to his home? How has Umuofia changed while Okonkwo has been away? Why have the clan members been unable to fight back against the white men and the church?

21. *Chapter 21:* How is Mr. Brown able to get his church and school established and keep them going? Is his approach a wise one? Why or why not? What benefits do the people in the clan feel they are receiving in this new era? Why isn't Okonkwo's return as triumphant as he had hoped?

22. *Chapter 22:* How is Reverend James Smith different from Mr. Brown? What problems do these differences cause? Why does Enoh try to start trouble? Why do the *egwugwu* spare Reverend Smith but burn down the church?

23. *Chapter 23:* How are the leaders tricked into being captured? What action do you think should have been taken by the clan? What action do they take?

24. *Chapter 24:* Why is Okonkwo unable to sleep? Are the plans he makes reasonable and possible? Why or why not? What determines the order of the speakers at the meeting? Why does Okonkwo kill the messenger?

25. *Chapter 25:* Why does Okonkwo kill himself? Why doesn't the clan handle his funeral and burial? Who is to blame for the fate of Okonkwo?

WRITING ACTIVITIES

1. In chapter 2, Achebe contrasts the dark nights with the moonlit nights. Try your hand at a couple of poems that explore this contrast. The first one could be general, beginning with dark nights and moving into moonlit nights. A diamante might be an appropriate form for such a poem (see Appendix A). You might then try some more personal poems, such as "How I feel in the dark" and "How I feel in the moonlight." Share these poems with a classmate and compare and contrast the feelings each of you presents in them.

2. Review the similes below and try rewriting them to express these same thoughts as we might convey them in contemporary English:

   "as slippery as a fish in water"

   "fame has grown like a brush fire"

   "tense like a tightened bow"

   "sharp as a razor"

   "bubbled with energy like a fresh palm wine"

   "rattled like a piece of dry stick in an empty shell"

   "busy as an anthill"

   "cast out of his clan like a fish onto a dry, sandy beach"

   Then rewrite each one with a fresh, new comparison, for example, "as slippery as a glaze of ice on the sidewalk." Survey five of your classmates to determine which of the three forms they like best. Write a paragraph drawing generalizations from your results.

3. In chapter 3, when Okonkwo asks for seed yams, Nwakibie says, "It pleases me to see a young man like you these days when our youth has gone so soft." Write an argumentative essay in which you either support or refute the claim that youth today has gone soft. You can take one of many approaches: (1) compare the youth of today to the youth in Okonkwo's era, (2) compare the youth of today with those of your parents' generation, or (3) set up your own standards for "soft" and pick any group of youth who may or may not fit into these standards.

4. Prepare a comparison/contrast paper in which you compare the gods of Okonkwo's culture with the gods of Greek mythology. This will require a thorough scanning of *Things Fall Apart* to locate all references to the various gods and a review of a mythology reference text. Prepare the paper for possible publication in a school literary magazine.

5. In chapter 4, Ogbuefi Ezeudu says that the village stopped killing people who broke the peace because it spoiled the peace it meant to preserve. Think about practices in our society that have similar ironies and yet are still continued. Write an argumentative paper opposing these practices that create the very result that they oppose. One example might be the payment of government subsidies to tobacco farmers to raise a crop that the government then spends millions to keep people from using.

6. *Things Fall Apart* contains a variety of folk tales. Examine one of the stories; for example, in chapter 9, Okonkwo tells about his mother's story of why mosquitoes buzz in people's ears. In these cases, folk tales are used to explain natural phenomena. Think of another natural phenomenon that Okonkwo's clan might need to explain. Write a folk tale to explain it. Collect all these folk tales and place them in your school library.

7. The title of this book comes from Yeats's poem, "The Second Coming." Find a copy of this poem, review it carefully, and prepare an essay explaining the relationship between the ideas in the poem and the ideas in this novel.

8. Search out the ironies in *Things Fall Apart* related to the missionaries and their goals. What do the ministers hope to accomplish? What do they destroy in order to accomplish their goals? For example, Christianity requires that followers honor their mothers and fathers; however, the introduction of this new religion broke apart families; even Okonkwo's son left his home and family. How are the two ministers—Mr. Brown and Reverend Smith—different in their approaches? Does one or the other create fewer ironic situations in his attempt to bring Christianity to these African people? Prepare a pamphlet or brochure exposing these situations and imploring understanding.

9. At the end of the novel, the Commissioner has plans to write a book about his work in Nigeria. At first, he thinks Okonkwo's story worthy of a chapter, but then relegates it to just a paragraph. Write a persuasive argument about how history might have been changed if one group of people had taken time to study another (i.e., at least write a chapter and hopefully a whole book) before making key decisions about their futures.

OTHER ACTIVITIES

1. The rules of Okonkwo's clan are often related to two principles of magic: homeopathetic and sympathetic. Homeopathetic magic states that things that look alike are alike; hence it is possible to make a doll that looks like a person and injure the person by injuring the doll. Sympathetic magic assumes that things that were once in contact are still in contact; therefore, it is possible to injure a person by using locks of hair or fingernail clippings from that individual. Prepare a chart classifying examples of these two types of magic that appear in the novel.

2. In chapter 6, the author describes the seven drums used for the wrestling matches. In other places in the novel, drums are played for various ceremonies and to provide information. Research musical instruments of Nigeria in the library or on the Internet. Using authentic materials wherever possible, construct one of these drums. Play the drum for your classmates while a narrator reads a scene in which these instruments were used.

How does this background help to increase understanding of the feelings of the people during these ceremonies?

3. "What is good in one place is bad in another." "The world has no end, and what is good among one people is an abomination with others." Set up debate teams that will use the idea in these two quotations as their proposition. This debate requires extensive research and long, careful thought. Is there nothing that is common among all people? Are there no rules that apply to everyone? Let the class judge the winners in this debate.
4. Mr. Brown and Akunna discuss their religious beliefs in chapter 21. Role play this discussion, beginning with the conversation in the novel but extending to other ideas related to these two religions. To conduct this role-playing activity, you must be well informed about the religion that you are espousing. When it is comfortable for you, present this role play before other members of your class and ask for their feedback.
5. Consider the roles of men and women in Okonkwo's clan. Prepare a split collage that shows the dividing line between the two. Examine the novel carefully for differences that are as subtle as men raising yams while women raise corn and other vegetables. Use pictures, drawings, real objects, or whatever else you find that will show the clear distinctions in the roles of these two genders.
6. Food is very important in the social life of Okonkwo's clan. Check the library or the Internet for recipes or make up your own recipes based on the descriptions in the novel. Prepare a mini-feast for the members of your class so that they will have a better understanding of the food so often described. (Find a suitable substitute for palm wine!)

SELECTED TEACHING RESOURCES

Media Aids

Internet

Things Fall Apart by Chinua Achebe. Available: http://www.windnet.com/mki/books/t/things_fall_apart.html (Accessed March 10, 2000).

The site lists ten links to sites about Achebe and *Things Fall Apart*, including questions, study guides, and background information.

Videos

Chinua Achebe. 30 min., color. Films for the Humanities & Sciences.

Chinua Achebe: The Importance of Stories. 57 min., color. Cinema Guild, 1996.

Printed Resources

Articles

Hathaway, James. "Using Chinua Achebe's *Things Fall Apart* in Introductory Geography Classes." *Journal of Geography* 92 (March/April 1993): 75–79.

Puhr, Kathleen M. "Things Come Together with *Things Fall Apart*." *English Journal* 76 (November 1987): 43–44.

Schur, Joan Brodsky. "From Fiction to Field Notes: Observing Ibo Culture in *Things Fall Apart*." *Social Education* 61 (November/December 1997): 380–384.

Teaching Aids

Things Fall Apart. Contemporary Classics series. Perfection Learning Corporation.

Things Fall Apart. Literature Unit Plans. Teacher's Pet Publications.

Things Fall Apart. Novel/Drama Curriculum Units. The Center for Learning.

Things Fall Apart. Novel-Ties. Learning Links.

Things Fall Apart. REACT series. Sundance.

Things Fall Apart. Perma-Guide. Perma-Bound.

Tests

Things Fall Apart. Essay, objective, and alternative assessment versions. Perfection Learning Corporation.

The Crucible

Arthur Miller

New York: Viking Press, 1952

Play: Available in paperback from Penguin USA.

SUMMARY

In the spring of 1692, life in Salem, Massachusetts, is in turmoil because Betty, Reverend Parris's daughter, is possibly bewitched and unable to move. Others from the village arrive, including Betty's friends, Abigail, Mercy, and Mary Warren. Abigail reveals that the girls were dancing in the woods and had conjured up spirits with the help of Tituba, Parris's slave from Barbados. John Proctor, who formerly had an affair with Abigail, tries to set aside the rumors of witchcraft, but when Reverend Hale arrives, Tituba and Abigail confess to witchcraft and name others to save themselves. The hunt for witches escalates so sharply that Elizabeth Proctor fears for her life for having turned Abigail out of her house because of her husband's lewd conduct. More and more villagers are arrested, including Elizabeth, and a trial is held, presided over by Deputy Governor Danforth and Judge Hathorne. In the end, all are condemned because the girls who are accusing control the courts. John Proctor goes to his death rather than sign his name to a false statement that would lead his neighbors to lie about their involvement in witchcraft.

APPRAISAL

The Crucible is a drama that has enjoyed increased critical acclaim through the years. First published in 1953, the play was viewed at that time as, in large part, a parallel portrayal of the contemporary events related to McCarthyism. (McCarthyism is a political attitude named for Joseph R. McCarthy, senator from Wisconsin, who ruthlessly persecuted people he suspected of being Communists. His personal attacks of the suspects were based on suspicion and not substantiated facts.) However, through the years this play has been successfully revived and is now viewed as a key dramatic work of art and an important component of Arthur Miller's legacy. It is most often taught at the eleventh-grade level.

THEMES

courage, mass hysteria, conformity, truth, honesty, religion, moral values, freedom, rights of free individuals

LITERARY CONCEPTS

irony, paradox, character development, historical fiction, setting, lighting, symbols, morality play

RELATED READING

Other plays by Arthur Miller that have been popular with young readers include *Death of a Salesman, A View from the Bridge,* and *After the Fall.* Students interested in the effects of Puritanism in colonial America may want to read *The Scarlet Letter* by Nathaniel Hawthorne. Students interested in reading further about the Salem trials might consider *Salem-Village Witchcraft: A Documentary Research of Local Conflict in Colonial New England*, edited by Paul Boyer. Those interested in the McCarthy controversy during the 1950s could read *The Age of McCarthyism* by Ellen Schrecker or *McCarthyism: The Great American Red Scare* by Larry Fried.

READING PROBLEMS AND OPPORTUNITIES

Students may experience difficulty with some of the vocabulary and the grammatical structures used in this play. Some possible words for study include:

Act I: *predilection, rankle, ingratiating, insoluble, theocracy, injunctions, quaking, dissembling, quavering, abominations, trepidation, partisan, calumny, titillated, stocks, tauntingly, congeries, incubic, succubi;*

Act II: *pallor, poppet;*

Act III: *contention, prodigious, effrontery, ipso facto, probity, guile, augur, accusatory, gulling, quailed;*

Act IV: *prodigious, contention, conciliatory, beguile, sibilance, incredulous.*

INITIATING ACTIVITIES

1. With your classmates, brainstorm the meaning of the term "witch hunt." Check the dictionary or the Internet for an etymology of the term. Supplement your definition by interviewing people of different ages regarding their understanding of the word and its meanings.
2. Research American history in the 1690s in Salem, Massachusetts. What precipitated the famous series of events known as the Salem witch trials? What were the outcomes of these trials? Who were the leading figures in the trials? What roles did they play? Present your information to the class and save it for a later activity.

DISCUSSION QUESTIONS

Act I

1. How were the Puritans able to survive and succeed in the colonies?
2. For what reasons is Parris so concerned about his daughter Betty? Which reason seems most important to him?

3. Why are the people of the village concerned about witchcraft? Why doesn't Parris go to talk with them?
4. How do the girls conspire together to save themselves? How does Abigail control the other girls?
5. Why do people fear John Proctor? What is the past relationship between John Proctor and Abigail? What is the present relationship between them?
6. Why does Rebecca say they should blame themselves? Why do the people of the village object to Reverend Parris's approach to religion? Why do Proctor, Giles, and Putnam argue over the lumber?
7. What is Hale's view of the devil? What is your view of the devil? What attitudes do Parris, Giles, Putnam, and Proctor have toward Hale?
8. Why does Tituba confess to being a witch? What might have happened to her if she hadn't confessed? How are Betty and Abigail selecting the names of those seen with the devil? Why are they doing this?

Act II

9. Why is it a good sign that the rabbit came into the house? What do the stage directions tell you about the relationship between John Proctor and his wife Elizabeth, that is, how is the way they say something different from the words they say?
10. Why is Goody Osburn accused and convicted of witchcraft? In her conversations with John and Elizabeth Proctor, how does Mary Warren show that she has changed? How is she the same?
11. Why does Elizabeth fear for her life? Why is John Proctor questioned by Mr. Hale? Are his answers satisfactory? Why or why not? Why does John forget the commandment about adultery? Why does John say that vengeance is ruling?
12. Compare and contrast the truth and fiction in the story of Mary Warren's poppet.
13. What does Proctor mean by "We are only what we always were, but naked now"?

Act III

14. How has Giles unwittingly condemned his wife? Why are Hathorne and Danforth so unwilling to hear evidence from Giles Corey and John Proctor?
15. Explain the irony in the arrest of those who signed the statement about the good character of Elizabeth, Martha, and Rebecca.
16. What types of responses does Parris consistently give to the claims that the children lied? Why does Danforth vacillate in his reactions to the claims that the girls are pretending?
17. How does Mary Warren react to Danforth's questioning? How does Abigail react? Why are their reactions different?

18. Why does John Proctor confess his affair with Abigail? Why does Mary Warren accuse John Proctor of being aligned with Satan? Why doesn't John Proctor deny the accusations? Why does Elizabeth lie about her husband's affair? Why does Mr. Hale quit the court?

Act IV

19. What is Tituba's attitude toward the devil and Hell? Why has Sarah Good joined Tituba in welcoming the devil?
20. What are Hale's motives for visiting those in jail? Are these motives selfless, selfish, or both?
21. What events have changed Parris's attitude toward and position on the witchcraft trials? Why does Danforth continue to insist on proceeding with the executions?
22. Are the issues between John Proctor and his wife resolved during their final meeting? Why or why not?
23. Why does John Proctor lie in confessing his sins and then tear up the confession he signed?
24. In what ways is the sunrise at the end of the play symbolic?

WRITING ACTIVITIES

1. An earlier title for this play was *Those Familiar Spirits*. Is this better than *The Crucible*? Write a letter to Arthur Miller urging him keep the title *Those Familiar Spirits* and abandon the idea of calling this play *The Crucible.* Explain why this would be a more effective title. *Or* take the opposite position and urge him to abandon the earlier title and adopt the new one.
2. In his description of Reverend Hale in Act I, Miller states, "The necessity of the Devil may become evident as a weapon, a weapon designed and used time and time again in every age to whip men into a surrender to a particular church or church-state." Prepare a description of the devil that includes your reactions to this picture of the devil. You may use any appropriate references in this position paper.
3. When this play was first presented in 1953, the United States was in the throes of its own witch hunt, precipitated by Senator Joseph McCarthy. Research this era and prepare a paper comparing and contrasting the Salem witch trials to the McCarthy era. Ask older friends and relatives to recall their experiences during the McCarthy trials to enable you to add personal testimony to your paper.
4. Several characters in this play are fairly flat, including Danforth, Hathorne, Herrick, and Parris. Choose one of these characters and prepare a character sketch of this individual. Search carefully for clues as to what motivated him to behave as he did and what prevented him from changing significantly throughout the play. Post these sketches on the bulletin board along with drawings of your own idea of the character's appearance.

5. This play clearly contains a lesson/warning for its readers/audience. What do you think that lesson/warning is? Prepare a statement beginning "*The Crucible* shows us that . . ." and conclude the sentence with the lesson/warning you found in the play. Collect these statements into a booklet, with one statement on each page. Place the booklet in your school library.
6. Check literary reference books in your library or the Internet to formulate a definition of a morality play. Then decide if *The Crucible* is or is not a morality play. Prepare your argument using sound reasoning and a carefully organized format.
7. Write a series of letters that a citizen in Salem might have sent to friends about the occurrences in his village during the course of the play. Write at least four letters, one for the events in each act. Keep in mind the prevailing moral and religious values of the time, as well as the prejudices and jealousies that existed.
8. Arthur Miller wrote a scene between Abigail and John that he later removed because it "seemed to deflect the tempo of the play." However, Miller continued to hope the scene could be retained and played without affecting the tempo because it showed the ambiguity in Abigail's mind: Is she capable of murdering for love? If your copy of the text does not include this scene, check your library for one that does. After you have read the scene, prepare an argument for or against including this scene in the next production of the play.

OTHER ACTIVITIES

1. Review the text for specific stage directions, such as "quaking with fear," "quavering as she sits," "sidles out" (all in Act I, but you will find dozens more). Write these directions on two sets of individual cards. As your partner enacts one of these directions, review your cards and determine which action is taking place. Place the cards in order and when your partner is finished, check to see how well you interpreted the action portrayed.
2. Conduct research on the names and titles used in the play. Are they realistic? Why are some of the women referred to as "Goody?" Prepare a chart for use by future readers of this play.
3. The cry of "witchcraft" arose in one case because one woman lost all her children except one, while another had many healthy children and grandchildren. Research medical practices at the time and incorporate that knowledge into our current understanding of gene pools and modern medicine to come up with reasonable explanations for the variations in living births and grown children experienced by these two women.
4. Role play the scene in Act III in which Abigail and the other girls pretend that Mary Warren is a bird that is about to fly down and attack them. Remember, you do not need to memorize lines word for word, but you should be familiar with the plot and the way the characters behaved. When you have finished with your role playing discuss how each of you felt and how your feelings changed as you continued the charade that you were bewitched.
5. Make a list of types of people today who are hunted down or persecuted and have no way to defend themselves. Make a chart listing the reasons that these witch hunts still prevail, as well as the attitudes and the fears that make humans behave in this manner. Prepare a website or a poster series to expose these behaviors.

SELECTED TEACHING RESOURCES

Media Aids

Cassettes (4)

The Crucible. Sundance.

CD-ROM

The Crucible. Macintosh and Windows versions. The Annenberg/CPB Project and Perma-Bound, 1995.

Internet

Arthur Miller's The Crucible. Available: http://www.ogram.org/17thc/miller.shtml (Accessed March 10, 2000).

This site is jam-packed with links to sites containing useful information on *The Crucible*, witch hunts, and Arthur Miller and even includes reviews of the film version.

Burns, Margo. *Arthur Miller's The Crucible: Fact & Fiction.* Available: http://www.ogram.org/17thc/crucible.shtml (Accessed March 10, 2000).

An interesting site that points out the historical discrepancies in the play.

Video

The Crucible. 123 min., color. Daniel Day-Lewis and Winona Ryder version. Sundance, 1996.

Printed Resources

Articles

Barlow, Dudley. "The Teachers' Lounge: 'Seeking the Spheres To Connect Them'." *The Education Digest* 61 (February 1996): 32–35.

About teaching Miller's play.

Cerjak, Judith A. "Beware the Loss of Conscience: *The Crucible* as Warning for Today." *English Journal* 76 (September 1987): 55–57.

Navasky, Victor S. "The Demons of Salem, With Us Still." *New York Times* 145 (September 8, 1996): sect. 2, p. H37, col. 1.

On Miller's adaptation of his play to the screen.

Book

Martine, James J. *The Crucible: Politics, Property, and Pretense.* New York: Twayne Publishers, 1993.

Teaching Aids

The Crucible. Contemporary Classics series and Latitudes series. Perfection Learning Corporation.

The Crucible. Literature Unit Plans. Teacher's Pet Publications.

The Crucible. Novel/Drama Curriculum Units. The Center for Learning.

The Crucible. Novel-Ties. Learning Links.

The Crucible. Novel Unit Guide, Novel Units Student Packet, and Perma-Guide. Perma-Bound.

The Crucible. REACT series, Dramatic Ideas Plus series, and Novel Ideas Classic series. Sundance.

Tests

The Crucible. Essay, objective, and alternative assessment versions. Perfection Learning Corporation.

The Great Gatsby

F. Scott Fitzgerald
New York: Scribner, 1925
Available in paperback from Scribner.

SUMMARY

Seen through the eyes of the young bond salesman Nick Carraway, Jay Gatsby is the mysterious owner of a lavish estate in West Egg on Long Island, New York, in the early 1920s. There he hosts extravagant parties to which the socially aspiring of the city, invited and otherwise, flock to observe and be observed. Gatsby, however, has a single compelling interest: the lovely, shallow, and vulnerable Daisy Buchanan (now married to a cad), whose love for Gatsby five years earlier has been fiercely rekindled. Their incandescent romance glows only briefly before it is extinguished by two violent events, which together lead Nick Carraway to conclude that the elusive American Dream is all but unattainable.

APPRAISAL

The Great Gatsby is the classic American novel of the 1920s, of the glittering world of wealth and extravagance, privilege, deception, and disappointment. Few novels have captured a time and place as vividly and memorably. When the book appeared in 1925, it was immediately praised by critics and the public alike as a work that fulfilled the earlier promise of Fitzgerald's first novel, *This Side of Paradise*. *The Great Gatsby* placed Fitzgerald in the forefront of modern American novelists, a position he has occupied ever since (except for a decline of his reputation in the 1930s). *The Great Gatsby* is most often taught in the eleventh grade.

THEMES

the American Dream, "the unreality of reality," pretension and hypocrisy, the unattainable, romanticism, wealth and privilege

LITERARY CONCEPTS

characterization, point of view, setting, imagery, symbol, irony, plot, foreshadowing, flashback, paradox, allusion

RELATED READING

Other works of fiction about the implications of wealth and privilege include *Tender Is the Night* by Fitzgerald, *Carriage Trade* by Stephen Birmingham, *Tales of Yesteryear* by Louis Auchincloss, *The Collected Stories of Louis Auchincloss*, and *The Age of Innocence* by Edith Wharton. More recently, *For Kings and Planets* by Ethan Canin also reveals the perceptions of a young man who travels from the Midwest to New York and comes under the spell of a charismatic figure. Students who like Fitzgerald might also like the novels of John O'Hara and John Updike (especially the Rabbit series) and the short stories of John Cheever.

READING PROBLEMS AND OPPORTUNITIES

The Great Gatsby is a gold mine of potential vocabulary enrichment. The first page alone has at least ten words that may be unfamiliar to most high school students. A list of words for possible emphasis could run for pages. The following are selected because most of them appear more than once and many (like *contemptuous*, *sumptuous*, *elusive*, and *hauteur*) so clearly reflect the atmosphere of the novel (page numbers are provided in parentheses):

riotous (5, 7),
proximity (8, 83),
reproach, reproachful (8, 66, 69),
turbulence, turbulent (9, 16, 77),
supercilious (9, 22),
imperceptibly, perceptible (11, 23),
ecstatically (11, 67, 70, 120),
desolate (11, 21, 86, 89),
incredulously, credulity (11, 30, 37, 52, 53, 69, 86, 95, 100, 101),
contemptuous (12, 18, 35, 77, 95),
languidly (13, 26),
unobtrusively (13, 84),
profound (14, 39, 75, 79, 97, 117),
complacency, complacent (14, 137),
impassioned (15, 31, 101),
skepticism, skeptical (16, 36, 38, 63),
cynical (17, 37, 90),
sauntered (21, 36, 82),
sumptuous (22),
sensuous (23),
vitality (23, 26, 54, 75, 107),
discreet (23, 26, 29),
haughty (25, 47, 55, 80),
apathetic (25),
incessant (26, 45, 106, 108, 115, 118, 130, 140),
hauteur (26),
disdain (27),
ambiguously (29),
innuendo (34, 37),
prodigality (34),
condescension, condescending (37, 41),
bona fide (38, 90),
vacuous (39),
florid (40, 78),
provincial (40, 140),
elude , elusive (41, 42, 47, 87, 98, 141),
jaunty, jauntiness (42, 43, 48, 63, 138),
indifferent, indifference (42, 77),
indignant (43, 45, 56, 132),
credibility (43),
tumultuous, tumult (44, 98, 106),
tentatively (45, 94),
subterfuge (48),
instinct, instinctive (58, 76, 77, 97, 128),
denizen (58),
scrutinize, scrutiny (66, 114, 132),
exhilarating (67),
distraught (68),
obstinate (69),
exultation, exulting (70, 106),
gaudiness (77),
debauchee (78),

oppressiveness, oppressively (81, 94),
profusion (81),
oblivion (82),
appalled, appalling (84, 87),
euphemisms (84),
dilatory (85, 88),
uncommunicable (87),
indiscreet (93),
inexplicable, explicable (97, 98, 115),
tangible (98, 105),
portentous (99, 106),
irreverent, reverent (99, 133),
libertine (101),
prig (101),
magnanimous (105),
presumptuous (105),
malice (115),
redolent (116, 118),
ravenously (116),
unscrupulously (116),
corroborate (120),
garrulous (121),
fortuitously (126),
amorphous (126),
protégé (126),
interminable (137),
inquisitions (137), and
transitory (140).

INITIATING ACTIVITIES

1. Complete the following "opinionnaire" and save your responses for a later discussion. For each statement, indicate *Strongly agree*, *Agree*, *Disagree*, or *Strongly disagree*:

   a. Contrary to conventional belief, wealth *can* bring happiness.

   b. Usually it is better *not* to get what you most fervently wish for.

   c. America is, always has been, and always will be a country of deep class divisions.

   d. It is all but impossible to be genuine at a large party.

   e. People spend great sums of money mostly to draw attention to themselves.

   f. At last, at the turn of a new century, America has become a country where anyone can achieve his or her dreams.

2. Read some background material on America's Roaring Twenties. (Possible sources include *Only Yesterday* by Frederick Lewis Allen, *The American Heritage History of the 20's and 30's*, edited by Ralph K. Andrist, and the Internet home page mentioned in "Selected Teaching Resources.") Pay particular attention to the social trends during the decade: the music, art, fashion, and fads that dominated the period, making it one of the most memorable in American history. Report your findings to the class.

DISCUSSION QUESTIONS

1. *Chapter I:* Who is the narrator of the book? From what distance? How does Nick Carraway present himself? What initial glimpse does he give us of Gatsby? How does Nick describe his surroundings on Long Island Sound? What do the following phrases suggest: "two old friends whom I scarcely knew at all"; "standing with his legs apart on the front porch" (about Tom Buchanan); and Daisy's comment, "I'm p-paralyzed with happiness" and her question, "Do they miss me?" What do we learn about the Buchanans and Miss Baker from their comments and movements and from Nick Carraway's comments about them? Does he like Tom and Daisy? Why do you think Daisy says about her daughter, "That's the best thing a girl can be in this world, a beautiful little fool"? Do you agree with Nick's

feeling that she is insincere? What does she mean by "our beautiful white [girlhood]"? What impression do we get of Gatsby from Nick's description of him at the end of the chapter?

2. *Chapter II:* What is suggested by the details of setting, like the eyes of Dr. Eckleburg, early in the chapter, and the valley of ashes? What more do we learn about Tom Buchanan in this chapter? What is Myrtle Wilson like? Why do you think Tom is attracted to her? Is there evidence that Myrtle is "above" her husband, as she says? What is important to her? What do we learn in the chapter from comments by Catherine and the McKees? Why do you think Fitzgerald includes details like the spot of dried lather on Mr. McKee's cheek? Afterwards in the Pennsylvania Station, how do you think Nick Carraway feels about the evening he has just spent?

3. *Chapter III:* What further impression do we get of Gatsby early in the chapter? Why do people come to his parties? How do they view Gatsby? Why is the man with owl-eyed glasses surprised that the books in Gatsby's library are real? What do the uncut pages suggest? After hearing and inferring so much about Gatsby, what is your first direct impression of him? Does Nick Carraway's view of him change? If so, how? In what ways is Gatsby mysterious? How does he seem to regard his guests? How do you view them? What does Jordan mean when she says of large parties, "They're so intimate"? Why do you think the evening dissolves into couples bickering? And why does Fitzgerald include the scene with the upended automobile? How does Nick view himself? How have you come to view him? What do you like and dislike about him? Do you sense that he is the honest person he claims to be? Why or why not? Of the characters encountered so far, whom do you feel you know best? Why?

4. *Chapter IV:* What kind of contrast is shown in the opening sentence? Why do you think Fitzgerald lists Gatsby's summer guests? What does the list imply? How does Nick Carraway's view of Gatsby continue to change? What is implied by Gatsby's frequent use of the phrase "old sport"? When Gatsby begins to describe his history, why does Nick not believe him at first? Can you imagine what Gatsby's "sad thing" and his request refer to? What does the conversation with Mr. Wolfshiem add to our sense of Gatsby? How does Gatsby contribute to the air of mystery and intrigue that surrounds him? Do you think Gatsby loves Daisy, or are there other reasons for his wanting to see her again? Why do you think Nick is attracted to Jordan Baker, especially given his perceptions of her as dishonest?

5. *Chapter V:* Why does Gatsby seem reluctant to accept Nick's offer to invite Daisy to meet him? Why does Nick in turn reject Gatsby's offer? At Nick's house, how do you account for Gatsby's behavior? When Nick returns to the house after the rain, why do you think Gatsby and Daisy are so joyful? Why does Gatsby want to show Nick and Daisy his house? How would you respond to Gatsby's display? Why does Daisy cry at the "beautiful shirts"? Do both Gatsby and Daisy have both money and love? Why does Gatsby possibly feel that the green light at the end of Daisy's dock has lost its magic, its significance? Why do both Gatsby and Daisy want Nick to stay? In what way is the song "Ain't We Got Fun?" so revealing? What does Nick mean by "the colossal vitality of his [Gatsby's] illusion"? Is Gatsby happy? Is he capable of happiness? Discuss.

6. *Chapter VI:* What do we learn about Jay Gatsby's origins? From the beginning, what motivated him? Why was Cody so impressed with the young Gatsby? What, ultimately, did Cody give Gatsby? In the exchange with Mr. Sloane and the unnamed lady, what does Gatsby learn, if he had not known it before? What does Nick mean by "it is invariably

saddening to look through new eyes at things upon which you have expended your own powers of adjustment"? What does Daisy's comment, "These things excite me *so*," tell us about her? Why does Gatsby insist on referring to Tom as "the polo player"? How does Daily respond to the party? What is meant by "She saw something awful in the very simplicity she failed to understand"? What more have we learned about Daisy in this chapter? Why does Gatsby feel she hasn't enjoyed the evening? Why does he feel that the past can indeed be repeated? What are Gatsby's "unutterable visions"? At the end of the chapter, what is Fitzgerald, through Nick, trying to convey?

7. *Chapter VII:* Do you think that Daisy and Gatsby are clearly in love with each other? Discuss. What does Daisy's reaction to her little girl say about her? Why does Daisy suddenly suggest going to town? What is there about Daisy's voice that seems so compelling to Nick, not only here but throughout? Why does he call it "indiscreet"? Why does Tom say it is "full of money"? Does he mean something different from what Nick means? Why does Tom want to drive Gatsby's car to town? What does the renting of the parlor at the Plaza Hotel tell us about the group? When Gatsby tells about his limited time at Oxford, why does Nick say he experiences a renewal of faith in him? Why is Gatsby so excited about telling Tom the truth about himself and Daisy? What is revealed in this scene about Gatsby and Daisy? Do they grow closer together in the scene, or farther apart? Explain. On the way home, why does Nick say, "So we drove on toward death through the cooling twilight"? What appears to have caused the death of Myrtle Wilson? How is everything complicated by this development?

8. *Chapter VIII:* Why does Nick seem to think that Gatsby is pursuing a hopeless cause? As Gatsby reveals his early attraction to Daisy, what more do we learn about him? What exactly was the nature of their attraction to each other? Do you think they were honest with each other? How would Gatsby have defined the word *nice*? What does Nick Carraway mean by "the youth and mystery that wealth imprisons"? After the war, why had Daisy rejected Jay Gatsby for Tom Buchanan? Why do you think Fitzgerald so often uses imagery of ghosts and shadows in the novel (as on p. 118)? As Nick leaves Gatsby, why does he call out, "You're worth the whole damn bunch put together"? Do you think Nick believes this? What does he like about Gatsby? Why does he believe Gatsby's dream is "incorruptible"? What message do you think Gatsby hoped for at the pool? Why do you think Nick thought "perhaps he [Gatsby] no longer cared"?

9. *Chapter IX:* What does Nick Carraway mean when he says, "I'll get somebody for you, Gatsby"? Why is it so important to him? What does the reaction to Gatsby's death suggest about him and his friends and acquaintances? Wolfshiem's reaction in particular? Mr. Gatz's? What does the schedule in the book about Hopalong Cassidy tell us about Gatsby as a boy? What do you think of Daisy's failure to respond, and of Nick's not resenting it? As Nick remembers his earlier returns to the Midwest from school, why does he "see now that this has been a story of the West, after all"? What might have been the "deficiency" possessed by all of them in the story that made them "subtly unadaptable to Eastern life"? How do you interpret the "night scene by El Greco" described by Nick? What does the scene between Nick and Jordan convey about the two of them, especially Nick's comment "I'm five years too old to lie to myself and call it honor"? How does Nick ultimately feel about Daisy and Tom? Is he fair in his assessment of them? Why does Nick decide to leave the East for home? What do you think he means by "the last and greatest of human dreams"? Why does Nick think such dreams are so elusive? What does he—and Fitzgerald—mean by the book's final, memorable sentence? As you look back at the

novel, why do you think Fitzgerald used the word *great* to describe Gatsby in the title? Was Gatsby in any way "great," or is Fitzgerald being ironic?

WRITING ACTIVITIES

1. Write a diamante about the book and its characters with the contrasting words *reality* and *illusion*. (See Appendix A.) Or substitute any other pair of contrasting words that seem appropriate for the novel.
2. One of the major influences on the writings of F. Scott Fitzgerald was his wife Zelda, who became almost as famous as he, sharing his flameout in the last half of the 1920s. It has been suggested by more than one biographer that Zelda was a source for Daisy. Read a biography of Zelda or parts of one (possible choices include *Zelda* by Nancy Mitford and *The Romantic Egoists* by Matthew J. Bruccoli). Then write a two- to three-page comparison between character and source.
3. In a sense, *The Great Gatsby* is a brilliant portrayal of the "lifestyles of the rich and famous" during the Jazz Age. In our own age, these lifestyles are routinely depicted in television programs and in magazines like *People* and *Us*. Using resources like these, write a paper entitled "Contemporary Lifestyles of the Rich and Famous: *The Great Gatsby* Revisited." Include pictures if you wish, copied from magazines, and comment on the extent to which you feel this age is as shallow as Nick Carraway felt the Twenties were.
4. Write a newspaper article on the deaths of Myrtle Wilson and Gatsby that might have appeared a few days later in the *West Egg Weekly*, based on interviews with everyone who knew about them. You will have to make your own decision about how forthcoming people like Nick Carraway would have been.
5. We see everything in the novel through the lens of Nick Carraway's narration. Write about one of the following scenes from a different point of view:
    a. the party scene in chapter III from Gatsby's perspective as the orchestra begins to play "Jazz History of the World"
    b. the scene in the room at the Plaza Hotel in chapter VII from Jordan Baker's perspective
    c. Daisy's thoughts at the funeral service for Gatsby in chapter IX, if she had been there
6. Write a brochure or article (or even a tongue-in-cheek list poem) entitled "How To Throw a Party" as Jay Gatsby might have written it.
7. The novel is obviously about the title character. It has been suggested, however, that it is as much about Nick Carraway. Write a persuasive paper contending that we end up knowing far more about Nick Carraway than we do about Gatsby.
8. *The Great Gatsby* is perhaps our greatest novel about "the American Dream," about what we as Americans seem so desperate to find and about its elusiveness. Write an essay about your American dream or dreams. What do you ultimately hope for, what do you think will be the difficulties in attaining it, and what might be possible reasons for its not turning out to be what you had hoped?
9. Note the famous Cugat illustration of a woman's eyes that served as the original book cover. Write a paper in which you explain how you think the painting relates to the themes and characters in the novel.

10. Write a research report on one of the following topics:
    a. fashion during the Roaring Twenties, especially styles of clothing likely to be worn to parties held by the wealthy
    b. the fads of the Jazz Age, especially those that might have appealed to the likes of the Buchanans and Jordan Baker

11. As we learn in chapter V, Jay Gatsby invented himself in "the service of a vast, vulgar, and meretricious beauty" when he was seventeen years old. Given what you have learned by reading the book and your own set of values, write a paper about how you would invent yourself.

OTHER ACTIVITIES

1. *The Great Gatsby*, of course, depicts the Jazz Age and makes numerous references to songs and other music, including titles like "The Sheik of Araby," "Three O'Clock in the Morning," and especially "Ain't We Got Fun?" Try to find recordings of these songs (and possibly others) that reflect the period and play them for the class. Speculate on why Fitzgerald chose these particular titles.
2. Draw or paint a picture of the Dr. Eckleburg road sign based on its description at the beginning of chapter II. Try to convey some of the symbolic qualities that Fitzgerald apparently intended.
3. With several other students, act out a scene of party conversation that suggests the shallowness, insincerity, and meaninglessness portrayed throughout the novel. You may write a script or improvise the scene (or try a little of both).
4. One critic has written that Fitzgerald's favorite word was *glitter*. Create a collage that employs the idea of glitter as the focal point of an effort to express the qualities of the Roaring Twenties conveyed in the novel.
5. Create an original art work (a painting, collage, mobile, etc.) based on one of the following quotes from the book:
    a. "The best thing a girl can be in this world [is] a beautiful little fool."
    b. "the youth and mystery that wealth imprisons" (chapter VIII)
    c. "the womb of ... purposeless splendor" (chapter IV)
    d. the final sentence in the book

6. Toward the end of the novel, Nick Carraway says that West Egg "still figures in my more fantastic dreams. I see it as a night scene by El Greco: a hundred houses, at once conventional and grotesque, crouching under a sullen, overhanging sky and a lustreless moon. In the foreground, four solemn men in dress suits are walking along the sidewalk with a stretcher on which lies a drunken woman" (p. 137). Try to locate this work (or one like it) by El Greco in a book of his paintings. Then share it with the class and explain the possible connection between the work and the novel as Carraway saw that connection.
7. The most famous dance of the Roaring Twenties was the Charleston. Learn the steps of the Charleston and teach it to your classmates using appropriate period music. As part of this activity, try to determine the cause of the dance's enormous popularity during this era of high times and uninhibited behavior.

8. In chapter VII, Daisy, impressed with Gatsby's look of coolness, tries to recall the advertisement of a man Gatsby reminds her of. Look through magazines like *Esquire*, *Gentlemen's Quarterly*, and *The New Yorker* for an ad that might satisfy her efforts to recall. Then write a paragraph explaining your choice and share it with the class.

SELECTED TEACHING RESOURCES

Media Aids

Cassettes (6)

The Great Gatsby and Other Stories. Read by Alexander Scourby. Contains the novel plus four short stories, all unabridged. Perma-Bound.

Filmstrip and Cassette/Record

Gatsby: The American Myth. Thomas S. Klise Co.

Internet

Board of Trustees of the University of South Carolina. 1997. *F. Scott Fitzgerald Centenary*. ©1997. Available: http://www.sc.edu/fitzgerald/index.html (Accessed March 10, 2000).

A tremendous resource on the author, including a brief life of Fitzgerald, a Fitzgerald chronology, facts about Fitzgerald, essays and articles, bibliographies, quotations, and even photographs and voice and video clips.

The 1920s Experience. n.d. Available: http://www.angelfire.com/co/pscst/index.html (Accessed March 10, 2000).

A useful home page on the Jazz Age, including sections on people, events, inventions, art, literature, music, entertainment, and fads and fashions.

A + LS/Media Weaver High School Novel Bundle, *The Great Gatsby*. Available: http://www.amered.com/curr/mwtgg.html (Accessed March 10, 2000).

Through varied activities and reading responses, students are introduced to *The Great Gatsby*.

Video

The Great Gatsby. 146 min., color. Robert Redford/Mia Farrow version. CLEARVUE/eav, Perma-Bound, and Sundance, 1984.

Printed Materials

Articles

Berman, Ronald. " 'Oh, Science and Art, and All That': Reflections on *The Great Gatsby*." *The Journal of Aesthetic Education* 23 (Fall 1989): 85–95.

Birkerts, Sven. "A Gatsby for Today." *The Atlantic* 271 (March 1993): 122ff.

Presents the novel as an American classic with special relevance for the 1990s.

Lukens, Margaret. "Gatsby as a Drowned Sailor." *English Journal* 76 (February 1987): 44–46.

Smiley, Jane et al. "To Be Continued . . . (Sequels to Famous Literary Works)." *Harper's Magazine* 285 (August 1992): 35–45.
Includes a brief sequel to *The Great Gatsby* written by Jay Parini.

Books

Bloom, Harold, ed. *Gatsby*. Major Literary Characters series. New York: Chelsea House Publishers, 1991.

Lehan, Richard Daniel. *The Great Gatsby: The Limits of Wonder*. A Twayne Masterwork Study. Boston: Twayne Publishers, 1990.

Peck, David. *Novels of Initiation: A Guidebook for Teaching Literature to Adolescents*. New York: Teachers College Press, 1989.
Includes a chapter on *The Great Gatsby*.

Teaching Aids

The Great Gatsby. Contemporary Classics series and Latitudes series. Perfection Learning Corporation.

The Great Gatsby. Literature Unit Plans. Teacher's Pet Publications.

The Great Gatsby. Novel Unit Guide, Novel Units Student Packet, and Perma-Guide. Perma-Bound.

The Great Gatsby. Novel/Drama Curriculum Units. The Center for Learning.

The Great Gatsby. Novel-Ties. Learning Links.

The Great Gatsby. REACT series, Novel Ideas Classic series, and Novel Ideas Plus series. Sundance.

Tests

The Great Gatsby. Essay, objective, and alternative assessment versions. Perfection Learning Corporation.

Death of a Salesman

Arthur Miller
New York: Viking Press, 1949
Available in paperback from Penguin.

SUMMARY

Willy Loman is a salesman who finds his life crumbling beneath him. He unrealistically places his hopes in his sons Happy and Biff, but when Willy is fired, Happy and Biff are unable to realize a business venture. Doubts and memories of past indiscretions cloud Willy's mind, and he begins to lose his ability to cope. Despite the concern of his loving, long-suffering wife and the offers of assistance from his friend Charlie, Willy finally—and tragically—chooses to end his own life.

APPRAISAL

Following its first production in 1949, *Death of a Salesman* was heralded as a major new contribution to American theater. For that year it won the Pulitzer Prize, the New York Critics Circle Award, the Antoinette Perry Award, the Theater Club Award, and the Front Page Award. The play remains as popular and significant as ever, seen by millions of viewers in film and television versions and translated into dozens of languages, including Chinese. The source of its enduring success is perhaps its presentation of an unforgettable character, Willy Loman, with whom so many can identify and empathize. In American high schools, *Death of a Salesman* is most often taught in the eleventh grade. In its effort to portray working-class Americans honestly and realistically, the play contains some profanity.

THEMES

self-deceit, self-knowledge, success, materialism, family loyalty and parental love, pride and self-respect, values, moral and social standards of contemporary America

LITERARY CONCEPTS

realism, expressionism, ambiguity, irony, pathos, tragic hero, symbolic use of lighting, music, and scenery, characterization, theme, symbolism

RELATED READING

The quest for and questioning of the American dream are explored in many twentieth-century American novels, among them *Babbitt* by Sinclair Lewis and *Winesburg, Ohio* by Sherwood Anderson. Two other plays by Arthur Miller explore similar concerns: *All My Sons* and *The Prize.*

READING PROBLEMS AND OPPORTUNITIES

Because much of the dialogue is written in the language of lower middle-class American speech, students should not have difficulty reading this play. They may, however, experience occasional problems that appear in the stage directions, such as:

> *mercurial, turbulent, enthralled, insinuates, laconic. trepidation. and stolid* (all in act 1); and
>
> *incredulously, raucous, sotto voce, ominously, and implacably* (all in act 2).

These words could easily be taught in advance.

Because the play combines realistic and expressionistic scenes, students may have some trouble visualizing the action. It may help to know that Miller originally intended to title the play *The Inside of His Head*, thus communicating his emphasis on one man's perception of the world. Hence, Willy Loman, like all of us, sees what he wants to see, remembers what he wants to remember, and dreams of things that can never be.

INITIATING ACTIVITIES

1. Make a list of the ten qualities you feel an individual must possess to be successful. In small groups of three to five students, compare your lists and try to reach a consensus on the ten items. Save the lists for later discussion.
2. Write a short paper (one to two pages) in which you compare the hopes and dreams your parents have for you with your own desires and aspirations. Discuss the similarities and differences between the two sets of goals.
3. With your classmates, discuss the role of the salesperson in our society. Consider these questions: What type of person makes a good salesperson? What are the advantages and disadvantages of being a salesperson? What kinds of satisfaction do salespeople obtain from their jobs?

DISCUSSION QUESTIONS

Act I

1. Read carefully the directions for the set at the beginning of Act 1. What parts of the set are realistic? What parts have a dreamlike quality? What is the purpose of the "imaginary wall-lines"? Why is Willy Loman called "the Salesman"—with a capital S?
2. Based on the description in the stage directions and Linda's opening conversation with Willy, explain how Linda feels about her husband.

3. How does Willy contradict himself when he talks about Biff? What does this tell you about Willy's current mental state? Is it possible to tell by this conversation how Willy really feels about Biff? Why or why not?
4. Biff and Happy's conversation in the bedroom reveals a good deal about their personalities, their hopes, their dreams, and their frustrations. Compare and contrast Biff and Happy. How does each of them feel about working in business? Which of the two has a better understanding of himself and his potential?
5. In the stage directions that set the next scene, leaves seem to appear over the house. What does this tell you about the time in which the next part of the play takes place? What might these leaves symbolize?
6. The car-polishing scene is part of Willy's memory. Examine this section of the play carefully. Which segments of dialogue indicate that Willy's reminiscences are not actually happenings, but rather are what Willy would like to believe is truth?
7. When Willy compares Bernard to his boys, he declares that they will get ahead in the business world. Why does he say this? What does this speech tell you about his values?
8. Willy's memories include his romantic interlude with another woman. Why do you think he had this affair? Could this be an indication that he does not love Linda, or does it satisfy some other need that he has? Why is he so upset that Linda is mending her stockings?
9. What is Willy's attitude toward his brother Ben? In what ways is Ben a symbol of the American dream? In what ways is Ben a phony? How has the American dream changed since Arthur Miller wrote this play? How does Willy's conversation with Ben reveal Willy's fears about his inadequacies and his uncertainties about himself?
10. What is Linda's attitude toward Biff and Happy? Why does she say of Willy, "But he's a human being, and a terrible thing is happening to him. So attention must be paid"? How do her sons react to her revelations about Willy's behavior?
11. Why has Biff been unsuccessful in his attempts to work in business? What does he believe his family should do? What does Biff tell Willy he actually is going to do? Why does he suggest that he may try to go into business? What is Willy's reaction to this proposal? In what ways is this reaction in keeping with Willy's character?
12. Throughout Act 1, Willy contradicts himself. What do you believe are the reasons for this? Is Willy mentally unbalanced, is his existence a contradictory one, or is there some other explanation? Defend your choice with examples of his behavior.

Act 2

13. What is Willy's problem with appliances and automobiles? Is this problem typical of American-made goods? Why or why not?
14. What relationship exists between Howard and Willy? What sections of dialogue and stage directions help to clarify this relationship?
15. Why does Willy admire Dave Singleman? Contrast Willy's name with the name of his hero. In what ways are these names symbolic of the character and fortune of each man?

16. When Howard leaves, Willy recalls a conversation with Ben. How do Ben and Willy view success? Do you think either of them is correct? Why or why not? What role does Linda play in Willy's decision?

17. How does Bernard's reluctance to mention that he is arguing a case before the Supreme Court contrast with the actions of Willy and his sons? Why wouldn't Willy accept help from his friend Charlie? What are the principal ways in which Willy and Charlie are different?

18. What factors make it difficult for Biff to tell his father the truth about his visit with Bill Oliver? What weaknesses does Biff display as he tries to face reality? Do you blame Biff for his behavior? Why or why not?

19. Willy's reminiscences of Biff's visit to Boston help to clarify some of the unexplained behavior of the characters in the play. How does this incident help to account for Biff's attitude toward his father? How does it help to explain Biff's position in life?

20. What is Linda's attitude toward her sons when they return? Is she right to blame Biff and Happy for their behavior toward their father? Why or why not?

21. What factors lead to Willy's decision to take his own life? Why does he hesitate at first? What finally causes him to make up his mind?

Requiem

22. Why does Arthur Miller call the final section of the play the "Requiem"? How does Willy's funeral serve to emphasize the contrast between appearance and reality in Willy's life?

WRITING ACTIVITIES

1. Review the list of qualities an individual needs to be successful. (*See* "Initiating Activity" 1.) Write an essay addressed to the other members of your class in which you evaluate the character of Willy Loman in terms of the items on the list. At the end of the essay, summarize your evaluation of Willy Loman. Compare your essay with others written by your classmates. In what ways do you agree in your evaluation and in what ways do you disagree? Discuss these differences and try to determine the reasons behind them.

2. Write an obituary for Willy Loman that he would like to have written about his life. Before you do this, check your local newspaper to determine the kind of information that should be included and the style that is most often used. Then rewrite the obituary as Linda or Charlie would have written it. What are the major differences?

3. Review the play and note the references to seeds and planting that you find. Write an essay in which you examine the symbolic significance of seeds in *Death of a Salesman.* Consider some of the following questions: Why is Willy so concerned about planting and growing something? Why is he unable to succeed in his gardening? How is Willy's life symbolized by the futility of his efforts to make something grow?

4. In the "Requiem," each of the major characters makes a statement that summarizes his role in the play. Write a brief character sketch of Biff, Linda, and Happy in which you use the statements that follow as a starting point.

a. Biff: I know who I am, kid.
b. Linda: I can't understand it, Willy.
c. Happy: Willy Loman did not die in vain. He had a good dream. It's the only dream you can have—to come out number-one man.

5. Although Willy does not leave any messages for his family, the dialogue, particularly his conversation with Ben, indicates his reasons for suicide. Write a suicide note that Willy might have left for his family. As you prepare the note, keep in mind Willy's inability to face the truth about himself and his family.
6. Write a short story in which you follow the fortunes of Biff or Happy Loman after the death of their father. In the story, explore their futures, but keep in mind all that you have learned about their characters throughout the play.
7. *Death of a Salesman* presents a contrast in values such as sources of happiness, importance of money, importance of family, and honesty. Prepare a chart on which you list the values of each of the following characters: Willy Loman, Ben, Charlie, Linda, Biff, and Happy. Compare your chart with those made by other members of your class. Discuss the similarities and differences that occurred in your charts.
8. Literary scholars have long debated whether or not Willy Loman is a tragic hero. Establish your own definition of a tragic hero by checking several sources that define literary terms. Then decide if you think Willy Loman is indeed a tragic hero. Write a persuasive essay to support your position. You may also want to read Arthur Miller's own views on the subject in "Tragedy and the Common Man" (*Theater Arts* 35 (March 1951), 48–50).

OTHER ACTIVITIES

1. Design the cover of a playbill for a production of *Death of a Salesman*. Your drawing should arouse interest in the play and suggest one or more of its themes.
2. Willy Loman was besieged by a number of forces, both internal and external, that shaped his life and destiny. Design a mobile that illustrates these forces and how they pulled Willy in different directions.
3. The stage directions for the play call for music to indicate time or to underscore mood. Prepare a tape of music you think would be appropriate for use in a production of *Death of a Salesman.* Play appropriate sections of the tape as your classmates read the play aloud. Ask your classmates to comment on the mood the music evoked in them.
4. Choose a scene from the play that illustrates Willy's tendency to function in the past and the present simultaneously. Act out this scene with your classmates. Afterwards, discuss the techniques Miller uses to help the audience sort out the action.
5. Prepare a collage that represents the character of Willy Loman. You may want to include pictures from magazines, clippings from newsprint, and real objects or bits and pieces of real objects.
6. From one of the following lines taken directly from the play, derive a resolution to be debated by several members of the class:

   a. "Be liked and you will never want."
   b. "Never leave a job till you're finished."

c. "A man who can't handle tools is not a man."
d. "Never fight fair with a stranger."
e. "Start big and you'll end big."
f. "Personality always wins the day."
g. "The only thing you got in this world is what you can sell."
h. "Nobody's worth nothin' dead."
i. "No man only needs a little salary."

Example of a resolution based on item i: American business must begin to make efforts to reduce the level of salary expectations among American workers.

SELECTED TEACHING RESOURCES

Media Aids

Cassette (1)

Death of a Salesman and The Crucible. Abridged. Sundance.

Cassette (2)

Death of a Salesman. Perfection Learning Corporation.

Internet

Death of a Salesman by Arthur Miller. Available: http://www.windnet.com/mki/books/d/death_of_a_salesman.html (Accessed March 10, 2000).
A link to a variety of sources on Arthur Miller and on *Death of a Salesman*.

Video

Death of a Salesman. 135 min., color. Dustin Hoffman version. Guidance Associates.

Printed Resources

Article

Zorn, Theodore E. "Willy Loman's Lesson: Teaching Identity Management with *Death of a Salesman*." *Communication Education* 40 (April 1991): 219–224.

Book

Bloom, Harold (ed.). *Arthur Miller's* Death of a Salesman. Bloom's Notes Series. Bloomall, PA: Chelsea House Publishers, 1996.

Teaching Aids

Death of a Salesman. Contemporary Classics series. Perfection Learning Corporation.

Death of a Salesman. Dramatic Ideas Plus series. Sundance.

Death of a Salesman. Literature Unit Plans. Teacher's Pet Publications.

Death of a Salesman. Novel/Drama Curriculum Units. The Center for Learning.

Death of a Salesman. Novel-Ties. Learning Links.

Death of a Salesman. Novel Unit Guide. Novel Units Student Packet, and Perma-Guide. Perma-Bound.

Tests

Death of a Salesman. Essay, objective, and alternative assessment versions. Perfection Learning Corporation.

Their Eyes Were Watching God

Zora Neale Hurston

New York: J. B. Lippincott, 1937

Available in paperback from HarperPerennial,
a division of HarperCollins Publishers.

SUMMARY

As a child, Janie Crawford is unaware that she is not like the white folks her grandma works for until she sees herself for the first time in a photograph. As she grows to young adulthood, she stretches beneath the blooming pear tree and is impatient for love. However, when Johnny Taylor comes along, her grandma is so concerned about her future that she marries Janie off to Brother Logan Killicks, an older man who owns a house and sixty acres. At first her husband worships her, but soon she is treated much like his mule. One day while Logan is gone, Joe Starks comes by the house and soon convinces Janie to run off with him to Florida and get married. Once Joe and Janie get to Eatonville, Joe proves himself a leader, opens a store, builds a home, and is proclaimed mayor of the town. Janie is then given another role to fill: As the mayor's wife she is allowed to work in the store but is not allowed to fraternize with the townspeople or enjoy their social activities. Joe grows fat and belligerent, and soon dies, leaving her a woman of property. When Tea Cake, a man younger than she is, comes into her life, she is cautious at first, but is quickly taken in by his charm. Tea Cake treats her as an equal; teaches her to fish, play cards, and enjoy life; and provides the blooming pear tree for her that she sought for so long. After they are married in Jacksonville, they move to the Everglades, where Tea Cake and Janie work the bean fields and host parties in their hut for the other workers. Only the threat of a hurricane disturbs their joyful existence, and when they fail to heed its warning signs, they must flee before the storm's rage. When Janie is nearly drowned and is attacked by a mad dog, Tea Cake jumps in to save her and is bitten himself. A few weeks later when Tea Cake shows signs of rabies, Janie seeks help from the doctor, but it is too late. In a rage brought on by the disease, Tea Cake threatens to kill Janie, so Janie must shoot him in self-defense. The trial is swift and Janie is released to bury Tea Cake in grand style and return to her home in Eatonville, satisfied with the one love that has given her what she had been seeking her whole life.

APPRAISAL

Their Eyes Were Watching God is Zora Neale Hurston's most highly praised novel; in fact, some critics have placed it alongside the works of Faulkner, Hemingway, and Fitzgerald. During her career, Hurston was often criticized for not writing protest fiction by her colleagues, including Richard Wright, who felt the novel was without message, theme, or thought. In 1972, Alice Walker was teaching the novel and discovered that Hurston was buried in an unmarked grave. Her essay, "Looking for Zora," marked the beginning of a new era in the critical evaluation and heightened appreciation of this masterfully written classic of Afro-American literature, which is most appropriate for eleventh and twelfth graders.

THEMES

love, success, friendship, racial relations, self-realization, self-fulfillment, happiness, empowerment, jealousy

LITERARY CONCEPTS

flashback, reverie, character development, dialect, symbolism, tall tales, metaphor, simile, personification, oxymoron, lyrical novel, first-person point of view, third-person point of view, free and indirect discourse, feminist novel

RELATED READING

Other books by Zora Neale Hurston include *Jonah's Gourd Vine, Tell My House, Mules and Men,* and *Dust Tracks on the Road.* Other strong African-American heroines can be found in *The Color Purple* by Alice Walker and *Beloved* by Toni Morrison. In addition, Virginia Hamilton has provided readers with such outstanding figures as *Zeely*. Students who appreciate Hurston's style might also relish the short stories in *Cane* by Jean Toomer.

READING PROBLEMS AND OPPORTUNITIES

Their Eyes Were Watching God is a treasure trove of opportunities for study of an author's exquisite use of language. The first hurdle that some students will have to overcome is the use of black dialect, slang, and some dated words and expressions. In addition, students must be ready to appreciate a novel that often reads like a poem. Figurative language abounds and while it may slow down the reader, its truth and eloquence make it worth the necessary contemplation. The following list contains only words that require dictionary study; later activities will focus on dialect and figurative language (chapter numbers are given in parentheses).

pugnacious, pugnaciously (1, 7)
languid (2),
lacerating (2),
desecrating (2),
conjecture (3),
mien (3),
incredulous (5),
temerity (5),
fractious (6),
gaiters (6),
discomfiture (6),
prostrating (7),
stolidness (7),
promontories (7),
ostentatiously (8),
excruciating (11),
languished (12),
transmutation (16),
defilement (16),
oblique (18), and
fetid (20).

INITIATING ACTIVITIES

1. Research the Harlem Renaissance to determine when it took place, what writers were key to its success, what caused this Renaissance, and what effects it had on later literary works. Prepare a report on the Harlem Renaissance for your classmates. You may choose to illustrate your report with pictures of important authors and/or short selections from their works. Be sure to include your appraisal of the importance of this Renaissance.
2. What do you think is the ideal relationship between a husband and wife? Should one direct the activities of the other? Is one partner better suited to make decisions than the other? Discuss these ideas with your classmates and attempt to arrive at a consensus.

DISCUSSION QUESTIONS

1. *Chapter 1:* Why does Janie Stark arouse so much interest on her return to town? What is the relationship between Janie and Phoeby? Who do you think Tea Cake is?
2. *Chapter 2:* Compare and contrast Janie's view of kissing Johnny Taylor with Nanny's view of the same act. What does the pear tree symbolize? Why is Nanny so set on Janie's marrying Logan Killicks? Why does Janie object? Why is Nanny "a cracked plate"?
3. *Chapter 3:* Why does Janie go to visit Nanny? What advice does Nanny give her? Is it good advice? Why or why not? How does Janie become a woman?
4. *Chapter 4:* How does Joe Starks seek to win Janie over? Why does Janie decide to go with him?
5. *Chapter 5:* Why is Joe Starks able to take charge in Eatonville? How does Janie feel about her so-called elevated status as the mayor's wife? How does Mayor Starks move the community forward? Why do some of the townspeople have both good and bad feelings about Joe Starks and his possessions?
6. *Chapter 6:* Why do the townspeople make up stories about Matt Bonner's mule? How does Mayor Starks use the mule and its death to his advantage? Why does Joe exclude Janie from the activities of the townspeople? How are the actions of the buzzards like the actions of the people of Eatonville? What are the real purposes of the dramas (discussions of nature versus caution, Daisy and her suitors) that are played out on the porch of the store? What does Janie come to realize about her relationship with Jody? How do you think this will affect their lives together in the future?
7. *Chapter 7:* Why does Jody verbally attack Janie? Why does Janie respond as she does? Why does Jody physically attack Janie?
8. *Chapter 8:* How does Jody deceive himself about his illness? Why is Janie unable to help him, even when he is near death? What are her emotional responses to his death?
9. *Chapter 9:* How does Janie cope with Joe's death and the onslaught of suitors that follows? Why does she believe that "mourning oughtn't tuh last no longer 'n grief"?
10. *Chapter 10:* Why is Janie able to get along so well with Tea Cake? In what ways does he treat her differently than her two first husbands did?
11. *Chapter 11:* Describe the emotions that Janie experiences as her relationship with Tea Cake develops. In what ways is he good for her? In what ways might he be bad for her?

12. *Chapter 12:* Why doesn't Phoeby understand Janie's love for Tea Cake? How has Janie's attitude toward life and marriage changed? Do you think Janie is making a mistake by going off with Tea Cake? Why or why not?
13. *Chapter 13:* Why is Janie afraid during the times that Tea Cake is gone? What character flaws does Tea Cake reveal? How does Janie respond to these flaws? How is it possible that Janie's soul "crawled out from its hiding place"?
14. *Chapter 14:* Why is Janie so comfortable with her life on the muck? Why does she agree to work in the bean fields?
15. *Chapter 15:* What does Tea Cake say about his relationship with Nunkie? What do you believe is his relationship with her?
16. *Chapter 16:* Why does Mrs. Turner want to be friends with Janie? Why does Tea Cake want her to stay away from Janie? How does Mrs. Turner establish a pecking order among her acquaintances?
17. *Chapter 17:* How does Tea Cake drive off Mrs. Turner? What is the irony in his plan?
18. *Chapter 18:* Why do Tea Cake and the others ignore the warning signs of an approaching storm? How are Tea Cake and Janie able to keep going and outrun the oncoming water? How does Tea Cake save Janie's life?
19. *Chapter 19:* Why does Tea Cake want to go back to the Glades? Why does Janie agree? How do Tea Cake and Janie cope with his illness? Why doesn't the doctor move him to the hospital? Why is Janie found not guilty of murdering Tea Cake?
20. *Chapter 20:* Why is Mrs. Turner's brother driven away? Why is Janie happy and contented after she returns to her home?

WRITING ACTIVITIES

1. Nanny explains Logan's actions to Janie in this way: "He ain't kissin' yo' mouf when he carry on over yuh lak dat. He's kissin' yo' foot and 'tain't in uh man tuh kiss foot long." Write a letter to Janie explaining why you think Nanny's advice is good or not so good. You may use examples from the book, but don't tell Janie how her life with Logan will turn out. You may also use examples from other novels or from your own experience.
2. In his conversations with Hicks, Coker observes, "Us colored folks is too envious of one 'nother. Dat's how come us don't git no further than us do. Us talks about de white man keepin' us down! Shucks! He don't have tuh. Us keeps our own selves down." Research the essays and speeches of Arthur Ashe and Jesse Jackson. Do you find a similar theme in their writings? Write a short speech that Ashe or Jackson might have given to Coker in response to his observation.
3. One of the favorite games at the store was to poke fun at Matt Bonner's yellow mule. Review some of the tales in chapter 6 and then try your hand at writing a tall tale about the mule. Get together with several of your classmates and tell your tales as if all of you were sitting on the front porch of the store.
4. In chapter 6 the men talk about the way to treat women. Why do some of the men feel that hitting women is justified? How does Janie respond to their ideas? Rewrite the scene and become a character in it. Respond to the men's ideas and to Janie's. The format should be

simple: Just list the character who is speaking, put a colon after the name, and then begin the dialogue.

5. Chapter 14 contains descriptions of the migrant workers who come to Florida to pick beans. Prepare an analysis of their lifestyle, using the information in this chapter and other information gathered from library and Internet sources, if necessary. Include in your analysis the following components: their value system, their needs, their hopes, their pleasures, and their dreams.

6. *Their Eyes Were Watching God* is written using free, indirect discourse, that is, a blend of first- and third-person point of view. Select one chapter from the novel and examine carefully the use of point of view. While the story appears to unfold as a third-person narration, various observations are from Janie's mind or come occasionally from the thoughts of other key characters. In an essay for your classmates, explain how the third- and first-person point of view can be separated, and then how Hurston smoothly ties them back together in a unified work of art.

7. Throughout the novel, figurative language (metaphors, similes, personifications, oxymora) abound. The following short list contains only some examples of Hurston's compelling uses of poetic language (chapter numbers are listed in parentheses):

   a familiar strangeness (5),
   like a hen on a hot brick (6),
   she was a rut in the road (7),
   eat out of a long-handled spoon (8),
   an oxen's foot on her tongue (8),
   good meat on yo' head (10),
   keep hisself in changing clothes (11),
   got de world in uh jug (11),
   stuffing courage into each other's ears (18), and
   tongues cocked and loaded (19).

   For each of these examples, and others that you find, list at least one common example of figurative language that means nearly the same thing; for example *an oxen's foot on her tongue* = *a cat got her tongue*. Choose five of these examples and write an essay explaining and justifying the author's choice of language over conventional forms.

8. Write a comparison/contrast essay of Janie's life with each of her three husbands. Focus on the traditional values that are associated with a successful marriage. Explore the values that Janie sought in her life. Explain how each of her husbands did or did not fulfill the traditional roles of husband and Janie's ideal of a husband.

9. Janie explains what love is in chapter 20: "Love is lak de sea. It's uh movin' thing, but still and all, it takes its shape from de shore it meets, and it's different with every shore." Try your hand at a definition of love from the viewpoint of the three main male characters in the book: Logan, Joe, and Tea Cake. Share these definitions with others in your class, but don't include the name of the character, to see how well you have captured the values and emotions of each.

10. Explore the ways in which this novel empowers women. In a letter to a friend, describe how this empowerment takes place through the course of the novel. Evaluate the author's success in presenting the quest for self-realization and empowerment that Janie pursued.

OTHER ACTIVITIES

1. Janie liked the way that people sat around the store and passed around pictures of their thoughts. In fact, she especially liked it because "the thought pictures were always crayon enlargements" (chapter 6). Try your hand at a "crayon enlargement" of one of the stories that is told in this novel. Ask your classmates to comment on how successful you were in creating a visual picture of a word picture.
2. Prepare a graph of the growth of the relationship between Janie and Tea Cake. Identify key points in their relationship along the high and low points of the graph. Ask your classmates to review your work and add to the graph if they feel it is warranted. Keep modifying the graph until everyone involved is satisfied that it is an accurate representation of the growth of their relationship.
3. The title of this novel is found in chapter 18 in the description of the beginning of the hurricane. Reread that section and create a visual presentation of that scene that could be used for the cover of the book or as a poster to market the book. Choose your medium carefully so that it is possible to depict the fury and strength of nature about to be unleashed against the people awaiting the storm's wrath, immobilized by the insignificance they felt.
4. The dialect used by the characters in the book serves a variety of purposes: It heightens the realism of the story, it adds flavor to the figurative language, and it underscores, in some cases, the world view of the characters. Select one of these purposes and find examples in the novel that illustrate this purpose. Prepare an audio or videotape in which you present your findings. For example, if you looked for realism, you might select terms such as *kerflommuck, boogerboo,* and *jook* (this sample represents just a few of the many terms to be found) and explain their meaning, as well as discuss why they were appropriate for the time and place in which they were used.
5. Many myths exist about animal behavior. Select a reputable source and determine if the behavior attributed to the animals before and during the hurricane is consistent with biological studies on animal behavior. Present your findings to the class in an illustrated talk.
6. Improvise Janie's trial (chapter 19), filling in some of the details omitted in the novel by providing dialogue that would be appropriate for the characters in this scene. Remember, it is not necessary to memorize any lines; simply understand the plot of the story and be very familiar with the character you are playing so you can consistently respond to others in an appropriate fashion. After the improvisation, discuss your thoughts and feelings about the character you portrayed with your classmates.

SELECTED TEACHING RESOURCES

Media Aids

Cassettes (2)

Their Eyes Were Watching God. Abridged. Perfection Learning Corporation and Sundance.

Internet

Zora Neale Hurston. Available: http://pages.prodigy.com/zora/content.htm (Accessed March 10, 2000).

An exciting site that contains interesting information about the author, as well as opportunities for interaction, and links to useful websites.

Printed Resources

Article

Greene, Brenda M. "Addressing Race, Class, and Gender in Zora Neale Hurston's *Their Eyes Were Watching God*: Strategies and Reflections." *English Education* 27 (December 1995): 268–276.

Book

Bloom, Harold, ed. *Zora Neale Hurston's* Their Eyes Were Watching God. New York: Chelsea House Publishers, 1987.

Teaching Aids

Their Eyes Were Watching God. Contemporary Classics series. Perfection Learning Corporation.

Their Eyes Were Watching God. Literature Unit Plans. Teacher's Pet Publications.

Their Eyes Were Watching God. Novel/Drama Curriculum Units. The Center for Learning.

Their Eyes Were Watching God. Novel Ideas Plus—New Voices series. Sundance.

Their Eyes Were Watching God. Perma-Guide. Perma-Bound.

Tests

Their Eyes Were Watching God. Essay, objective, and alternative assessment versions. Perfection Learning Corporation.

Lord of the Flies

William Golding

New York: Coward, McCann & Geoghegan, 1955

Available in paperback from Perigee.

SUMMARY

When a group of young boys find themselves stranded on an island following a plane crash during an atomic war, they form a society of their own. Ralph and Piggy summon the others by blowing on a conch shell, and the former is elected chief over Jack, whose choirboys are declared hunters. After a signal fire is lit, Ralph sets the reluctant group to building shelters, but the split between him and Jack widens when the fire is allowed to die because the boys go off to hunt pigs. The group is further divided by the fear of an unknown beast, in reality the body of a dead airman. When Simon returns from climbing a mountain to discover the true identity of the beast, he is accidentally killed by the group during a frenzied dance. The society continues to degenerate as Jack and his followers adopt a more savage appearance and behavior. When Ralph and his few remaining followers approach Jack's fortress, they are scorned, Piggy is killed, and Ralph becomes a fugitive hunted by Jack's young savages. Ralph is finally saved from a conflagration intended to flush him out by the crew members of a passing naval ship, who spot the smoke and rescue the boys.

APPRAISAL

After a slow beginning, *Lord of the Flies* became a runaway best-seller on college campuses in the early 1960s, required reading for most students. Like many other novels, it has since filtered down to high schools where the book has become a modern classic. Its popularity was newly enhanced in 1983 by Golding's selection as a Nobel Prize laureate. Although the novel may have less impact today than it did in 1955, many students still feel the influence of its terror and suspense and wonder about the human savagery it depicts as well as its grim avowal of original sin as the root of social problems. The novel is taught throughout high school (and sometimes below), but seems most appropriate for the upper grades.

THEMES

good versus evil, savagery versus civilization, original sin, survival, fear, friendship, initiation

LITERARY CONCEPTS

symbol, allegory and fable, plot, characterization, setting, foreshadowing, metaphor, deus ex machina

RELATED READING

Perhaps the most compelling recent novel to compare with *Lord of the Flies* is *John Dollar* by Marianne Wiggins, the story of eight schoolgirls who are similarly shipwrecked on an island and forced to develop a structured society. There are many other books about survival, of course, from *Robinson Crusoe* by Daniel Defoe and the young adult novel *Sweet Friday Island* by Theodore Taylor to nonfiction like *Alive! The Story of the Andes Survivors* by Piers Paul Read. Other novels depicting the loss of youthful innocence in a world where evil is dominant are *Billy Budd* by Henry Melville and *The Chocolate War* by Robert Cormier. *Lord of the Flies* was adapted for the stage in 1996 by Nigel Williams and published as a play by Faber and Faber.

READING PROBLEMS AND OPPORTUNITIES

Related by an omniscient narrator, *Lord of the Flies* is a far-from-easy book. The compelling plot, however, will enable many readers to overcome the stumbling blocks posed by difficult words, many of which can be profitably used for vocabulary study. They include the following (chapter numbers are provided in parentheses):

effulgence (1),
enmity (1),
fronds (1, 8, 12),
strident (1),
incredulous (1, 3, 4),
furtive (1, 3, 7, 8),
pallidly (1),
mortification (1),
suffusion (1),
pliant (1),
hiatus (1),
gesticulated (2, 3, 5, 10),
conspiratorial (2),
errant (2),
ebullience (2),
recrimination (2),
tirade (2),
festooned (3, 9),
abyss (3),
inscrutable (3),
vicissitudes (3),
declivities (3),
blatant (4),
incursion (4),
detritus (4),
myriad (4),
tacitly (4),
gyration (4),
ineffectual (5, 11),
perilous (5),
tempestuously (5),
tremulously (6, 8, 9),
embroiled (6),
diffidently (6),
impenetrable (6, 11),
stupendous (6),
leviathan (6),
infuriatingly (7),
covert (7, 8, 12),
succulent (9),
torrid (10),
assimilating (10),
multitudinous (11),
ludicrous (11),
derisive (11),
truculently (11),
cessation (11),
talisman (11),
inimitable (12),
antiphonal (12),
cordon (12),
elephantine (12), and
ululate (12).

INITIATING ACTIVITIES

1. Imagine that you and a group of your friends have been stranded on a desert island without provisions. Make a list of the ten most important things that would need to be done to assure your survival and comfort. When you have created the list, place your procedures in priority order. Save the list for a later activity.
2. With your classmates, debate the following premise: Humans are basically and inherently evil. You may defend the position, pro or con, from any of a number of stances: social, religious, political, historical, and so forth.

DISCUSSION QUESTIONS

1. *Chapter 1 (The Sound of the Shell):* Where do the boys land? What circumstances bring them there? What is Piggy like? What is Ralph's attitude toward him? Cite specific actions and bits of conversation to support your answer. Why is Ralph pleased with their situation? What effect does the sound of the conch have? How do the members of the choir react to Jack Merridew? Why is Ralph elected chief? What do you consider to be the qualities of a good leader? What does Ralph say to placate Jack? Why does Jack want the choirboys to become hunters? What does he seem to be obsessed by? Why is he unable to kill the pig? In general, how do the boys feel about being on the island?
2. *Chapter 2 (Fire on the Mountain):* What becomes the function of the conch? What does it symbolize? Why do the boys fear the beast? Why do you think Golding includes it here as a topic of concern among them? Do you think the fire is a good method to assure a rescue? Why or why not? What rational actions do the boys take? What irrational actions? What role does Piggy take in evaluating the actions of the group? What do you think happened to the boy with the birthmark?
3. *Chapter 3 (Huts on the Beach):* Up to this point, what do you know about Ralph? About Jack? Why do they conflict with each other? In what ways is Ralph slightly critical of the others? What problems does he encounter in trying to get the shelters built? Why is Jack so intent on hunting? What aspects of life on the island do the boys like? What do they dislike? Are their actions typical only of children or of people in general? Why? Recall the fable of the ant and the grasshopper. How are the boys like the insects in the story? At this point, is the society they have established functioning smoothly? Why or why not? What kind of person is Simon? How do the others view him?
4. *Chapter 4 (Painted Faces and Long Hair):* How do the "littluns" occupy their time? What do the actions of Maurice and Roger toward them suggest about their basic nature? Do you believe that most people would act like this? Why or why not? When Roger throws the stones at Henry, why doesn't he aim to hit? Why is Piggy an outsider? Why is the fire allowed to die out? How does Jack rationalize his behavior in allowing this to happen? What are the possible ramifications of his action? How does Ralph try to deal with this problem? What else might he have done? Jack defends himself by saying, "We needed meat." Is this true? What mood are the boys in as the chapter ends?
5. *Chapter 5 (Beast from Water):* How does Ralph come to appreciate Piggy despite his physical defects? Why does Ralph try to establish some fixed rules for the group? Why doesn't the assembly go the way he had planned? What does Ralph consider most important? How do the boys respond to the talks about the beast? What does Simon mean when he says, "Maybe it's only us"? Why is it impossible for the boys to decide on the possibility of

the beast's existence? What forces are working in their minds? What does Ralph mean when he says the rules are the only thing the group has? Piggy believes that the presence of grownups would make things all right: "Grownups know things; they ain't afraid of the dark. They'd meet and have tea and discuss. Then things 'ud be all right." Do you agree with him? Why or why not?

6. *Chapter 6 (Beast from Air):* What elements of nature help to create the beast that the boys so greatly fear? How does Jack taunt Ralph into joining the hunt for the beast? Should Ralph have allowed Jack to do this? Why or why not? How do Jack's speeches show that the democracy is breaking down? Simon is the only one who rationally considers what the beast might be. Why is he unable to communicate his deductions to the others? Why does Jack join Ralph on his exploration? Why do the two of them view the half-cave so differently? Why is Ralph so adamant about continuing the climb up the mountain?

7. *Chapter 7 (Shadows and Tall Trees):* At this point, it is clear that Ralph is losing his control over the boys. Why? Why is he content to abandon the climb for a while to allow time for the hunt? What purpose does the inclusion of Ralph's daydreams about home serve? How does he react to the hunt? Is this an indication of a change in his priorities? Why or why not? What urges does he feel during the game with Robert? Do you think these urges are universal? Why or why not? What forces influence Ralph in his decision about whether or not to continue up the mountain? What would you have done in his place? Why? How do Ralph, Jack, and Roger express their fear of the beast?

8. *Chapter 8 (Gift for the Darkness):* Why does Jack call a meeting? Throughout the novel, although the characters and events represent something larger than themselves, Golding is careful to have his youthful characters behave like children. How is Jack's behavior after not being elected chief like the behavior of children in general? What is Simon's plan for dealing with the beast? Why don't the others accept it? How does Piggy save the day with his suggestion? Why do the boys so readily agree to it? What definite split has now taken place in the society? What two ideas do these two groups represent? If you had been on the island, which group would you have joined? Why? In what ways does Jack prove himself a capable leader? In what ways is he ineffective? What is the Lord of the Flies? In what ways is this object a symbol? Ralph is puzzled about why "things break up like they do." Why do they and how could such breakups be prevented? Why does Jack steal the fire rather than the conch? Does the Lord of the Flies actually speak to Simon? If not, in what ways is this gruesome object able to speak? Why is the chapter called "Gift for the Darkness"?

9. *Chapter 9 (A View to a Death):* Why does Simon continue to climb the mountain? Why is he alone? Why do Ralph and Piggy decide to attend Jack's feast? Point out the primitive elements in the feast scene. Compare and contrast the advantages that Jack and Ralph offer the other boys in their effort to gain support. After he triumphs, why does Jack suggest that the boys begin the dance? What is the outcome? What has been Simon's function in the novel?

10. *Chapter 10 (The Shell and the Glasses):* In what ways does Piggy try to rationalize the killing of Simon? Is this a typical way people deal with their own evil deeds? Why do Ralph and Samneric join in this practice of rationalizing and making excuses? What clues indicate the extent of Jack's authority? Why do the others allow him to have this power? Can you think of current or historical figures who have had similar power? Why does Ralph despair for the future of his little band and the hope of a rescue? Why do Jack and his hunters attack Ralph and Piggy?

11. *Chapter 11 (Castle Rock):* What basis of right and wrong is Piggy planning to use in his appeal to Jack to give back his glasses? Is this a realistic approach for him to take? Why or why not? What vestiges of civilization do the members of Ralph's group hope to use to win Jack and his followers over? Why does Piggy cling so to Ralph? How does Jack deter Ralph from his original purpose? Why is the group silent when Piggy holds up the conch? Is Piggy's death an act of deliberate murder or a childish prank? Discuss.
12. *Chapter 12 (Cry of the Hunters):* What realities is Ralph forced to face? Why do Samneric refuse to help him? Would you have behaved in the same way? Why or why not? In what ways is Ralph still able to think rationally? In what ways does his reasoning fail him? How does Golding build suspense throughout the chase scene? How has Ralph become like the boys who are chasing him? A fire is built to flush Ralph out, but what, ironically, does the fire do? How does the behavior of the boys change upon the arrival of the naval officer? Are the boys now returning to a world that is more moral and civilized than the one they are leaving? Discuss.

WRITING ACTIVITIES

1. Review the list you made in Initiating Activity 1. Compare your list with the actions taken by the boys in the book. Write a comparison/contrast essay that points out and explains the similarities and differences in the two lists.
2. Jack and his hunters engage in chants during their hunts and ritual dances, such as "Kill the pig! Cut his throat! Kill the pig! Bash him in!" Write at least three chants that Ralph and his followers might have used to counter those of the other group. The chants should reflect the concerns of this group and they should be catchy.
3. Often, the boys on the island choose to have fun and ignore their responsibilities. In particular, the boys who are supposed to tend the fire elect to go off and hunt, thus letting the fire go out and foregoing a chance for rescue. Write about a time when you ignored responsibilities to satisfy an immediate desire.
4. Throughout the novel, symbols are evident. Choose one of the following and explore its possible meanings:

   a. the pig's head on a stake—Lord of the Flies

   b. fire

   c. Piggy's spectacles

   d. the conch

   Explain your conclusions in an essay.
5. When Ralph decides to climb the mountain at night, the group is convinced that the beast exists because the boys do not get a good look at the dead airman. Prepare an outline of another ending for the novel, including events that might have occurred if Ralph had chosen to climb the mountain in the daylight.
6. Write two eulogies for Simon or Piggy: one as Ralph might have composed it and the other as Jack might have.

7. Write an imaginary television interview that might have taken place after the boys returned home. Choose at least two of the major characters to take part in the interview and formulate at least ten sets of questions and answers. Remember that the responses of the boys to the questions may be based more on what they want others to know than on what really happened.

8. Several parallel incidents occur in the novel. Choose one of these from the list below:

   a. the fire set by the boys when they first arrive and the fire set at the end of the novel

   b. the rock that the three boys send smashing over the cliff in chapter 1 and the rock that kills Piggy in chapter 11

   c. Ralph's dance in chapter 4 and the dance by the group in chapter 9

   Write a paper in which you compare and contrast these parallel events. Explain why the author included them in the novel.

9. We aren't sure how much the naval officer believes of what Ralph tells him at the end of the book. Write a letter the officer might have written home to his wife that evening describing the incident and his feelings about it.

10. You are Ralph twenty years after the book ends. The family of Simon has requested that you contribute a brief written remembrance of the boy to be made part of a memorial tribute. Write your memories and thoughts of Simon.

OTHER ACTIVITIES

1. Construct a mask to show how Jack paints his face to look like a savage. Refer to chapters 4, 9, and 11 for suggestions regarding form and color. Papier-mâché would be an effective medium to use.

2. With several other students, enact the assembly that occurs in chapter 5. Add dialogue and group responses as appropriate. It is more important that the mood of the meeting be conveyed than the exact lines from the book.

3. Prepare two drawings of the beast (the dead airman): one as Ralph, Jack, Roger, and Samneric see it and the other as Simon sees it. You may wish to use two different media to create different effects.

4. Prepare a collage that represents the darker side of humanity. Use pictures from newspapers and magazines, clippings of words and phrases, headlines, and so forth.

5. Act out a conversation between Ralph, Jack, Samneric, and Roger at a reunion of the group twenty-five years after their experience on the island. What would they have to say to each other? What comments would they make about such issues as nuclear disarmament? How would Ralph and Jack relate to each other after the lapse of time? Keep in mind their basic natures as presented in the novel.

6. Assume that Ralph is killed and the ship does not arrive. Design a flag that Jack might have created for his tribe or society. Use design and color to convey the group's priorities.

SELECTED TEACHING RESOURCES

Media Aids

Cassettes (6)

Lord of the Flies. Unabridged. Read by the author. Listening Library and Perma-Bound.

Internet

Fischer, Hans G., 1999. *Golding, William: 1911–1993*. Available: http://educeth.ethz.ch/english/readinglist/golding,william.html. (Accessed March 10, 2000).

A useful resource for teachers, with a biography, bibliography, photograph, character sketches, and analyses as well as comments from students and teachers.

Videos

Lord of the Flies. 100 min., color. Clearvue/eav, Perma-Bound, and Sundance, 1963.

William Golding. 55 min., color. Films for the Humanities & Sciences.

Printed Materials

Articles

Ely, Sister M. Amanda. "The Adult Image in Three Novels of Adolescent Life." *English Journal* 56 (November 1967): 1127–1131.

Gulbin, Suzanne. "Parallels and Contrasts in *Lord of the Flies* and *Animal Farm*." *English Journal* 55 (January 1966): 86–88, 92.

Lederer, Richard H. "Student Reactions to *Lord of the Flies*." *English Journal* 53 (November 1964): 575–579.

Lederer, Richard H., and Rev. Paul Hamilton Beattie. "*African Genesis* and *Lord of the Flies*: Two Studies of the Beastie Within." *English Journal* 58 (December 1969): 1316–1321, 1337.

Martin, Jerome. "Symbol Hunting: Golding's *Lord of the Flies*." *English Journal* 58 (March 1969): 408–413.

Saldivar, Rhonda. "Piggy's Spectacles: A Unifying Element in *Lord of the Flies*." *English in Texas* 26 (Spring 1995): 52–53.

Veidemanis, Gladys. "*Lord of the Flies* in the Classroom: No Passing Fad." *English Journal* 53 (November 1964): 569–574.

Yorke, Malcolm. "Two Popular Books with One Unpopular Message: Man Is a Beast." *Use of English* 25 (Summer 1974): 307–311.

Books

Bloom, Harold, ed. *William Golding's* Lord of the Flies. Bloom's Notes series. Bloomall, PA: Chelsea House Publications, 1996.

Reilly, Patrick. *Lord of the Flies: Fathers and Sons*. New York: Twayne Publishers, 1992.

Teaching Aids

Lord of the Flies. Contemporary Classics series and Latitudes series. Perfection Learning Corporation.

Lord of the Flies. Literature Unit Plans. Teacher's Pet Publications.

Lord of the Flies. Novel Unit Guide, Novel Units Student Packet, and Perma-Guide. Perma-Bound.

Lord of the Flies. Novel/Drama Curriculum Units. The Center for Learning.

Lord of the Flies. Novel-Ties. Learning Links.

Lord of the Flies. REACT series, Novel Ideas Classic, and Novel Ideas Plus series. Sundance.

Tests

Lord of the Flies. Objective, essay, and alternative assessment versions. Perfection Learning Corporation.

Hamlet

William Shakespeare

1603

Play: Available in paperback from several publishing companies.

SUMMARY

The untimely death of his father summons Prince Hamlet from his university studies to the Danish court at Elsinore Castle. On arrival, he is further disturbed by the news that his mother, Gertrude, has hastily married his uncle, Claudius, who has already seized the throne and is trying to prevent the Norwegian prince Fortinbras from invading Denmark. With his friend Horatio and others, Hamlet sees the ghost of his father on a castle rampart, follows him, and learns of his father's murder at the hands of the treacherous Claudius. Hamlet is horrified and vows revenge. To learn the cause of Hamlet's increasingly erratic behavior, Claudius enlists the aid of Hamlet's friends, Rosencrantz and Guildenstern. He also seeks help from Polonius, his vain and pontificating Lord Chamberlain, whose daughter Ophelia has rejected Hamlet's affection at her father's request. The despairing Hamlet confounds them all with "antic behavior," meanwhile considering his means of revenge against Claudius with great anguish and deliberation. When he contrives a "play within a play" to test Claudius, the king implicates himself by bolting from the scene. With this, Hamlet's motivation for vengeance—if not his ability to effect it—is intensified. In a meeting with Gertrude, he kills the eavesdropping Polonius and escapes after disgustedly berating his mother for her sexual attraction to Claudius. Hamlet and Claudius proceed to thrust and parry with each other, the latter finally planning Hamlet's demise by dispatching him to England with Rosencrantz and Guildenstern. Meanwhile, partly in response to her father's death, Ophelia goes mad, and her brother Laertes returns from France, vowing, in stark contrast to Hamlet, to gain immediate revenge. Hamlet, who continues to wrestle with the morality of his actions, manages to escape Claudius's plot against him and returns to Denmark. He requests a meeting with the king, who by now knows of his return and is planning with Laertes to murder him in a duel. When Hamlet discovers at a grave site that Ophelia has killed herself, he confronts Laertes, then regains his self-control and leaves. The final scene includes a fencing duel between Hamlet and Laertes contrived by the latter and Claudius to result in Hamlet's death. In the match, however, the plan is upstaged: Hamlet and Laertes wound each other with the same poisoned sword, which Hamlet then uses to kill Claudius, and Gertrude drinks a cup of poison also intended for Hamlet. Before dying, Hamlet asks Horatio to tell his story and explain his actions. "The rest is silence."

APPRAISAL

This is Shakespeare's longest and most provocative play. Considered by many the greatest literary masterpiece ever written (and Hamlet the most compelling character), the drama has generated more critical commentary than any other Shakespearean play, indeed than any other work. Schools of thought surround it; bibliographies of its criticism run scores of pages. In the word of one critic, the tragedy is "bottomless" in its potential for interpretation and analysis. With scholars and critics unable to agree on its meaning, the play offers high school students (surely seniors for the most part) unlimited opportunities for worthwhile discussion and writing. They may lack the depth of experience to plumb the deeper implications, but with a teacher's help they can productively explore the issues of revenge, guilt, and paralyzing deliberation, among others.

THEMES

revenge, moral behavior, thought versus action, melancholy and depression, evil and treachery, hypocrisy, grief, madness, guilt, honor, death, love, sexuality

LITERARY CONCEPTS

tragedy and the tragic hero, blank verse, imagery, soliloquy, pun, metaphor, symbol, irony (including dramatic irony), setting, plot structure, characterization, reversal, play within a play, aside, allusion, comic relief, foil, synecdoche, hyperbole, stagecraft

RELATED READING

After *Hamlet*, other works of literature may seem almost superfluous. For some students, nonfiction books suggested by some of the play's themes may prove interesting, works like *A Brilliant Madness: Living with Manic-Depressive Illness* by Patty Duke and Gloria Hoffman and *The Moral Animal: Why We Are the Way We Are* by Robert Wright. Certainly other Shakespearean tragedies would serve as compelling reads, especially *King Lear* and *Macbeth*. Some students may also find Tom Stoppard's play *Rosencrantz & Guildenstern Are Dead* worth reading.

READING PROBLEMS AND OPPORTUNITIES

Any of Shakespeare's plays can be counted on to present reading challenges for all but the most discerning and motivated students. Given the length of this play and of some of its scenes, the complexity of the protagonist, and Hamlet's fondness for obscure word play, *Hamlet* is particularly demanding.

As one might expect from any play by Shakespeare, *Hamlet* offers numerous opportunities for vocabulary enrichment. Among the many words to consider for teaching are the following, some of which may be missing from some versions of the play (act and scene numbers are given in parentheses):

apparition (1:1)
usurp (1:1)
brazen (1:1)
invulnerable (1:1)
malicious (1:1; 2:2)
(in)discretion (1:2; 2:1; 2:2; 3:2, 5:2)
auspicious (1:2)
impotent(ce) (1:2; 2:2)
obsequious (1:2)
obstinate (1:2)
dexterity (1:2)
imminent (1:3)
libertine (1:3)
perilous (1:3)

beguile (1:3)
charitable (1:4)
sepulchre (1:4)
enmity (1:5)
fretful (1:5),
pernicious (1:5)
arrant (1:5)
ambiguous (1:5)
perusal (2:1, 4:7)
rebuke (2:2)
promontory (2:2)
pestilent(ce) (2:2, 5:1)
affectation (2:2)
vengeance (2:2)
oppression (2:2)
remorseless (2:2)
lecherous (2:2)
repugnant (2:2)
insolence (3:1)
resolution (3:1)
abominably (3:2)
inexplicable (3:2)
judicious (3:2)
boisterous (3:3)
repentance (3:3)
compulsive (3:4)
abstinence (3:4)
convocation (4:3)
oblivion (4:4)
craven (4:4)
importunate (4:5)
incensed (4:5, 5:2)
negligence (4:5)
abate, abatement (4:7)
circumvent (5:1)
imperious (5:1)
ingenious (5:1), and
palpable (5:2)

INITIATING ACTIVITIES

1. Have students discuss any situation in which they have been confronted with a moral dilemma and delayed their decision. What was the dilemma? What contributed to the difficulty in making the decision? Did anyone help with the problem? How was it finally resolved? What effect did the delay have on the final decision? To what extent was there satisfaction with the outcome? What did you learn from the experience? In general, do you think it is better to make a decision quickly or slowly and carefully?
2. Have students complete, and afterwards discuss, an "opinionnaire" with the following quotes modified from the play (for each statement, indicate *Strongly agree*, *Agree*, *Disagree*, or *Strongly disagree*):
   a. A sin is a sin regardless of how some people may regard it. ("There is nothing either good or bad but thinking makes it so.")
   b. The most important quality a person can have is being honest with himself. ("To thine own self be true.")
   c. Sometimes even irrational or "crazy" behavior can be rooted in logic or common sense. ("Though this be madness, yet there be method in it.")
   d. The worst of people are sometimes those who seem most attractive. ("The devil hath power to assume a pleasing shape.")
   e. The passion of love inevitably weakens with time. ("Time qualifies the spark and fire of [love].")

DISCUSSION QUESTIONS

(*Note: Hamlet* presents several textual problems caused by its early evolution through numerous transcripts and quartos from 1601 to 1623. Thus, scholars disagree on what is the authentic *Hamlet*. The following questions are based on the version of the play edited by Philip Edwards and presented in The New Cambridge Shakespeare series [Cambridge University Press, 1985]. Teachers and students reading other versions should omit questions accordingly.)

1. *Act 1, scene 1:* What do you think Marcellus means by "this thing"? What is Horatio's view of their sightings? When the ghost appears again, who does it seem to be? Why would a "scholar" (i.e., Horatio) know how to address it? Why might it seem "offended"? What does Horatio think the appearance forebodes? What is Marcellus concerned about? Horatio answers his concerns with background information. What is this background that involved "our last king," Fortinbras of Norway, and the latter's young successor? When the ghost reappears, what do you make of its spreading its arms while remaining silent? How do the sentinels react? Why do they plan to tell young Hamlet? What purposes has this introductory scene served?
2. *Act 1, scene 2:* In Claudius's introductory speech, who is the Hamlet to whom he refers? What does he mean by "one auspicious and one dropping eye"? For what does he express gratitude? What is the situation he explains involving Fortinbras? What early thoughts do you have about this new king? What does Laertes want? In his first line, spoken aside, what does young Hamlet mean by "a little more than kin, and less than kind"? What do Claudius and Gertrude ask of Hamlet? How does he explain the nature of his despondency? Describe the relationship that exists at this moment between Hamlet and the royal couple. In Hamlet's soliloquy, what does he wish for? What does he mean by "frailty, thy name is woman"? Do you think his distress is justified? Why or why not? At the end of the scene, what does Hamlet suspect?
3. *Act 1, scene 3:* How does Laertes view Hamlet? Why does he caution his sister Ophelia against him? How does she react? Describe Polonius. How is he like many parents even today? Is his advice to Laertes sound? How do you think Polonius views himself? How does Shakespeare want us to view him? Is his advice to Ophelia regarding Hamlet different from that of Laertes? If so, how? Why does he not want Ophelia to see Hamlet? At this point, how would you describe Ophelia?
4. *Act 1, scene 4:* Before the ghost appears, what feelings does Hamlet reveal about Claudius? About men in general? What is "the stamp of one defect" he speaks of? Do you agree that men and women who are otherwise strong and admirable sometimes have a "tragic flaw"? Why does Hamlet wish to follow the ghost? Why do Horatio and the others try to hold him back? At this point, to what extent is Hamlet behaving rationally? How many different attitudes toward ghosts have we seen thus far in the play? Which one does Hamlet have?
5. *Act 1, scene 5:* What does the ghost reveal? Why and how has he been doomed? What frame of mind is the ghost in? What expectations does he have of Hamlet? Do you think they are reasonable? What might he mean by "taint not thy mind"? In his response, how does Hamlet place these dishonorable acts in a larger context ("this distracted globe")? How does he promise to "set it down"? When Horatio and Marcellus return, why is Hamlet so insistent about their keeping the secret of what they have seen? Why does the ghost cry out, "Swear"? What does Hamlet mean by "There are more things in heaven and earth, Horatio,/than are dreamt of in your philosophy"? What final request does Hamlet make of his companions, and why? Hamlet seems to believe what the ghost has told him. Do you?
6. *Act 2, scene 1:* What do Polonius's instructions to Reynaldo reveal about the former? How do they relate to previous developments in the play? What do they reinforce? What do we understand about Polonius that he does not understand about himself? On the basis of Ophelia's report, how has Hamlet changed? How does Polonius misread these changes?

Do you agree with Polonius that "it is as proper to our age/ To cast beyond ourselves in our opinions/ As it is common for the younger sort/ To lack discretion"? Why or why not?

7. *Act 2, scene 2:* Why has Claudius sent for Rosencrantz and Guildenstern? How much time would it appear has passed between Act 1 and Act 2? Do Claudius and Gertrude fear Hamlet? Why? If what the ghost said in Act 1, scene 5 is true, do you think Gertrude knows about the murder? What might suggest that she does not? In response to Polonius, what does she mean by "more matter with less art"? As Polonius relates his story to the king and queen, what concerns him besides Hamlet's madness? In his conversation with Hamlet, what does Polonius sense? How would you describe Hamlet's remarks? What does he think of Polonius? What does he mean by "there is nothing either good or bad but thinking makes it so"? Why are Rosencrantz and Guildenstern so focused on ambition? How does Hamlet view these two? How does he explain to them the cause of his change in behavior? How do you feel about Rosencrantz and Guildenstern? Is it ethical for a parent to secretly enlist the aid of their children's friends? Why or why not? What might be the purpose of the discussion about the theater prior to the players' arrival? What does Hamlet mean by "I am but mad north-by-northwest"? How does he make fun of Polonius? What seems to be Hamlet's purpose in speaking lines from "Aeneas' tale to Dido" and calling for its enactment by the players? In particular, how is "Pyrrhus's pause" fraught with meaning? To what extent does Polonius understand Hamlet's purpose here? In his concluding soliloquy, of what does Hamlet despair? Why is he reluctant, impotent? Is he less—or more—certain here of the treachery of Claudius? What plot does he devise to get at the truth? Why did Shakespeare choose to rhyme the last two lines of the soliloquy?

8. *Act 3, scene 1:* What does Claudius ask of Rosencrantz and Guildenstern? How does the question differ from the one asked at the beginning of Act 2? How would you compare Claudius and Gertrude in their expressed concern for Hamlet? Do they seem equally open and genuine? What do you make of Claudius's aside: "How smart a lash that speech doth give my conscience"? What does he seem to reveal here? In the famous soliloquy that follows, what choices does Hamlet wrestle with? What does he mean, "Thus conscience does make cowards of us all"? Do you think Hamlet lacks courage? Why or why not? In his talk with Ophelia, who is the more honest? Why does Hamlet tell Ophelia to "get thee to a nunnery"? At this point, what motivates him? Is he more concerned that his father has been murdered, or that he was not named king? Does he see himself as honest and virtuous? Do you? Why or why not? How does he view the world? What is his frame of mind? In this scene, do you think he knows he is being watched? Why or why not? Why did Shakespeare convey Hamlet's feelings here in prose and Ophelia's in verse?

9. *Act 3, scene 2:* Do Hamlet's instructions to the players reflect his larger concerns in any way? How does he feel about Horatio? Does he see qualities in Horatio that he himself lacks? Explain. When Claudius, Polonius, and Ophelia arrive, how and why does Hamlet engage in word play? Over the years critics have puzzled over the inclusion of the dumb show. Can you suggest what its purpose might have been (given the fact that *The Murder of Gonzago* virtually repeats it)? How successful is the latter? What lines do you think Hamlet inserted into the play? Is Hamlet certain now of the king's guilt? Of his mother's involvement? Does he now feel justified in seeking revenge? Do you feel he is justified? Why or why not? Do you believe he is prepared to carry out the revenge? Throughout this scene, why does Hamlet persist in his "antic behavior"? How does he compare Rosencrantz's and Guildenstern's actions to playing a musical instrument? How has he been "played on" like a pipe? In his brief soliloquy, how does Hamlet wish to approach his

meeting with his mother? What does this imply? Do you think at this point that Hamlet finally and truly understands himself? Why or not?

10. *Act 3, scene 3:* How does Rosencrantz justify—or pretend to justify—the king's orders to send Hamlet off to England? In Claudius's soliloquy, what do we learn? What is uppermost in his mind? How does he bring himself to pray, and for what? Do you agree that a horrible deed repented is therefore made less horrible? Why or why not? Where do we see similar examples of this in our own times? Here, is Claudius's villainy fully confirmed, or do we have any inkling of sympathy for him? As Hamlet observes him, why is Hamlet reluctant to act? Is he more—or less—ethical here than Claudius? What does Claudius conclude in the final couplet?

11. *Act 3, scene 4:* In this famous "closet scene," what does Hamlet mean by "set you up a glass/ Where you may see the inmost part of you"? Does Gertrude seem to reveal her guilt here—or her innocence? If she is guilty, what is the nature of it? How does Hamlet see her? In his accusations, how does he compare the two brothers? What concerns him about the reappeared ghost? What concerns the ghost? When Gertrude accuses Hamlet of madness, how does he respond? Does he regret having killed Polonius? How does he justify his actions ("but heaven hath pleased it so")? What does he mean by "I must be cruel only to be kind;/Thus bad begins, and worse remains behind"? What instructions does he give his mother, and why? Explain why this scene is often called the turning point in the play: In what ways have the plot and the characters changed?

12. *Act 4, scenes 1–4:* In your view, is Gertrude true to Hamlet in her explanation to Claudius, or does she betray him? Describe Claudius at this point. What concerns him most: his own safety, his reputation, his marriage to Gertrude, his crown? In his exchange with Rosencrantz and Guildenstern, what does Hamlet's banter imply? In Claudius's remarks at the beginning of scene 3, what are the implications of "diseases desperate grown"? What seem to be Hamlet's purposes in his antic comments to the king? In the final few lines, to what or whom does Claudius appeal? To what end? In Hamlet's soliloquy in scene 4, what does he again debate within himself? What does he mean by "a thought which quartered hath but one part wisdom/And ever three parts coward"? How does he contrast his own cause with that of Fortinbras? To what does he renew his commitment?

13. *Act 4, scene 5:* What does Gertrude mean by "So full of artless jealousy is guilt, /It spills itself in fearing to be spilt"? Describe Ophelia's state of mind. Who occupies her thoughts? What do you think is the primary cause of her distraction? How does Claudius react? In his speech and afterwards, what do we learn that complicates the plot even more? Do you agree that Claudius is, as he says, guiltless of the death of Polonius? Why or why not? In this scene, is he still the manipulating Claudius, or has he changed? How does the behavior of Laertes here contrast with that of Hamlet throughout the play?

14. *Act 4, scene 6:* What dramatic purposes does Hamlet's letter to Horatio serve? What do you think is communicated in Hamlet's letters to the king?

15. *Act 4, scene 7:* What two reasons does Claudius give Laertes for not moving against Hamlet? What does he hide from Laertes? How does the king react to Hamlet's letter? What do you think is Hamlet's purpose in writing it? Why do you think Claudius tells Laertes the story about the skillful horseman? What does he implore of Laertes, and how is this ironic? What quality of Claudius is emphasized in the plans he devises for Laertes?

16. *Act 5, scene 1:* What is the purpose of the scene with the two gravediggers (clowns)? Why is it not written in blank verse? What are the implications of Hamlet's remarks to Horatio

as they watch the first gravedigger? Explain the pun with the word *lie* in Hamlet's bantering with the gravedigger. Why is Hamlet so taken with the idea of the great being transformed in death to such base uses ("the noble dust of Alexander . . . stopping a bunghole")? In the scene at Ophelia's grave, how and why does Hamlet question Laertes's grief? Does Hamlet feel guilt for Ophelia's death? Should he? Is Laertes justified in hating Hamlet? At this point in the play, to what extent does your sympathy lie with Hamlet? With anyone else?

17. *Act 5, scene 2:* How had Hamlet managed to escape from the plot to have him murdered? In what way did he turn the tables? Does Hamlet now seem certain of the action he must take? How have his feelings toward Laertes changed, and why? What is the outcome of the bantering conversation between Hamlet and Osric? As he contemplates the match, what is Hamlet's attitude? Is he confident? Fatalistic? At last committed? What does he mean by "the readiness is all"? In his comments to Laertes, how does Hamlet explain his actions? Is he sincere? How does Laertes react? Is he sincere? Why or why not? In what ways is the mayhem that follows ironic? What request does the dying Hamlet make of Horatio? Why? What does Hamlet want the world to know? Finally, what has been the nature of his inaction? Over the course of the play, has Hamlet changed? If so, how? What do you think Shakespeare intended playgoers and readers to take away from the play?

WRITING ACTIVITIES

1. In Act 1, scene 2, after his father's ghost departs, Hamlet writes down in a tablet his thoughts about what he has heard so that he will not forget. Write what you think he would have entered into his book: thoughts, feelings, misgivings, plans.
2. In Act 1, scene 4, Hamlet explains the concept of a "tragic flaw" that often undermines the noblest efforts of a person. Write a paper in which you explain not your tragic flaw—let's not get carried away—but a weakness you see in yourself that you would like to improve. *Or,* explain the tragic flaw in another literary character (e.g., Dimmesdale in *The Scarlet Letter* or Heathcliff in *Wuthering Heights*).
3. Conduct research on one of the following topics: the Elizabethan view of ghosts; "the Divine Right of Kings" mentioned by Rosencrantz and Guildenstern in Act 3, scene 3, and later by Claudius; or the original source of the Hamlet story. Write up what you learn in a paper.
4. Write several entries in a diary kept by Gertrude that reveal, perhaps more than the play itself reveals, the nature of her thoughts and concerns. You may want to include entries that she might have written at the end of each act.
5. There are several references in *Hamlet* to a society that is rank and sullied; as Marcellus says, "Something is rotten in the state of Denmark." Write a paper about our own "distracted globe," the extent to which the world today seems "out of joint." Be sure to provide specific examples.
6. Write a paper in which you compare Hamlet at the beginning of the play with Ophelia toward the end. Focus on the losses each experiences and the ways in which each deals with those losses.
7. Write a paper supporting the contention by the literary critic Harold Bloom that Hamlet is perhaps the most intelligent character in all literature. Cite specific evidence of your point of view from the play itself. You may need to begin by defining "intelligence."

8. Write a blues song that might have been composed by Hamlet on the day after the end of Act 5, scene 1 (assuming that scene 2 is delayed). Begin the song with the traditional blues opening, "Woke up this morning . . . ."
9. Find either an astrology chart or a Myers-Briggs personality chart with its sixteen profiles. Using either resource, try to see where Hamlet would best fit. Write a paper in which you present your conclusions.
10. With his vacillations between melancholy and "antic behavior," some might consider Hamlet a precursor of the contemporary manic-depressive. Read about this psychological condition in at least two reference sources and write a paper in which you argue that Hamlet was or was not a manic-depressive.
11. Examine a moral dilemma—for example, the question of whether a very young child who has been reared by a family for one or two years should be returned to the birth parents, who had originally given him or her up for adoption but now want the child returned. In a paper of three to five pages, examine the issue from an objective, balanced perspective that acknowledges the complexity of the question and the difficulty in reaching a decision. Begin the paper with a reference to Hamlet and his dilemma; finish it by making a recommendation for the issue you have written about.
12. Read the play *Rosencrantz & Guildenstern Are Dead* by Tom Stoppard. Then write a paper in which you answer the question, "Is it better to be the hero of your own life or a supporting player in the life of someone who is himself heroic?"

OTHER ACTIVITIES

1. Polonius is well-known for his vain advice. Write and then perform a monologue in which a modern Polonius gives advice to his teenaged children about such matters as drugs and alcohol, driving, curfews, and schoolwork. Try to convey his pomposity and hypocrisy.
2. Hamlet is surely one of literature's most complex characters. Design a mobile or a collage that represents the complexity of the choices faced by Hamlet and the anguish he expressed in facing them.
3. Listen to Tchaikovsky's "Incidental Music to *Hamlet*," which is available on *Orchestral Music*, a compact disc from Chandos that may be found in your city or county library. Then write a one- to two-page paper on ways in which you think the music reflects the conflicts, characters, and themes in the play.
4. Draw a timeline for the play indicating when the major events take place and the lapses of time between acts and scenes. In some cases (e.g., between Act 1 and Act 2), where there is no clear indication, you can offer approximations.
5. Pretend that you have been assigned the task of drawing the illustration for the cover of *Playbill* to be used in a new Broadway version of *Hamlet*. Draw a picture of a scene that you think best captures the essence of the play. (One possibility would be Hamlet holding a raised sword over the head of the praying Claudius, but there are many others.)
6. With several other students, act out the "play within a play" scene in Act 3, scene 2. You can read the lines, improvise them, or pantomime the action. Have students take the parts of not only the actors in the troupe, but the observers as well (Hamlet, Claudius, Gertrude, Horatio, etc.).

7. Write and enact another "play within the play" that, had the drama troupe performed it, might have made Hamlet believe that Claudius was innocent.
8. Pretend that Hamlet is arrested upon his return to Denmark after he thwarts the plot of Claudius to have him killed. Try him for the murder of Polonius. You will need students to play the parts of a prosecutor, a defense attorney, character witnesses, Gertrude, and others. One of the early decisions for the defense team will be how to plead (i.e., innocent on the grounds of mental anguish, innocent on the grounds of self-defense, guilty, etc.).

SELECTED TEACHING RESOURCES

Media Aids

Cassette

A Study Guide to William Shakespeare's Hamlet. 1 hour. Time Warner Audio Books, 1998.
Includes historical background, reviews, and a plot overview plus accompanying booklet.

Cassettes (2)

Hamlet. 186 min. Modern Library/BBC AudioBooks, 1996.

Cassettes (4)

Hamlet. 205 min. Caedmon, 1979.

Cassette (1) and Filmstrip

Hamlet. 20 min. Thomas S. Klise.

CD-ROM

Hamlet on CD-ROM. Windows or Macintosh. Films for the Humanities & Sciences.
Includes searchable text, dramatizations of key scenes, commentary by scholars, examination of major themes, click-on glossary, bibliography, and Internet connection to Shakespeare websites.

Illuminated Books and Manuscripts: Hamlet. Windows. EduQuest.
Contains complete text, scenes from Olivier film, and commentaries by scholars.

Internet

Bayne, Kathryn. 1997. *Teacher CyberGuide: The Tragedy of Hamlet, Prince of Denmark*. 1997. Available: http://www.sdcoe.k12.ca.us/score/ham/hamtg.html (Accessed March 10, 2000).
An online teaching guide to the play, developed by the San Diego County Office of Education.

Delaney, Ian. 1997–1999. *A Short Course on Hamlet*. 1997. Available: http://server1.hypermart.net/hamlet/ (Accessed March 10, 2000).
A guide from England with numerous links to other useful sites.

Gray, Terry A. 1997. *Mr. William Shakespeare and the Internet.* 1995–1999. Available: http://daphne.palomar.edu/shakespeare/. (Accessed March 10, 2000).

Contains numerous links to wonderful home pages devoted to Shakespeare, several on the teaching of the Bard.

Videos

A Taste of Shakespeare: Hamlet. 37 min., color. Bullfrog Films, 1994.

Discovering Hamlet. 53 min. PBS Video, 1990. Interpretation.

The Great Hamlets. Two programs, each 56 min., color. Films for the Humanities & Sciences. Interviews of great actors discussing their interpretations of the role.

Hamlet. 135 min., color. Mel Gibson/Glenn Close version. Clearvue/eav and Warner Home Video, 1990.

Hamlet. Two parts (216 min.), color. BBC and Time-Life Production featuring Derek Jacobi and Kenneth Branagh. Ambrose Video Publishing, 1988.

Hamlet. 147 min., b & w. Lawrence Olivier version (1948). Hallmark Home Entertainment, 1995.

Hamlet. 30 min., color. Films for the Humanities & Sciences. Interpretation.

Shakespeare and His Stage: Approaches to Hamlet. 45 min., color. Films for the Humanities & Sciences.
Hamlet as portrayed by Barrymore, Olivier, Gielgud, and Williamson.

Shakespeare Explorations with Patrick Stewart—Hamlet: *Polonius.* 24 min., color. Barr Films, 1992.
An actor's interpretation of the Lord Chamberlain.

Printed Resources

Articles

Farrer, F. "Telling a Hawk from a Handsaw." *Times Educational Supplement* 4051 (February 18, 1994): X.

Felter, Douglas P. "Exploring Shakespeare Through the Cinematic Image: Seeing *Hamlet.*" *English Journal* 82 (April 1993): 61–64.

Gavin, Rosemary. "*The Lion King* and *Hamlet*: A Homecoming for the Exiled Child." *English Journal* 85 (March 1996): 55–57.

McKenna, John J. "Using Learning Styles to Put Hamlet on Trial." *Contemporary Education* 61 (Winter 1990): 81–86.

Sowder, William H., Jr. "The Thing's the Play: Doing *Hamlet.*" *English Journal* 82 (April 1993): 65–67.

Walizer, Marue E. "Adolescent Experience as Shakespearean Drama." *English Journal* 76 (February 1987): 41–43.

Books

Evans, Bertrand. *Teaching Shakespeare in the High School.* New York: Macmillan, 1966.

Levin, Harry. *The Question of Hamlet.* New York: Oxford University Press, 1970.

O'Brien, Peggy, ed. *Shakespeare Set Free: Teaching* Hamlet *and* Henry IV, Part 1. New York: Washington Square Press, 1994.

Wells, Stanley. "A Reader's Guide to *Hamlet*" in *Hamlet,* edited by John Russell Brown and Bernard Harris, 200–207. Stratford-Upon-Avon Studies 5. New York: St. Martin's Press, 1964.

Wilson, John Dover. *What Happens in* Hamlet. 3d ed. New York: Cambridge University Press, 1951.

Abridged Text

Hamlet. Shakespeare for Young People series (text shortened, language unchanged). Learning Links.

Parallel Text

Hamlet. Original text and modern language text side-by-side. Perfection Learning Corporation.

Posters

Hamlet. Set of five, 17" x 22", color. Sundance.

Teaching Aids

Hamlet. Cliff's Teaching Portfolio. Perma-Bound.

Hamlet. Dramatic Ideas Plus series and REACT series. Sundance.

Hamlet. Literature Unit Plans. Teacher's Pet Publications.

Hamlet. Masterprose series and Latitudes series. Perfection Learning Corporation.

Hamlet. Novel Unit Guide, Novel Units Student Packet, Perma-Guide. Perma-Bound.

Hamlet. Novel/Drama Curriculum Units. The Center for Learning.

Hamlet. Novel-Ties. Learning Links.

Tests

Hamlet. Essay, objective, and alternative assessment versions. Perfection Learning Corporation.

Wuthering Heights

Emily Brontë
1847
Available in paperback from several publishing companies.

SUMMARY

When Catherine and Hindley Earnshaw are six and fourteen, respectively, their father brings home to Wuthering Heights an unruly urchin named Heathcliff whom he has found homeless on the streets of Liverpool. Hindley grows to despise the foundling and to persecute him, but the spirited Catherine, and Heathcliff, who is sullen and quiet, develop a strong attachment. After Hindley returns home from college with a new wife to become master of the house when his father dies, his alienation from Heathcliff and Catherine increases. Catherine is then injured during an excursion to the neighboring Thrushcross Grange and remains there for five weeks, during which she falls in love with the peevish Edgar Linton. When she returns to the Heights, Heathcliff is confused and resentful, although Catherine insists that she cares for him as much as ever. When Heathcliff overhears her say she plans to marry Edgar, he leaves Wuthering Heights; and three years later Catherine and Edgar are wed—despite the fact that she (as she has confided to the housekeeper, Nelly Dean) and Heathcliff are permanently inseparable. Meanwhile, Hindley's wife has died in childbirth, leaving him a son, Hareton, and in despair he drowns his sorrows in drink.

Shortly after Catherine and Edgar settle at Thrushcross Grange, Heathcliff returns. He sets out to gain control of Wuthering Heights by gambling with Hindley and to resume his passionate relationship with the receptive Catherine. Edgar resists, but his attention is diverted by his sister Isabella's sudden infatuation with Heathcliff. Although Heathcliff despises the girl, he sees an opportunity for further control and marries her. His passion, however, remains for Catherine alone—and hers for him. When Catherine's health fails, Heathcliff visits the Grange in secrecy, where the two express an intense and destructive devotion to each other. That night, Catherine dies after giving birth to a daughter, whom Edgar names for her mother.

Suffering intense anguish because of Catherine's death, Heathcliff plots for even more control over those he despises. When Isabella leaves him to live in London (where she gives birth to their son, Linton), Heathcliff vows he will someday have the boy. As the years pass the young Cathy grows up; when Isabella dies, Cathy falls in love with the weak and whining Linton, who has been claimed by his father. Although Heathcliff hates his son, he forces a marriage between the two cousins to gain control over Thrushcross Grange upon the death of Edgar. Linton then dies, leaving the bitter Cathy to live with Heathcliff and Hareton at Wuthering Heights.

Now in complete control, Heathcliff begins to lose interest in anything but a final spiritual union with his beloved Catherine. He dies at the Heights during a violent rainstorm and is buried beside Catherine and Edgar, leaving Cathy and Hareton to build from the emotional wreckage a hopeful new love between them.

APPRAISAL

This is one of the greatest English novels, considered a masterpiece of plot, structure, characterization, and setting. The book was written in 1845 by the daughter of a Yorkshire parson, Emily Brontë, who died at the age of thirty in 1848, a year after *Wuthering Heights* was published. In its intensity and mysticism, its powerful portrayal of two strong and willful characters (especially the brooding, unforgettable Heathcliff), and its compelling descriptions of the Yorkshire moors, the novel is unsurpassed. It is most appropriate for the twelfth grade.

THEMES

love and passion, revenge, evil and hatred, pride and selfishness

LITERARY CONCEPTS

characterization, setting, mood, plot, flashback, structure, symbol, figurative language

RELATED READING

The most logical book to recommend may be *H: The Story of Heathcliff's Journey Back to Wuthering Heights*, a sequel written by Lin Haire-Sargeant in 1992. Otherwise, students might consider *Rebecca* by Daphne du Maurier, a modern romance of passion and intrigue, and Stephen King's recent gothic romance *Bag of Bones*. Some students may wish to consider the popular gothic romances by writers like Mary Stewart and *Jane Eyre* by Emily Brontë's sister Charlotte.

READING PROBLEMS AND OPPORTUNITIES

Written over a century and a half ago, *Wuthering Heights* offers a considerable challenge to most high school students. Although the sentence structure seems comparatively modern, the connections among the Earnshaws and Lintons are involved (see the diagram below), the dialect of the servant Joseph often requires translation, and the level of vocabulary is high.

For those who are ready and able to appreciate it, the novel offers a wealth of opportunities for word study, including the following examples (the numbers in parentheses are the chapters in which the words occur):

misanthropist, misanthropical (1, 13, 31),
peevish (1, 5, 8, 9, 10, 17, 18, 21, 23, 24, 26),
morose, moroseness (1, 2, 8, 13, 26, 32),
physiognomy (1, 10, 18),
copious (2, 21),
obviate (3, 13, 20),
reproach, reproachful (3, 17, 21, 33),
writhe (3, 14, 15, 17, 23, 24),
caprice (3, 9, 15),
insolent, insolence (4, 5, 6, 9, 10, 11, 33),
reproof, reprove (5, 7, 8, 18, 21, 32),
abominable (8, 9, 17),
annihilate (6, 9, 13, 27, 29, 34),
execrated, execrations (6, 8, 13),
culpable (6, 18),
equanimity (7, 8),

obstinate, *obstinacy* (7, 9, 10, 14, 17, 20, 22, 32, 34),
ingenious, *ingenuity* (8, 13, 32),
antipathy (8, 9, 18, 21, 33),
ignoble (8, 17),
petulant, *petulance* (8, 10, 15, 18, 21),
imperiously (8, 10),
livid (8, 15),
consternation (8, 12),
indifferent, *indifference* (9, 10, 12, 34),
indignant, *indignation* (9, 10, 11, 13, 15, 18, 19, 20, 21, 31),
judicious, *injudicious* (9, 10, 17),
indulgent, *indulgence* (9, 11, 14, 25, 26, 27),
avarice, *avaricious* (10, 25),
abhor, *abhorrence* (10, 13, 17, 33),
malevolence (10, 17, 18, 21),
apparition (11, 13, 32),
propitiate (11, 18),
presumptuous (11, 12, 17),
apathy, *apathetic* (11, 12, 26, 28),
despondency (11, 13, 20),
peremptory (11, 19),
pertinacious (12, 17, 26),
paroxysm (12, 15, 16, 27),
lamentation (12, 13, 18, 21, 23, 25),
sanguine (13, 19, 20),
doleful (13, 17, 23),
iteration, *reiteration* (14, 18, 20, 23),
asunder (15, 25, 33),
trepidation (19, 20),
supplicate (21, 27),
magnanimity (27, 33), and
monomania (33).

Many of these words could be grouped and taught under the heading "Words of Gloom and Doom."

Concerning the relationships of the characters, teachers may wish to reduce student confusion by providing the following diagram before assigning the novel:

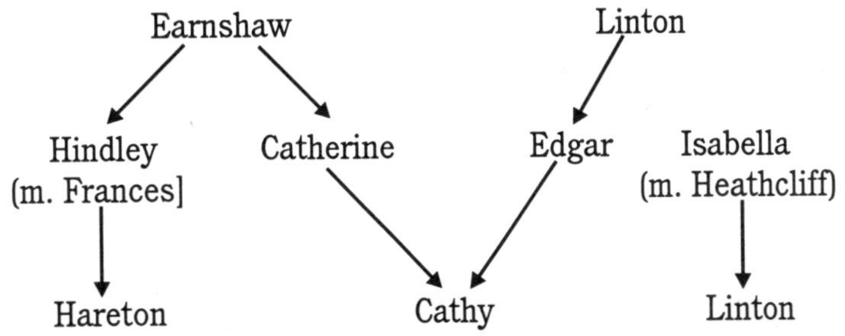

INITIATING ACTIVITIES

1. With your classmates, discuss the nature of love and passion. How would you define the two terms? What is the relationship between them? Can either exist without the other? Is either destructive of the other? Which of the two is more likely to change in the course of a long relationship? In what ways? What colors would you associate with each? Would you rather be known as a warm and loving person, or a passionate person? Can a person be both?

2. Consider the following situation: You are ten or eleven years old. Without discussing the matter with you, your parents decide to adopt into the family an underprivileged child of about your age. When he or she arrives, you discover that the child is sullen and resentful and unresponsive to your efforts to talk and play. When you persist, he or she says, "Leave me alone." Write a brief paper explaining how you would react to this problem and how you might work to find a solution. Be honest and specific.

DISCUSSION QUESTIONS

1. *Chapter 1:* Who is the narrator? Whom is he visiting? Why? Describe Wuthering Heights. Describe Heathcliff. How does the narrator compare himself to Heathcliff? In what ways do they seem different?

2. *Chapter 2:* Why does Mr. Lockwood return to Wuthering Heights? Whom does he find there this time and what is the mood that prevails? How are the inhabitants of the place related, if at all? How does Mr. Lockwood feel about his visit?

3. *Chapter 3:* What do Catherine Earnshaw's inscribed volumes reveal, especially about past conflicts? Who, apparently, was Hindley? What might be the implications of Mr. Lockwood's dream about the sermon on 490 sins? Who dominates his second dream? What does Mr. Lockwood learn (or think he learns) from the dream? Does he seem to take the dream seriously? Why do you think Heathcliff responds so emotionally to Mr. Lockwood's account of his dream? What is Hareton like? What are the attitudes of Heathcliff and his daughter-in-law, Cathy, toward each other? What might be the reason for his reluctant charity toward her?

4. *Chapter 4:* Why does Mr. Lockwood strike up a conversation with Mrs. Dean? What does he learn? When he first arrived at Wuthering Heights, how had Heathcliff been received? (Note the word *it* in reference to him.) According to Mrs. Dean, how did Cathy and Hindley differ as children—in particular, in their reaction to the newcomer? With whom do your sympathies lie at this point in the story?

5. *Chapter 5:* Describe Cathy as she is pictured by Mrs. Dean. Why do you think she and Heathcliff were so attracted to each other? Why does Mrs. Dean say "she was much too fond of Heathcliff"?

6. *Chapter 6:* Upon Heathcliff's return, how did the relationship of Hindley to Catherine and Heathcliff change? Despite this, why did the latter say he would not have changed places with the Linton children? What did the incident at Thrushcross Grange tell you about Cathy? Why did Heathcliff think she was "immeasurably superior"?

7. *Chapter 7:* When Catherine returned to Wuthering Heights after five weeks, to what extent was she different? How did Nelly Dean suggest that Heathcliff change his nature? She said, "A good heart will help you to a bonny face, my lad." Do you agree? Do you agree that this was Heathcliff's problem? Why or why not? Why hadn't the effort to reform Catherine affected her attitude toward Heathcliff? Having listened to Nelly Dean tell her story, why is Mr. Lockwood insistent upon hearing more? Is his interest merely that of a gossip?

8. *Chapter 8:* According to Mrs. Dean, why did Cathy develop a "double character"? At this point, what were Cathy's virtues? Her shortcomings? Why did Heathcliff settle into "unsociable moroseness"? To what extent was he the cause of his own sullenness? To what extent was he a victim? What did Cathy's actions during Edgar's visit reveal about her?

9. *Chapter 9:* What did Catherine's conversation with Mrs. Dean in the kitchen reveal about her? Why did she have misgivings about agreeing to marry Edgar? What were her reasons for agreeing? Do you agree with Mrs. Dean that they were foolish reasons? Why or why not? Why didn't she feel she could marry Heathcliff? Did she love him? Why? Was her reason for loving Heathcliff more rational than her reasons for loving Edgar? What do you think she meant by saying, "Whatever our souls are made of, his and mine are the same"? Is this a good basis for a happy marriage? Why or why not? At this point, whom

do you think Catherine loved more, Edgar or Heathcliff? How would you describe her love for each of them? Through chapter 9, how has the author used the setting of the novel to reinforce or underscore meaning?

10. *Chapter 10:* What effect did Heathcliff's return have upon Catherine? Upon Edgar? Was Edgar justified in feeling upset? Why or why not? Where had Heathcliff been during his three years' absence? How was he different? How was he the same? What seemed to be his intention in returning? In light of her telling Edgar that Heathcliff "was now worthy of anyone's regard," account for Cathy's later contradictory description of him to Isabella. Do you think that Cathy's description of her friend was honest? If so, why was she so attracted to him? Why did she choose to humiliate Isabella before Heathcliff? How did the latter respond? How had Nelly Dean's feelings for Heathcliff changed since his return? What were her fears?

11. *Chapter 11:* Why did Nelly Dean decide to visit Wuthering Heights? Why was she disturbed? When Heathcliff next visited the Grange, why did he and Catherine argue? Why do you think he compared her with a tyrant? Why did he seek revenge? Against whom? Why was Catherine so upset at Edgar's reaction? Do you agree with her that Edgar was a coward? Why or why not? Was Heathcliff brave? Or did his behavior reflect something less than courage? Discuss. The chapter ends with everyone at Thrushcross Grange in anguish. Who was most responsible? Why?

12. *Chapter 12:* Why did Catherine grow so distraught? Do you think she was genuinely ill or feigning illness? Why? "I'm sure I should be myself were I once among the heather on those hills." Why did she feel this way? Why did she seem especially upset over Edgar's seeking consolation in books? Why was Edgar so conciliatory? At this point in Ellen Dean's story, what did each of the main characters want?

13. *Chapter 13:* In her letter to Ellen, what changes did Isabella reveal in her feelings? Early in the letter, what might she have meant by "*I can't follow it through*"? What could Joseph possibly mean by "Weel done, Miss Cathy"? Describe what life at Wuthering Heights had become for those who resided there. Why did Isabella want Ellen to visit?

14. *Chapter 14:* When Ellen Dean visited the Heights, how was she received? How did Heathcliff draw distinctions between himself and Edgar? What did he feel was the nature of his and Catherine's attraction to each other? Why do you think Isabella had been so attracted to him? Had she, as Heathcliff suggested, been entirely responsible for her infatuation? Or had Heathcliff encouraged it? What might have been his motive for doing so? "The more the worms writhe, the more I yearn to crush out their entrails." Is Heathcliff totally despicable? Why or why not?

15. *Chapter 15:* Describe the meeting between Catherine and Heathcliff. In what ways did they consider each other responsible for their anguish? Do you sympathize with either? Why or why not? Heathcliff cried out: "I love *my* murderer—but *yours*? How can I?" What did he mean? Were Heathcliff and Catherine unwilling—or unable—to part? Discuss.

16. *Chapter 16:* Ellen Dean remembers "how much selfishness there is even in a love like Mr. Linton's." Do you agree that there is always selfishness in love? Why or why not? How do you account for Heathcliff's response to Catherine's death? For the intensity of his feelings? In the last three paragraphs of the chapter, there are two possible symbols. What are they?

17. *Chapter 17:* According to her account of the evening before her escape from Wuthering Heights, why didn't Isabella agree to let Hindley kill Heathcliff? The next morning, how did she move Heathcliff to attack her? Why did Heathcliff vow that he would eventually have their child? Later, why did he say regarding Hareton, "And we'll see if one tree won't grow as crooked as another, with the same wind to twist it"? Now that Catherine was dead, what motivated Heathcliff's behavior?

18. *Chapter 18:* How did Cathy appear to be like her mother? How was she different? What was Hareton like? Why do you think Heathcliff treated him as he did? Do you agree with Ellen Dean that the boy, at age eighteen, could have been changed into something better, more refined at this point? Why or why not? How do you feel toward Hareton?

19. *Chapter 19:* Why did Edgar give up Linton so easily? Did he have any choice? Discuss. Describe Joseph's attitude toward Heathcliff. Did he in any way respect him?

20. *Chapter 20:* What was Heathcliff's purpose in intending to be kind toward Linton? Why did he want to monopolize the boy's affection? Why did he hire a tutor? Why did he despise the boy? What kind of person do you think Heathcliff truly respected?

21. *Chapter 21:* What kind of young man did Linton become? Why did Heathcliff wish him to marry Cathy? Why did Heathcliff prefer Hareton to Linton? Do you think he actually liked, or even loved, Hareton? Why or why not? At age sixteen, what kind of person did young Cathy seem to be? Why was she so attracted to Linton? What did Ellen Dean's actions regarding the letters reveal about Ellen?

22. *Chapter 22:* "I care for nothing in comparison with Papa," said Cathy. Do you believe her? Why or why not?

23. *Chapter 23:* Obviously Linton and Heathcliff were contrasts. Was the son like the father in any way? Discuss. Cathy said she was less childish than Linton. Compare them in other ways. Why was she unable to see him for what he was?

24. *Chapter 24:* Why did Hareton behave as he did during Cathy's visit to see Linton?

25. *Chapters 25 and 26:* "I must persevere in making her sad while I live, and leaving her solitary when I die." What did Edgar mean? What motives of the fathers led to the resumption of meetings between Cathy and Linton? At their first meeting, why do you think Linton was so different? What did their meeting reveal or confirm about Cathy?

26. *Chapter 27:* Linton told Cathy: "I'm a traitor too, and I dare not tell you." What did he mean? Why did Heathcliff hope that Edgar would die before Linton? Why did Heathcliff despise anything that seemed afraid of him? Do you think he despised Cathy? Why or why not?

27. *Chapter 28:* Was Linton, as Nelly Dean observed, a "wretched creature"? What was his greatest weakness?

28. *Chapter 29:* What did Heathcliff mean when he told Cathy, "I don't like you well enough to hurt [Linton]"? Do you think Heathcliff was at all affected by Cathy's comment that "*Nobody* loves you—*nobody* will cry for you when you die! I wouldn't be you!"? Why or why not? On the day before, why had Heathcliff opened Catherine's coffin? What else had he done to it? Why? Why do you think Heathcliff told these things to Nelly Dean?

29. *Chapter 30:* When Linton died, why did Heathcliff ask Cathy how she felt? Later, why was she so offended by Hareton's efforts to be friendly?

30. *Chapter 31:* Mr. Lockwood resumes the narrative with a visit to Wuthering Heights. What are his feelings toward Hareton? Why does Cathy treat her cousin so rudely? Why do you think Heathcliff is described as having "a restless, anxious expression" on his face?

31. *Chapter 32:* As Mr. Lockwood approaches Wuthering Heights, what changes does he notice? In Nelly Dean's account, why did Catherine change her mind with regard to Hareton? Did she act from the goodness of her heart or for selfish reasons? Why did Joseph disapprove?

32. *Chapter 33:* Why did Heathcliff release Catherine from his grasp? Why did he fear that Catherine's love would make Hareton "an outcast, and a beggar"? Why did Hareton support Heathcliff? In what ways did Nelly Dean see potential in Hareton? Why did Heathcliff feel there was "a strange change approaching"? Was his lingering love and grief for the dead Catherine natural? Was it good? Why or why not? Heathcliff claimed that he did not hope for death. Yet he said, "I have a single wish, and my whole being and faculties are yearning to attain it." Did he contradict himself? What was his wish?

33. *Chapter 34:* "As to repenting of my injustices, I've done no injustice, and I repent of nothing." Taking into account all of his experiences, do you agree with Heathcliff? Why or why not? What did he mean by, "My soul's bliss kills my body, but does not satisfy itself"? Did Heathcliff die happy? Fulfilled? Revenged? Discuss. Does the book end on a positive or a negative note?

WRITING ACTIVITIES

1. Write an account of how you think Heathcliff spent his three years away from the moors. Keep in mind the perceptions that Nelly Dean and others have of him upon his return (his "upright carriage" and dignified manner; his apparent supply of money; etc.).

2. After reading the conversation between Nelly Dean and Catherine about love in chapter 9, write a paper entitled "Reasons Good and Bad for Falling in Love."

3. Write the letter from Heathcliff to Catherine that Nelly Dean delivers in chapter 15.

4. Write a comparison/contrast paper on one of the following:

    a. Edgar and Hindley as fathers

    b. Edgar and Linton as weak men

    c. the two Catherines

5. In chapter 24, Linton and Cathy quarrel over "the pleasantest manner of spending a hot July day." Read their two ideas on this topic and then write your own response. Try to be descriptive.

6. In the final chapter, Nelly Dean wonders about Heathcliff's origins: "But where did he come from, the little dark thing?" Keeping in mind the facts about Heathcliff presented in the book, write a paper that speculates on his boyhood in Liverpool or elsewhere.

7. On Heathcliff's gravestone, "We were obliged to content ourselves with the single word, 'Heathcliff.' " Write an appropriate epitaph for him.

8. "The persons most responsible for the tragedies that befell the inhabitants of Wuthering Heights and Thrushcross Grange were. . . ." Write a paper in which you identify the three characters you consider most worthy of blame.

9. With its drama, passion, and mystery, and its involved relationships between characters, *Wuthering Heights* often calls to mind that contemporary genre, the soap opera. Write a soap opera parody of a specific scene from the novel. Call your scene "As the Heights Wither" and write it in script format.*

10. In chapter 34, Heathcliff tells Nelly Dean: "I have not written my will yet; and how to leave my property I cannot determine! I wish I could annihilate it from the face of the earth." Write Heathcliff's will. Keep in mind the above comment as well as his relationships with Hareton, Cathy, Nelly Dean, and others who remain behind.

11. Like many novels, *Wuthering Heights* has a number of turning points where the plot could have taken a different direction had something different happened. Write a paper on three of these significant moments in the book.

12. Write a review of the musical version of *Wuthering Heights* by Bernard J. Taylor. (See "Selected Teaching Resources.") *Or,* write a comparison between the musical and the novel, indicating where the musical remains true to the book and where it departs.

OTHER ACTIVITIES

1. In chapter 3, Mr. Lockwood finds "an excellent caricature of my friend Joseph" sketched by Catherine on a page in her Testament. Draw a caricature of Joseph or one of Heathcliff. (Descriptions of the former occur in the early chapters; of the latter, in chapter 10.) Keep in mind that a caricature exaggerates one or more of the dominant physical features of the subject.

2. Few novels are as inextricably rooted in their setting as *Wuthering Heights*. With this in mind, complete one of the following activities:

   a. Draw a picture of the house and grounds of Wuthering Heights, using the description in chapter 1 as a starting point. Try to capture the "atmospheric tumult" of the place in your drawing.

   b. Draw a map of the moors that includes Wuthering Heights and Thrushcross Grange.

3. "Nelly, I am Heathcliff! He's always, always in my mind: not as a pleasure . . . but as my own being." Using collage, paint, or other media, design an artistic representation of the oneness that Catherine and Heathcliff felt.

4. Role play a scene involving Hareton, Cathy, and their two children, ages twelve and fifteen, seventeen years after the novel ends. While the family visits the cemetery where Edgar, Catherine, and Heathcliff lie buried, one of the children asks, "Who was Heathcliff and why is he buried here?" How would Cathy, and especially Hareton, respond? What other questions might the children ask?

5. When Nelly Dean accuses Heathcliff of injustices in chapter 34, he denies them. With several other students, conduct a mock trial of Heathcliff. One student should play the role of prosecutor; another, the role of defense attorney. Other students should play the parts of characters called upon to testify: Catherine (the mother), Edgar, old master Earnshaw, Hareton, Nelly Dean, and so on. The remainder of the class should decide on Heathcliff's guilt or innocence with regard to whatever charges are brought against him.

---

*This activity was written by Barbara Friend Davis, an English language arts teacher in South Carolina.

SELECTED TEACHING RESOURCES

Media Aids

Cassettes (2)

Wuthering Heights. Abridged. Perfection Learning Corporation.

Cassettes (8)

Wuthering Heights. 11 hrs. Recorded Books.

Cassettes (9)

Wuthering Heights. 13.5 hrs. Books on Tape.

Internet

Eagle Intermedia Publishing, Inc. N.d. *Bronte Country*. Available: http://www.bronte-country.com/ (Accessed March 10, 2000).

A commercial British site with numerous photographs of the Yorkshire Dales (including Top Withins, the alleged setting of the novel) as well as information on books about the Brontës and several links.

Scoggins, Dene. 1996–1997. *Wuthering Heights*. 1996–1997. Available: http://www.cwrl.utexas.edu/~scoggins/316british/WutheringHeights/index.html (Accessed March 10, 2000).

Includes material on Victorian society, women in Victorian society, Victorian architecture, and a message forum on the novel.

Videos

The Brontë Sisters. 52 min., color. Films for the Humanities & Sciences.

Wuthering Heights by Emily Brontë. 27 min., color. Critical interpretation. Films for the Humanities & Sciences.

Wuthering Heights. 104 min., b & w. Olivier-Oberon version. Perma-Bound, 1939.

Wuthering Heights. 107 min., color. Juliette Binoche and Ralph Fiennes version. Paramount Home Video, 1992.

Wuthering Heights: The Musical. color. Written by Bernard J. Taylor. Silva Screen Records (available from Dress Circle), 1992.

Wuthering Heights Package. 50 min., color. Corporation for Public Broadcasting/ Annenberg/CPB Project.
Discussion of themes, imagery, structure, and style.

Printed Materials

Articles

Gold, Linda. "Catherine Earnshaw: Mother and Daughter." *English Journal* 74 (March 1985): 68–73.

Ohmann, Carol. "Emily Brontë in the Hands of Male Critics." *College English* 32 (May 1971): 906–913.

Book

Bloom, Harold, ed. *Wuthering Heights*. Bloom's Notes series. Bloomall, PA: Chelsea House Publications, 1996.

Teaching Aids

Wuthering Heights. Literature Unit Plans. Teacher's Pet Publications.

Wuthering Heights. Masterprose series. Perfection Learning Corporation.

Wuthering Heights. Novel/Drama Curriculum Units. The Center for Learning.

Wuthering Heights. Novel Unit Guide, Novel Units Student Packet, and Perma-Guide. Perma-Bound.

Wuthering Heights. REACT series. Sundance.

Tests

Wuthering Heights. Essay, objective, and alternative assessment versions. Perfection Learning Corporation.

Appendix A

DIAMANTES

Several response guides include an activity requiring students to write a diamante poem. A diamante is a diamond-shaped poem based on contrasts. Although there are variations, the most common pattern produces a seven-line poem with the following form:

Line 1—one word, usually a noun

Line 2—two adjectives that describe the noun

Line 3—three participles (*-ing*, *-ed*, *-en*) also describing the noun

Line 4—four nouns that provide a transition from the word in line 1 to the word in line 7; or a long phrase that provides the transition

Line 5—three participles that describe the noun in line 7

Line 6—two adjectives that describe the noun in line 7

Line 7—a noun that contrasts with line 1

Fire

orange and yellow

licking, leaping, lighting

caught between desire and indifference

staring, glaring, glistening

silver and blue

Ice

Appendix B

COMPANIES

Many of these companies can be accessed through Internet websites located through search engines.

Ambrose Video Publishing, Inc.
1290 Avenue of the Americas, Suite 2245
New York, NY 10104
1-800-526-4663

Audio Bookshelf
161 Collins Town Road
Union, ME 04861
1-888-792-2100

Bantam Doubleday Dell Audio Publishing
1540 Broadway
New York, NY 10036

Barr Films
Video Division
100 Wilshire Boulevard, Floor 3
Santa Monica, CA 90401-1121

Books on Tape, Inc.
P.O. Box 7900
Newport Beach, CA 92658
1-800-626-3333

Bullfrog Films
P.O. Box 149
Oney, PA 19547-0149
1-800-543-3763

Caedmon
Division of Harper Audio
10 E. 53rd Street, Suite 420
San Francisco, CA 94103

California Newsreel
149 Ninth Street, Suite 420
San Francisco, CA 94103

The Center for Learning, Teachers/Authors/Publishers
Box 910
Villa Maria, PA 16155
1-800-767-9090 (Operator 21)

Christopher-Gordon Publishers, Inc.
480 Washington Street
Norwood, MA 02062
1-800-934-8322

Cinema Guild
1697 Broadway, Suite 506
New York, NY 10019-5904
1-800-723-5523

CLEARVUE/eav
6465 N. Avondale Avenue
Chicago, IL 60631-1996
1-800-CLEARVUE

Coronet/MTI
4350 Equity Drive
P.O. Box 2649
Columbus, OH 43216

Corporation for Public Broadcasting
Annenberg CPB Project
901 E Street NW
Washington, DC 20004-2037
1-800-532-7637

Dress Circle
57/59 Monmouth Street
Upper St. Martin's Lane
London, England WC2H 9DG

EduQuest
P.O. Box 610787
San Jose, CA 65161-0787

Filmic Archives
The Cinema Center
Botsford, CT 06404
1-800-366-1920

Films for the Humanities & Sciences
P.O. Box 2053
Princeton, NJ 08543-2053
1-800-257-5126

Grace Products
1761 International Parkway
Richardson, TX 75081

Guidance Associates
Box 1000
Mount Kisco, NY 10549
1-800-431-1242

Hallmark Home Entertainment
6100 Wilshire Boulevard, Suite 1400
Los Angeles, CA 90048

Learning Corporation of America
4350 Equity Drive
P.O. Box 2649
Columbus, OH 43216

Learning Links
2300 Marcus Avenue
Dept. A96
New Hyde Park, NY 11042

Listening Library
One Park Avenue
Old Greenwich, CT 06870-1727
1-800-243-4504

Live Home Video
P.O. Box 10124
Van Nuys, CA 91410-0124
1-800-326-1977

Modern Library/BBC Audiobooks
c/o Random House
201 E. 50th Street
New York, NY 10022

PBS Video
1320 Braddock Place
Alexander, VA 22314

Paramount Home Video
5555 Melrose Avenue
Hollywood, CA 90038-3197

Penguin Electronics
375 Hudson Street
New York, NY 10014
1-800-253-6476

Penguin Highbridge Audio
Attn: Order Department
1000 Westgate Drive
St. Paul, MN 55114
1-800-782-5756

Perfection Learning Corporation
1000 N. Second Avenue
P.O. Box 500
Logan, IA 51546-1099
1-800-831-4190

Perma-Bound
617 E. Vandalia Road
Jacksonville, IL 62650
1-800-637-6581

Public Media Video
5547 N. Ravenswood Avenue
Chicago, IL 60640
1-800-323-4222

Random House Audio
201 E. 50th Street
New York, NY 10022

Recorded Books
270 Skipjack Road
Prince Frederick, MD 20678
1-800-638-1304

Sundance
Dept. 13
P.O. Box 1326
Littleton, MA 01460-9936
1-800-343-8204

Teacher's Pet Publications
11504 Hammock Point
Berlin, MD 21811

Thomas S. Klise
P.O. Box 317
Waterford, CT 06385

Tim Podell Productions
Box 244
Scarborough, NY 10510

Time Warner Audio Books
1271 Avenue of the Americas
New York, NY 10020

Voyager
578 Broadway, Suite 1106
New York, NY 10012

Warner Home Video, Inc.
4000 Warner Boulevard, No. 19
Burbank, CA 91522
1-800-626-9000

Author/Title Index

About the Authors

Janet Evans Worthington is the dean of the Center for Lifelong Learning at Plattsburgh State University of New York, Plattsburgh. She holds a B.A. in English from the University of Chicago, an M.A. from the University of Iowa, and a Ph.D. in English education from Florida State University. Her career has included teaching at both secondary and college levels. She has written numerous articles on teaching English, and is co-author of *Response Guides for Teaching Children's Books*, and *Candles and Mirrors* and *Novels and Plays* with Albert B. Somers, and *Practical Robotics* with Bill Burns. Dr. Worthington is the mother of three children.

Albert B. Somers is emeritus professor of education at Furman University in Greenville, SC. A native of North Carolina, Dr. Somers earned a B.A. in English and an M.A. in education from the University of North Carolina at Chapel Hill, and a Ph.D. in English education from Florida State University. His professional experience includes teaching high school English, working as an English language arts consultant at district and state levels, and teaching English and education in college. With Dr. Worthington, he has co-authored *Response Guides for Teaching Children's Books*, and *Candles and Mirrors*, in addition to *Novels and Plays*. Dr. Somers is also author of *Teaching Poetry in High School* published by the National Council of Teachers of English.